'The biggest problem and barrier [...] that people simply struggle to con[...] [...] them. This is where *Click or Clash?* comes in, from the [...] d author Dr Ali Walker. Ali demystifies relationships and the book is full of great practical tips and personal stories to help you create strong connections and relationships. If you want to know how to get the best out of people who are in your life, then read this book.' – **Janine Allis, founder of Boost Juice and part owner of Retail Zoo**

'I have the pleasure of working with Ali Walker at the Change Room program and watching her speak on connection types. I highly recommend *Click or Clash?* to better your understanding of people and how they learn, understand and react to information. But more importantly, to understand yourself, to become more conscious and have better relationships in your life.' – **Anthony Minichiello, NRL ambassador and former captain of the Sydney Roosters**

'After reading *Click or Clash?*, suddenly the world made a lot more sense. I wish I had this book when I was at uni, in my first job, when I was dating, changing careers, or starting my company. It's mandatory reading for life, love, or work.' – **Bec Brown, author of *You've Got This* and founder of PR company The Comms Department**

'If you've ever wondered why you click or clash with someone, this book will shed light on why. More importantly, if you want to have more clicks in your life, *Click or Clash?* is full of practical ways to do so.' – **Dr Amantha Imber, author of *Time Wise***

'As an academic leader I have had occasion to reflect on many different leadership models. It was not until I undertook the survey for Dr Walker's Connection Type model that I could finally say, "Yes, that's me, I'm a Water type (Ripple Effect) leader!" The model has provided me with a powerful narrative to speak to how I connect with others, my strengths and my weaknesses, in both my personal and professional life. An excellent toolkit.' – **Professor Leanne Piggott**

Also by Dr Ali Walker

Get Conscious: How to stop overthinking and come alive

Dr Ali Walker

click or clash?

Discover the new connection and compatibility types that will transform your relationships – in love, friendship and work

PENGUIN LIFE

UK | USA | Canada | Ireland | Australia
India | New Zealand | South Africa | China

Penguin Life is part of the Penguin Random House group of companies whose
addresses can be found at global.penguinrandomhouse.com.

Penguin
Random House
Australia

First published by Penguin Life, 2023

Cover design by Alex Ross Creative © Penguin Random House Australia
Typeset in 11.5/15.5 pt Berkeley LT by Midland Typesetters, Australia
QR code is a registered trademark of DENSO WAVE INCORPORATED

Printed and bound in Australia by Griffin Press, an accredited
ISO AS/NZ 14001 Environmental Management Systems printer.

A catalogue record for this
book is available from the
National Library of Australia

ISBN 978 1 76104 703 9

penguin.com.au

*We at Penguin Random House Australia acknowledge that Aboriginal and Torres Strait
Islander peoples are the first storytellers and Traditional Custodians of the land on which we
live and work. We honour Aboriginal and Torres Strait Islander peoples' continuous connection
to Country, waters, skies and communities. We celebrate Aboriginal and Torres Strait Islander
stories, traditions and living cultures; and we pay our respects to Elders past and present.*

Contents

To Raph, our Mountain Type

part one
What makes us click?

introduction

The awkward first date

Have you ever been on an awkward first date?

I have.

Did you marry the person you had an awkward first date with?

I did.

My husband and I had our first date at a pizza restaurant back in 2007. He is a chef and he had just opened his first restaurant a couple of months earlier. That week, he had worked over 80 hours. As you can imagine, he was very tired.

The first awkward moment happened when the food arrived. He had ordered a tomato dish and asked if I'd like to try some.

(In my head): *This is my chance to impress him! I'll demonstrate my extensive knowledge of food by throwing in the variety of tomato!*

Me (out loud): 'No thanks, I don't like *Roma* tomatoes.'

Him: 'That's okay, because these are *cherry* tomatoes.'

Me (mortified): 'Oh sure, I'd love some.'

At this point I had to eat the cherry tomatoes to demonstrate that it's only a certain species of tomato that I don't like.

Undeterred, I moved on to my next attempt to impress him. I started talking about my research in collective consciousness. Yes, you read that correctly – I thought it was a great idea for this social scientist to talk to a very tired person about my theories of relationships and group dynamics.

It started off with some meaningful nods.

Then, after about a minute, his eyes glazed over.

Then his blink rate went down.

I powered on, much like someone running with a stitch who's determined to cross some imaginary finish line.

A minute after that, he did the unthinkable (for a first date).

He looked down at his watch for at least 3 seconds – which is *ages* in this context – and then looked back up at me with an expression I couldn't read. But, let's be honest, that expression was probably a mixture of boredom, panic and a little bit of desperation.

I was shocked and also convinced at this point that there wouldn't be a second date (or any kind of future interaction). Specifically, my thought was: *I am never seeing this guy ever again.*

Mortified (again) and feeling defensive, I asked, 'Is there a problem?'

Yes, you read that right. I did ask that question, in the tone you probably guessed and with my arms crossed and eyebrows raised.

He took a (tired) breath. 'I really want to have this conversation with you . . .' he began.*

I sat there, bemused.

'. . . But I've been working all week and I'm really tired. I'd rather talk about it when I've got more energy.'

Me: 'Okay then, conversation police.' [Yes, I actually said that, still all guns firing]. 'What would you like to talk about instead?'

'Something light and easy,' he replied.

For most people, I'm sure this request would be straightforward. But if you've read this far, you've probably gathered that I'm a bit more intense than the average person, and so a request for 'light and easy' conversation actually put me on edge. I wasn't sure I could deliver. And also, you know when someone asks you not to do something, and then all you can think about is doing that particular thing?

Our mains hadn't even arrived yet!

---

* Author's note: this statement was a complete fabrication. He has never raised this topic again with me since that night and, several years later, when I asked him to read the **one-page summary** of my PhD, he finished the first paragraph and said, 'Do I have to read all of it?'

I thought we had completely clashed and dismissed any future romantic prospects, but the date recovered to the point where I offered to drive him home from the restaurant. It was a Sunday night in winter and there were no cabs around, and Uber wasn't invented yet. As I turned my car into his street, it dawned on me that we were going to have to do the awkward first date goodbye. I ran through the options in my mind. Do I leave the engine running or turn it off? If I leave it running, do I activate the handbrake? Do I leave my glasses on?

I settled for leaving the car running, with my foot on the brake. I left my glasses on.

I turned to him, expecting some form of 'I had a good time,' or 'Let's do this again,' or at the very least 'Thanks for the lift home!'

He leant over, kissed me on the cheek, said, 'Good night,' and then proceeded to get out of the car.

I reversed out of his driveway (after he was out of the car of course, I think) saying 'Oh my god. *So* awkward,' under my breath.

About thirty seconds later, as I drove down his street, still flushed from embarrassment, my phone started ringing. I saw his name on the caller ID.

'Oh no,' I thought with dread, 'He's left something in the car! I'm going to have to turn around and do the awkward goodbye all over again.'

'Hello?' I said, trying to sound casual.

'Was that really awkward?' he asked.

I burst out laughing. 'Yes! So awkward!'

That question changed everything.

We talked all the way as I drove home and saw each other two days later and two days after that, and again, and so on. We were married in 2011 and now have two sons and a dog. We are still married. The small emotional risk he took to make that phone call and ask that question has shaped our lives. The courage to connect asks us to take these emotional risks. Sometimes I wonder if we are still happily married because we started from such a low bar, with few to no expectations of one another. If it's not awkward, we're doing well!

I didn't know it at the time, but on that first date we were having a classic interaction between a Light Connection Type (that's me) and a Shapeshifter Connection Type (that's my husband). If you're new to my work, don't worry – this is not a science fiction book. With the Light/Shapeshifter reference I mean that we both have radically different ways of approaching human connection and this was a typical interaction between our types.

My way of bonding with someone is through intense, engaged, occasionally over-sharing conversations (you probably aren't surprised by this, and halfway through the introduction I'll bet you feel like you know me already). My husband prefers light and easy interactions over time as a way of establishing connection. Yes, okay 'normal people', I hear you saying, 'Doesn't everybody prefer that type of connection?' Actually, it turns out that there is no 'best way' to connect – only our way.

My husband builds closeness gradually, by being together and sharing enjoyable experiences over months and years, while I build closeness quickly by talking and sharing emotions. I'm looking for a union of hearts and minds in an hour. He's looking for fun and ease. What you will discover in this book is that, when it comes to connection, there is no right or wrong approach, only different paths and preferences. Both my husband and I have equally fulfilling relationships and connections with other people – we just have radically different ways of getting there.

In a nod to our first date story, he recently gave me a card that said, 'I love you from my head to-ma-toes'.

Click or clash: what does it mean?

Whether we click or clash with a person, group or place is one of *the* most important human experiences. It affects whether we ultimately thrive at school, university, work, sports, in community, love and in friendships. Identifying the people and the social environments that produce a click in us can guide our life decisions towards belonging and away from loneliness. Whenever we meet a new person, the first priority for our brain is to establish if they are a friend or an enemy, as well as whether we are going to experience belonging with them. We have evolved ways to read body language to work out if we are physically and psychologically safe in another person's presence.

I want you to imagine that we all have plugs (similar to electrical plugs) extending out from our heart, mind and gut constantly looking for connection with other people, places and groups. Once we plug into a connection source, we instantly experience an exchange of emotional energy.

When the exchange of energy is dull, we tend to simply acknowledge the lack of compatibility and politely avoid each other, with no hard feelings. We accept our differences and move on with our lives.

In negative exchanges of emotional energy we are gripped by the interaction – we feel offended or insulted or agitated.

When we experience a positive connection, it's as though our plug has found a match. It allows us to receive a nourishing flow of energy from another source; that source can be nature, another person, a group of people, or a sensory or contemplative experience like music, meditation or movement.

Sometimes connection can be stimulating but also toxic. We *need* to experience connection and belonging, so we will always choose malnourished connection over none at all, just as we do with food (when we're hungry we'll eat just about anything!). Examples of malnourished connection include mindless scrolling on a phone for extended periods, being mistreated in a relationship, smoking or drinking alcohol to numb pain, or gossiping with other people to feel connected to them.

This book is about the different types of clicks and the different types of clashes we all experience as we go about our lives – and why they happen.

What does it mean to 'click' with someone?

I know you know what it feels like, but just so we're on the same page: clicking with a person, group or place means that we feel instantly comfortable in that person's company or in that social environment. A click signifies a positive connection. This emotional energy feels safe and familiar, and we are at ease. Our brains produce neurotransmitters such as oxytocin, serotonin, dopamine and endorphins, which promote positive feelings like happiness and pleasure, while reducing anxiety and depression. When we click with a person or a place, we want to maximise the time we spend together.

We have phrases for when we click: we hit it off, we got along like a house on fire, we are kindred spirits, the time flew, we warmed to each other, we were on the same wavelength, we 'gelled', we took to each other, we had an instant rapport, we got on well, we were very compatible, or we had a lot in common. These phrases indicate that there is something welcome and familiar in our connection with a person or place; that they feel like home. When we click we find both comfort and joy in that environment – it produces a reaction in us that we enjoy. We click with a person or place when we experience belonging.

What does it mean to 'clash' with someone?

In contrast, clashing with someone means that we feel *lonely* in someone else's company. This isn't normally a word we associate with a personality clash but that's exactly what's happening. Loneliness is simply the absence of belonging – it's the gap between how we want to connect and how we are connecting. When we feel uncomfortable or agitated in someone's company, it's because their emotional energy feels unsafe, unfamiliar and unpredictable to us and we find it challenging to communicate with them. This simply means that we don't 'match' with them. We want to minimise the time we spend with this person or in this place. We can even clash with ourselves if we feel uncomfortable or lonely on our own. We can clash with a place or a group if we don't feel at ease or comfortable in that environment. When we feel lonely with another person or on our own, our brains suppress the activation of serotonin and dopamine, the pleasure chemicals. We have phrases for when we clash: we avoid them like the plague, we can't stand them, we fight like cats and dogs, we don't see eye to eye, all hell breaks loose, we have a war of words, and we agree to disagree. Like magnets that repel each other, a clash feels like an instant negative reaction.

Why do we click or clash?

To answer this question, we need to understand that compatibility can occur on different levels:

1. Instant click – we feel at ease
2. Intuitive click – we want to be friends
3. Intimate click – it becomes romantic

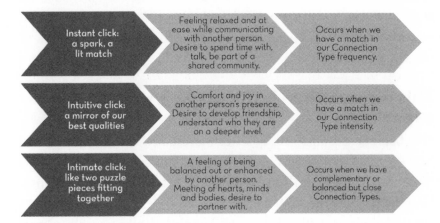

Clashes can also occur on different levels, which this book will explore:

1. Instant clash – the connection feels forced and unnatural
2. Intuitive clash – the person represents or worst qualities and gets under our skin
3. Intimate clash – the person triggers our trauma

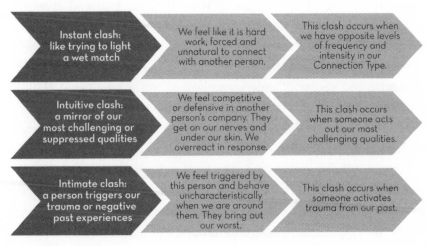

Human connection is an art and a science and this book presents my original models and research on how each of us attempts to achieve closeness and belonging. I want to help you understand every relationship you've ever had (or will ever have). As an academic who has worked in a university setting and as a consultant on culture and leadership, I am constantly exposed to the theory and the practice of human connection in my work. And like you, I am constantly exposed to the raw, messy and deeply emotional side of human connection in my personal life. I want to give you the tools and the strategies to process all of this.

This is more than just a book: it's an experience

This book is accompanied by a free personality assessment that will help you discover your Connection Type. You can access the assessment using the QR code inside the front cover or by going to https://bit.ly/connectiontype. Your Connection Type identifies how you relate and communicate with other people and the role you typically play in teams. It reveals your leadership style, how you experience belonging and loneliness, and how you communicate.

Once you have discovered your Connection Type, you can use the book to understand why you click or clash with other people, and who you are most compatible with. This process will help you identify those who bring out your best in friendship, in love and at work. When you understand *why* you click or clash with the people in your life, you will be able to identify the relationships and careers that best suit your Connection Type. You will have a narrative for your leadership style and you will understand how to avoid loneliness. Half of the value of the book comes from being able to understand yourself better, and the other half comes from being able to understand other people better.

I invite you to experience this book with your partner, friends and family. It will work best if they take the assessment as well, so you can compare your results. I have observed that, when groups of people develop a shared language around my model and as we view relationships through the prism of frequency and intensity of connection, everyone in the group benefits from the increased levels of awareness. I have seen this play out in intimate relationships, within families and in a variety of organisations – from mining to real estate companies, education to finance departments, and hospitals to corrective services.

As a social scientist, I've chosen to focus my work on relationships and human connection for this reason: because they are the number one predictor of physical and mental health.

Throughout my career I've seen how improving our connections with others can be the difference between:

- Intimate relationships that last and others that fall apart
- Close and engaged versus distant and detached families
- High-performing and struggling teams
- Successful leadership and absent or toxic leadership

Here is some feedback I've had from people working with the models:

- 'The model saved me twelve weeks of meetings.'
- 'You made sense of the issues in our relationship and gave us a shared language to deepen our connection.'
- 'I feel recalibrated.'
- 'I now know why I react so differently to my colleagues at work.'
- 'I thought something was wrong with me, but it's just my Connection Type.'
- 'You helped our team understand each other better and not take things personally. Our ways of working have improved.'
- 'I'm now looking through my history at every relationship I've had and every place I've worked and seeing it through the lens of my Connection Type.'

Not just another personality profile

'Of course,' I hear you say, 'I know about models like this – I've taken the DiSC profile and I know my Myers–Briggs type!' First of all,

I believe that *any* tool or model that helps to build our self-awareness is worthwhile. We can always take insights from personality profiles to enhance our connections with others. My philosophy is that there's enough room for everyone and I welcome the range of different approaches people use to profile personalities.

My model is different from assessments such as Myers–Briggs or the DiSC profile because it has a different objective. The aim of existing profiles is to reveal personality traits and tendencies in individuals. Additionally, the aim of psychometric tests is to assess intelligence, personality traits and aptitude for a particular context: for example, to ascertain whether an individual is a good fit for sales, law or banking.

The Ality Connection Type model takes a different approach. Instead of focusing on our personality traits, it focuses on the environment we need in order to experience belonging and avoid loneliness. It identifies the emotional habitat we need for mental, emotional and physical thriving. Most personality tests tell us about our strengths and aptitudes, whereas this model reveals the social settings we need to relate best to others. It uses the environment rather than the individual as its reference point. As far as I know, this is the first model to use this approach, allowing us to identify the optimal 'connection environment' for each individual.

Introducing the concept of emotional intensity to the Ality Connection Type model is also original and adds a powerful factor to our understanding of belonging and communication. The measurements of frequency and intensity of human connection are combined to identify your ideal role in relationships and teams, and as a leader. Once we understand the connection environments that bring out our best, we have our Connection Type. We can draw conclusions about how we behave in relationships and teams.

The research

After completing a PhD in group dynamics and collective consciousness in 2013 through the Australian National University, I founded my company Ality and developed original models of connection and motivation. Since 2018, thousands of people have taken the

assessments and, with their permission, my company Ality undertook research on 5000 people who had completed the AlityConnect
assessment between 2018 and 2021. My team collected anonymised
research data based on their responses. The tables below show the
demographics of the research sample:

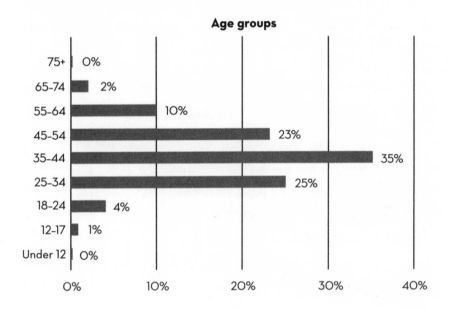

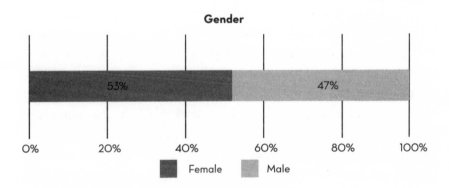

We had an option to select 'Other' from the Gender category. No one
from the research sample selected this, so the sample was 53 per cent
female and 47 per cent male.

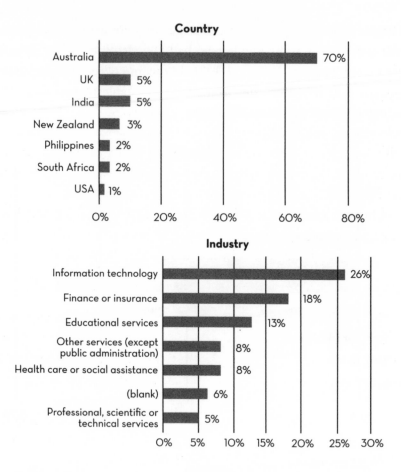

I have been able to draw some fascinating conclusions based on my research: for example, that men born before 1955 are more likely to be introverted and reserved (aka 'the strong silent type'), or that women in general are more likely to be high intensity and bond and connect through talking. Throughout *Click or Clash?*, I explore how these conclusions explain how we operate in the world: for example, how parents shape the Connection Type of their children and how leaders can use the Connection Type to bring out the best in their people.

Why this book?

I have had a lifelong interest in group dynamics. This fascination developed because I realised over time that the atmosphere of a room – whether it's a courtroom, a classroom or a dining room – often affected me in a more overpowering way than it affected many others. I used to absorb the emotional energy of the room like I was a sponge. I usually came away from other people feeling what they were feeling. Whether positive or negative, other people have always had a huge impact on my emotions. I used to think this was normal because I didn't have any other frame of reference. Just like when I needed glasses in my early twenties, it took me time to realise that everyone else could see something that I couldn't.

When it comes to human connection, it turns out that I don't have the same boundary that many people have between 'me' and 'we'. I have done a lot of emotional work to get a clear sense of where I end and where someone else begins, particularly in close relationships. This can feel like a blessing and a curse at the same time.

My experience of group dynamics used to feel as if I were a ball dropped into a pinball machine, as I bounced around when I was relating to people. It's taken me a lot of training, research, therapy and awareness to transform this into a skill and a science. It's been a long road to convert this experience of high sensitivity and being over-whelmed into a power and a strategy. And now I want to help you use these tools to transform your relationships, your family, your teams and organisations into flourishing ecosystems.

In 2018, I was contacted by the TEDx organisers of UNSW Sydney; the university where I worked as a senior lecturer. Did I want to give a TEDx talk? I still remember receiving the email. Let's go with the answer 'Yes!' I was on campus and just about to get some lunch. I went to the university cafe as though I was walking on air, grinning from ear to ear.

I was going to give a TEDx talk!

I thought to myself, *What will I talk about?* It had to be a culmina-tion of my life's work (yes, I know, a bit dramatic) and it had to be on the topic that I am most passionate about.

I arrived at the cafe feeling inspired and elated. After I ordered my lunch, the man behind the counter said to me, 'You look happy. Having a good day?'

'A very good day.' I beamed.

'Anything special happening?' he asked.

'I was just asked to give a TEDx talk!' I replied, unable to hold back the high intensity.

'What's that?' he asked.

'Oh,' I said, ever so slightly deflated, 'it's a conference where you talk for 18 minutes about an original topic and your speech is put on the internet.'

'That sounds great,' he replied. 'You must get paid a lot of money for that!'

'Oh,' I said, now officially deflated, 'you don't get paid for it.'

'Right,' he said, now just puzzled by my enthusiasm. 'Okay then, well, good luck with it.'

As I returned to my office, I silently berated myself for sharing my news with a stranger. *Why do I always do that? Why do I act as though everyone I meet is my best friend? And why do I care so much about a speech that I won't even get paid for?*

And then it dawned on me.

I had no boundaries. I couldn't even go out into the world without telling a stranger my life story.

Joke. I already knew that.

I realised in that moment that this was exactly the subject matter of my TEDx talk. I decided then and there to speak about how all of us connect differently.

> **We are all defined by how we connect:**
> **with ourselves, with place, with each other.**

I've had the privilege of speaking to over 100,000 people about human connection and culture over the last twenty years across all sectors and industries. My experience has consistently reaffirmed that belonging is our greatest psychological need, and that the core problems we face as people and as organisations are always connection problems: how we connect and what we value define us. The worries that keep us up at night are always about people and values. Even issues that don't seem on the surface to be about connection and values are nevertheless still about connection and values: money issues are linked to providing for others and affording a lifestyle to stay connected to the people around us; work issues are related to how we connect and what we value; even body-image issues are people issues because they are related to our social identity. Our greatest inspirations and greatest stressors therefore come down to two questions:

> **Where do I belong?**
> **What do I value?**

Some of the common questions I'm asked are:

- How do I stop taking the behaviour of other people personally?
- How do I stop absorbing the emotions of other people?
- How do I express empathy but avoid burnout?
- How do I integrate who I really am with who I have to be at work?
- How do I handle rejection or feeling left out?
- What do I do when someone at work undermines or excludes me?
- How do I lead in an authentic way?
- My partner and I fight all the time. Should we break up?
- Are emotions really contagious?
- How do I overcome social anxiety?
- How do I choose the right career for me?
- I want to move on in my career/relationship/life but I'm scared to change. What do I do?

All of these questions can be answered when we understand our Connection Type. Once you discover your Connection Type, it's my hope that you are able to:

1. Transform your relationships so that you can be yourself and no longer play roles to be loved and accepted by others

2. Stop taking the behaviour of other people personally as you realise that we are all acting out unconscious programs of our original attachment and bonding patterns
3. Accept the people you love for who they are and start connecting with them using radical acceptance and radical honesty.

Here's your quick guide to the book:

Part One – What makes us click? I begin with my story, the science of human connection and loneliness, and why belonging is the foundation of a happy life.

Part Two – Discover your Connection Type and connection environment. I then give the background to the Ality Connection Type model and its two measures: the frequency and the intensity of human connection. I'll also give you instructions on how to analyse your Connection Type results.

Part Three – The 17 Connection Types is where you'll read the reports about each type in the Ality Connection Type model. You will gain a deep understanding of your approach to connection and you will be able to compare this with those of your friends, family and co-workers.

Part Four – Who do you click or clash with? This part identifies which Connection Types you are compatible with and explains why we find some people more challenging to connect with than others. It explores the concept of instant, intuitive and intimate clicks and clashes and what to do when we experience them. It shares my research on harmonious romantic relationships and gives recommendations on choosing friends and intimate partners.

Let's get started. Understanding my Connection Type changed the course of my life and I can't wait to share it with you!

chapter 1

The gun story: connect as though your life depends on it

In April of 1997 my brother threw a party for his eighteenth birthday. I was fifteen. It was held in our family home and he'd invited about eighty people. Throughout the night, as the guests celebrated and danced, a few groups of gatecrashers arrived at the front gate, trying to get in. This was a common occurrence in the area we lived in. As we were close to the railway station, house parties like ours were targets for groups of teenage boys who caught the train up and down the line looking for somewhere to go on Friday and Saturday nights.

At approximately 10 pm someone came running into the house and shouted, 'There's a guy at the front gate with a gun!'

Mum grabbed the phone to call the police and my dad dashed up the driveway, with me close behind.

Outside the gate was a group of young men, all looking to be between sixteen and twenty years old – and all holding big sticks. The leader of the group had dark hair that was slick with gel and addressed my dad in a deliberately slow and threatening tone: 'Let us into the party.'

'No, go home, you're not invited,' Dad replied.

'Maybe this will change your mind,' the young man said, pulling a small gun out from his jumper pocket and aiming it at my dad's chest.

At that point, time slowed down for me, almost to a complete stop. The scene became very quiet as everyone waited to see what would happen.

Out of the stunned silence my intoxicated brother came charging up the driveway. 'He's bluffing!' he yelled. 'It's not a real gun! Let me out there!'

I silently gasped. Even though I had no idea of how to react to someone pointing a gun, I was sure that it was important to *not do* exactly what my brother was doing.

Along with some others I was able to restrain my brother and convince him to go back inside to the party.

I returned to stand next to Dad. I remember looking into the eyes of the guy on the other side of the gate and wondering how someone I had never met could potentially change my life in an irreversible and horrible way. I tried to connect with him, to read him and understand him, but he was locked on my dad in a cold and unfeeling stare.

The young man repeated, 'Let us into the party,' still pointing the gun at my dad's chest.

I wanted to laugh at the absurdity of the situation. Did he honestly think that my dad was going to open the gate and invite him in for a drink? 'Oh of course, now that you mention it, come in!' My mind reeled with a comical image of this person, armed with a gun, mingling with guests and raising a toast to my brother with champagne.

My dad replied in the calmest voice I had ever heard him use. 'Put that thing away. Don't do something stupid that you will regret for the rest of your life. The police are on their way; you're in enough trouble as it is.'

At this point, the young man's friends started pleading with him to leave. 'C'mon man, let's go, the cops will be here soon!'

I remember wondering, *Where are the police? Why can't I hear sirens?* My mum had dialled 000 as soon as we knew about the gun. We discovered later that the police had taken their time because they thought the young men were just another group of gatecrashers at a house party.

With one final scowl the young man said, 'You're lucky,' to my dad and lowered his gun. Then the group sprinted across the road back to the railway station.

On the surface, the behaviour of this man and his friends seems insane. Why would you come to a party that you aren't invited to and demand entry so violently?

But when we dig a bit deeper we realise that we all do crazy and irrational things to find connection (though this guy's behaviour was extreme). Have you ever called, messaged or emailed someone who is not interested in you multiple times in an effort to kickstart the relationship?

Oh, you haven't? Yeah me neither . . .*

Have you ever changed yourself in order to fit into a group or impress someone?

Well, I already know the answer to that one.

Have you ever been in love with someone or wanted to work for someone who didn't treat you very well?

Have you ever bought something you couldn't really afford or dressed differently in order to signal to a group of people that you are 'one of them'?

I repeat: we all do irrational things to find connection.

Psychologist Matthew Lieberman explains in his book *Social* that 'our need to connect is as fundamental as our need for food and water.'[1] The research on human connection demonstrates that relatedness is one of our greatest psychological needs.[2] As I explain to my two sons whenever they say that they *need* a biscuit, a need is something that will eventually kill you if you don't have it.

As belonging and relationships are a need, whether we realise it or not, we approach them with as much urgency as our drives to eat, drink and be housed. If I ask you to think about the significant mile-stones in your life, the story you tell will most likely be in terms of connection to others: your family, where you grew up, your education, your core relationships, your work and the places you have lived. We are defined by our relationships to other people, groups and places.

The gatecrashers at my brother's birthday weren't trying to connect with the people at the party. They were trying to connect with *each other*. When we are part of a group, we form a dynamic together and that

---

* Cue me looking away, raising eyebrows and whistling.

dynamic hardens like concrete. We all play our various roles within the group and we act out the patterns established by the group. Just as my friends and I go out for dinner these days and talk for hours, the gatecrashers achieved belonging with one another by causing trouble and trying to get into parties. Their sense of connection to each other was strengthened when they had these experiences together. Their group was acting out one of the most primal forms of connection in human evolution: us vs them. They were chasing the rush of connection and that high we all enjoy when we belong with other people. We reinforce belonging when we are in a group pursuing a common goal. Coming together in a group to fight or to unite against 'a perceived threat' is a strong motivator in social groups.[3] This is why we play or watch sport, gossip and consume sensationalised news media: we want to achieve belonging, even if it feels toxic.

We are all looking for ourselves in each other

As we go through life, we are looking to be witnessed, recognised and validated. Connecting with others is more powerful than just having someone to call at the end of the day or being part of a group that spends holidays together. It's not just about collaborating with colleagues or sharing a meal. It's much deeper than that and it's about survival – both physical and emotional. Such is our dependence on one another for safety and security that throughout human history, being socially isolated would inevitably lead to death. Recent research has been carried out on the effects of loneliness on our physical health, showing that a lack of human connection and social isolation can lead to ill-health, depression, addiction, antisocial behaviour and, in some cases, early death. A study from 2015 showed that loneliness and social isolation have more negative impacts on our health than obesity, smoking or substance abuse.[4]

I'm going to say that again.

> **Loneliness is worse for our health than smoking, obesity or substance abuse.**

I don't know about you but, when I was growing up, I learnt that smoking and substance abuse were bad for me. I also learnt that eating nutritious food was good for me. I never learnt about the powerful impacts of loneliness on my health and wellbeing, because the research didn't exist yet. A 2012 study showed that loneliness increases the risk for early death by 45 per cent and the chance of developing dementia in later life by 64 per cent.[5]

The flipside

On the flipside, there's a striking impact on our health and wellbeing when we have positive relationships. People with strong ties to family and friends have as much as a 50 per cent less risk of dying early than those with fewer social connections.[6] The benefits are enhanced when we *belong* to social groups, rather than simply engaging socially as individuals.[7] An analysis of data collected from a longitudinal survey of New Zealand residents showed that, when we make positive new social group connections right across our lifespans, we are less likely to develop depression (citing research from 2013), and group connections also create an enhanced sense of wellbeing during transitions such as retirement (2016) and university (2010).[8] Children who have regular family meals are more likely to perform better academically and be healthier, according to the National Center on Addiction and Substance Abuse at Columbia University (2005).

In 1998, 42 per cent of fifteen- and sixteen-year-olds in Iceland reported being drunk in the previous month, while 17 per cent had used cannabis and 23 per cent smoked every day. After some radical policy changes, these numbers have reduced dramatically. In 2016, only 5 per cent of fifteen- and sixteen-year-olds reported being drunk in the previous month, 7 per cent had used cannabis and only 3 per cent smoked every day.[9]

What caused these changes? After researchers analysed the problem and identified protective factors for the prevention of alcohol and substance abuse, a national program was introduced, called Youth in Iceland. The plan had four main elements:

1. **Family factors**: parents were educated about the importance of spending quantity time with their children (not just quality time). Parents were asked to sign an agreement to adopt the new regulations. Families and communities were mobilised to support the new program.

2. **Extracurricular activities and sports**: state funding was increased for organised sport, music, art, dance and other clubs (and some disadvantaged families were given leisure vouchers to pay for these activities).

3. **Peer group effect**: laws changed so that only those eighteen and over could purchase tobacco and only those twenty and over could purchase alcohol. Advertising for these products was banned. Children under sixteen were prohibited from being outside after 10 pm in winter and after midnight in summer.

4. **Evaluation**: the impact of these changes was accurately measured in annual surveys.[10] In short, Icelandic adolescents were given boundaries and healthy alternatives for how to spend their free time. The basis for these new structures was *human connection*.

The Harvard Study of Adult Development has been running since 1938 and currently has 1300 participants who tell us about the life cycle of health and happiness. What do you think is the sole predictor of health and happiness in our eighties? The quality of our social relationships. The people who fare the best are those who prioritise their relationships with family, friends and community. This is why I chose to focus on Connection Types, because, when we determine our types and how best to click with others, then we have the tools to elevate social engagement to social belonging.

There is now an abundance of research that links happiness to the quality of our social connections and relationships. Human beings are programmed for connection, which means that our brains are primarily designed for social interaction and relationships. We grow by observing and imitating each other. We relate through empathy. We have evolved based on safety in numbers. Being excluded or socially rejected has even been shown to activate the same part of our brain that processes physical pain. And, get this – these pain circuits are activated when we experience social rejection ourselves *and* when we experience social pain vicariously as an empathic response to someone else's pain.[11] Social exclusion or rejection sets off alarm bells in our brain, communicating that we are in danger.

It turns out that a sense of belonging is the juice that keeps us alive and vital. I think of a strong sense of belonging as being like the net underneath a tightrope walker, with life as the tightrope. If I were walking along a tightrope with no net, I wouldn't be walking; I would be clinging to the rope for dear life. With a strong net beneath me, I would walk tall and confidently, even perhaps taking risks, attempting to quicken my pace and having fun. Our relationships and community give us a sense of purpose in life. So, if we want to be happy and live well into our eighties (past the average life expectancy and beyond), it's actually more important for us to build community and strong relationships than anything else. Belonging to social groups where we feel secure and accepted is the number one thing we can do for our mental and physical health. What's more, it creates a positive feedback loop: the more connected we feel, the more we enjoy ourselves and love life, and then the more others want to be around us, too.

If you want to know how happy someone is, ask them how many social groups they are a part of that give them a positive sense of belonging. A social group can comprise a family, a relationship, a friendship group, a work team (this can literally just be having a job – you don't need to have friends at work, though this helps), a community organisation, a sporting club or a spiritual/faith-based community. My mother and mother-in-law are two of the happiest people I know. My mum still plays netball twice a week in her mid-sixties, is still married after forty years, has a coffee every morning with different people, walks with friends each week and has five children and eight grandchildren. Once a week my mum cooks dinner for her children and grandchildren – sometimes up to twenty people!

My mother-in-law also belongs to several social groups. Every week she sees a combination of her nursing friends, her high school friends, her golf friends, her card-playing friends and her art gallery friends.

She's also still married after forty-plus years and has four children and eight grandchildren.

Nourishing connection

The headline is that a sense of belonging promotes wellbeing and health across the entire life cycle:

- Children who belong are happier and do better at school. ·
- Teenagers who belong handle transitions better and are less likely to develop depression and addictions.
- Adults who belong have stronger mental health and are more likely to report strong life satisfaction.
- Older people who belong experience better physical health and attribute their happiness to their relationships.

'But!' I hear you saying (like so many of the people who attend my workshops), 'What if I spend a lot of time on my own? Does that mean I'm unhappy? Does that mean I should start socialising more, even if I don't want to?'

At this point I need to clarify that it's *loneliness* that is bad for us, and not simply being on our own. If you enjoy your own company and like spending time by yourself, that's not loneliness, that's *solitude*! Being alone and being lonely are very different experiences. For some people, being alone is lonely. For others, being alone is delightful. We each have our own emotional habitat that is unique to us – that's exactly what this book is about: discovering your emotional habitat, or Connection Type, as I call it.

Loneliness is a malnourished experience of connection. It's when there's a gap between expectation and reality, when your experience of connection does not meet your desire for connection. That's why we can feel lonely in a room full of people, or we can feel lonely sitting on the couch next to one other person. We can feel lonely when we haven't received a text we've been waiting for, or we can feel lonely when we're not invited to a party – loneliness results from any unfulfilled experience of connection. We can feel lonely whenever we have a connection desire that isn't met. You could be surrounded by a thousand people and feel a malnourished sense of connection. My research shows that we can even feel lonely if we want to be with a range of different people but are constantly with the same group of people. Or we can feel lonely if there's one particular person we want to spend quality, one-on-one time with, but they don't focus exclusively on us. Our connection needs are unique. Because we *need* to experience connection and belonging, we will choose malnourished connection over no connection, just as we will consume food that isn't nutritious if we are hungry. But these are false forms of connection – they might give us an initial rush like a sugar high, but they won't sustain us.

Connection money part one

Imagine that we all need to earn $100 of connection money by the end of every day in order to feel nourished. If you love being on your own, then time on your own will earn you connection money, such as an hour of pottering at home that gives you $20. But if you love being in the company of other people, then extended time on your own will deplete your connection money.

If you love connecting with people frequently, then you could even start earning connection money while you're grabbing your morning coffee. The other day I was placing my coffee order – a quarter-strength decaf latte (yes, yes, roll your eyes: I know it's just coffee-flavoured milk). The barista teased me about my order, as is his right. When he eventually handed me the coffee, it had 'Y Bother' written on the top of the cup. We laughed and this conversation earned me $5 of connection money. Then, as I was drinking my coffee, a friend called and we chatted for 10 minutes – that's another $10 of connection money. It was only 9 am and I had $15 of connection money! These incidental and unpredictable social interactions have more of a positive impact on us than we realise.[12]

Loneliness is the state of not earning enough connection money. Chronic loneliness is the state of consistently not earning enough connection money. When we are nourished by connection, we earn connection money, and, when we are drained by connection, we spend our connection money. One person can spend the whole weekend on their own and feel that their connection bank account is full, while another needs to cram their schedule with social activity after social activity. We all earn our connection money in different ways, just like we earn actual money in different ways.

Here's the thing: connection and belonging are *subjective experiences*. It's about the sense of belonging we feel in social relationships and groups. If I join a walking group and I always feel great after we walk together, then this is good for my health and longevity. But if I join a walking group that always leaves me feeling drained and annoyed afterwards, then this is not optimal for my sense of belonging, nor will it boost my health.

That's why we all respond differently to experiences of connection. Even two people at the same party have vastly different experiences. My husband tells me that he's ready to leave a party and what I hear is that I now have one hour to say goodbye to everyone in the room. I've learnt that he actually means he's ready to leave, as in walk out the door, immediately.

Two people in the same situation can respond as if they are on different planets. Recently I met two women at a conference. I was chatting to the first about whether or not we liked working from home. Amreeta told me she loved working from home because she could wake up an hour later than normal and go to the gym before starting. When she works from home she is always astounded by how productive she is, as she feels that she is in charge of her time. The sense of autonomy and accomplishment Amreeta feels from independently working from home earns her plenty of connection money.

Another woman, Marissa, joined the conversation at this point. 'We're just talking about how Amreeta likes working from home,' I said.

'Oh, I can't stand working from home!' exclaimed Marissa. 'I get so distracted when I'm on my own and my thoughts go out of control. By the end of the day when my family gets home, I'm so grumpy because I've just been in my head all day. It's such a relief to go back to work and see other people.' When 5 pm rolls round at Marissa's house, her connection money is depleted.

These were a typical Light type (Marissa) and Water type (Amreeta) connections. I marvelled at the difference between two people in their response to the same activity. It happens all the time as we react to people and events in unique ways. Connection compatibility is vital for our happiness. This doesn't just refer to compatibility between two people – it's our compatibility with our work, our lifestyle, our environment, where we live and how we set up our days.

Connection money part two

And even if you are ready to dismiss human connection as being touchy-feely and inconsequential despite the evidence, there are clear ways to measure its impact in numbers and actual dollars. Consider, for example:

- The builder who charges a 10 per cent margin instead of the standard 20 per cent because we get on so well, openly communicate and trust each other.
- The couple who stays married and therefore experiences the associated financial benefit of two financial contributions into one household.
- The friend who invites us to stay overnight when we are visiting, so we don't need to pay for accommodation.
- The person you phone at the internet provider who helps because we are kind and courteous, and who then restores our connection sooner, enabling us to work.
- The real estate agent going the extra mile to achieve a better sale price because we have established a positive connection.
- The work we might get from friends and family who want to recommend us, and the work we might get from strangers because of our positive reputation.
- The school that attracts higher enrolments because of the connection between the principal and parents.

Word-of-mouth can be translated as 'the effort you put into human connection'. You may not want to accept the emotional reasons for putting human connections first, but there are nevertheless concrete and quantitative reasons why it's logical and beneficial to make our relationships and communication our highest priority.

chapter 2

Four ways to belong, three ways to be lonely

In the early 1990s, evolutionary biologist Robert Dunbar declared that human beings are only capable of maintaining stable relationships with a maximum of 150 people.[13] This has become known as Dunbar's number. The theory is based on Dunbar's observations of a range of communities between 100 and 200 people from such diverse sources as hunter-gatherer societies, eleventh-century English villages, military units, online social networks, companies, government departments and even Christmas card lists.[14] According to Dunbar, we have five loved ones, ten close friends, and between thirty-five and fifty friends within the 150 meaningful contacts in our social network. These are 150 people characterised as people you would stop to say hello to if you passed them in the street or in a cafe. In addition, we have 500 people who are social acquaintances, and 1500 people we recognise and know the names of.[15] Dunbar's number explains not just the quantities but the types of relationships we can sustain.

It's important for us to experience belonging at each level Dunbar describes. We can't have 150 intimate partners, and we can't have 150 close friends. We need to have different experiences of belonging in order to have robust physical and mental health, as the following example demonstrates.

Hana's story of belonging

Hana moved from regional New South Wales to Sydney in 2021. It was always her dream to study at university in Sydney. Hana was temporarily renting a studio apartment near campus – her parents said they would help her with rent until the second semester when she was confident enough to move in with some fellow students. At the end of the first semester, instead of Hana making friends and moving out, Sydney was plunged into lockdown, which lasted for three months.

Hana felt very lonely. The campus shut down and she was studying alone in her studio apartment. Her grades started to suffer. She called her mother after one very long day and said that she was on the brink of failing her courses and that she wanted to give up her degree.

Hana's mother was devastated for her. She reminded Hana that it had always been her desire to study in Sydney. She urged her to stay until the end of the year. Hana agreed to see out the year, and passed the time by numbing her loneliness with a combination of bingeing TV series, scrolling through social media and drinking more alcohol than usual.

When lockdown ended, Hana's mother suggested that she join the campus gym. Feeling very unmotivated, Hana reluctantly went along to an exercise class. The first time she attended a class, she felt her energy levels rise. The second time she attended a class, she felt positive and hopeful for the first time in months. At the third class, she recognised a girl from one of her courses in the first semester. Her name was Violet. At the end of the exercise class, nervous and heart racing, Hana decided to ask if Violet wanted to get a coffee. Violet enthusiastically agreed and they had an engaged and interesting conversation. It turned out Hana and Violet were studying the same degree. After a few more exercise classes and coffees, Violet invited Hana to join a study group she had formed with some students she knew from school. Hana felt better than she had in months.

Now, almost a year later, Hana is thriving at university. She has a handful of strong friendships with people studying her degree and has moved into an apartment with Violet and another friend near the beach. Hana has even started playing the guitar again, after her friends started taking her to see live bands. Hana's sense of belonging in her social group has changed all of the outcomes in her life and has transformed her mental and physical health.

As Hana's story demonstrates, we experience belonging in four key ways:

1. **Natural belonging to self and nature:** we experience this element of belonging when we feel a sense of solitude and ease in our own company, when we feel a sense of place in our environment, and when we commune with nature and animals.
2. **Belonging with others through intimacy and close relationships:** we experience this element of belonging with intimate partners, individual family members and close friends.
3. **Belonging to social groups:** we experience this element of belonging with close social connections – for example, groups of friends we socialise with regularly, and sports or work teams.
4. **Belonging to the world:** we experience this element of belonging as we go about our day-to-day encounters in our community. We might interact with social acquaintances, family friends, local businesses or online communities.

Belonging is the click we feel when a connection is easy, familiar and comfortable

What many people don't realise is that we can, and must strive to, experience a *click* in each different element of belonging:

1. We can click with ourselves, animals and nature (natural belonging).

2. We can click with other people in one-to-one relationships (belonging with others).
3. We can click in social groups (social belonging).
4. We can click in our community through day-to-day encounters and identification with teams, symbols and institutions (belonging in the world).

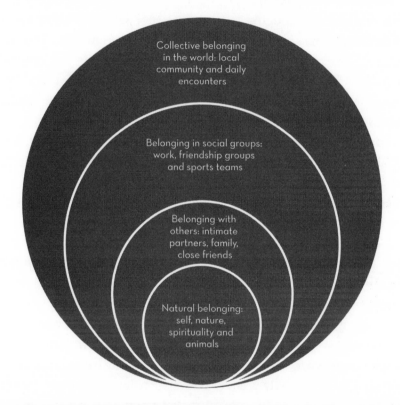

Collective belonging in the world: local community and daily encounters

Belonging in social groups: work, friendship groups and sports teams

Belonging with others: intimate partners, family, close friends

Natural belonging: self, nature, spirituality and animals

Belonging is so fundamental to our mental and physical health that if you are feeling flat or down, I suggest that you ask yourself these four questions:

- When was the last time I felt joy in silence and solitude, in nature or with animals?
- When was the last time I had a meaningful one-on-one connection with someone I care about, where I felt heard and understood?
- When was the last time I celebrated with a group of people, where I laughed, sang or danced?

- When was the last time I felt like I was part of something larger than myself, in a community of like-minded people?

These questions are linked to the four types of belonging, which I'll explain now.

1. Natural belonging

This element of belonging is the experience we have when we are connecting alone, in nature, spiritually or with animals. This is a uniquely personal experience that can feel inspiring and uplifting or profoundly lonely (or both). Growing up as one of five children, I never really experienced natural belonging as a key factor in my life, because I was always surrounded by people.

Until I learnt how to master it, time alone for me never felt comfortable because this wasn't a comfort zone when I was growing up. For me, time alone felt lonely, as if something was wrong. In the rare moments of it, uncomfortable feelings I'd been avoiding would rise to the surface. I would respond to time alone with a kneejerk reaction to see someone, call someone or organise a social activity. Without a clear sense of natural belonging, I started to identify myself through the eyes of other people – I existed because they made me real, or I was lovable because they loved me.

It wasn't until I moved out of home that I regularly spent a lot of time on my own, even though I was living in a share house with three other people. Then, when I started a relationship with my (now) husband, he worked *a lot* in the early years of our relationship, often from Tuesday morning to Sunday night, early in the morning until late at night. He only had Mondays off and I worked on a Monday. It was strange – I was in a relationship with someone in my city but it felt more like a long-distance connection because he was always at work.

This forced me to get comfortable with being in my own company, and eventually I learned to love it. I even remember the first time I went to see a movie on my own. It felt revolutionary. I saw *As It Is in Heaven*, and it was sublime. There was even a standing ovation in the cinema at the end of the film, something that has never happened before or since and it made it more profound that I was on my own.

In fact, being forced to spend time on my own at that point in my life is also one of the key reasons I completed a PhD. When you spend a lot of time on your own you become very clear about your passions and what you want out of life. Also, you have time to do what you might otherwise avoid doing!

I am increasingly experiencing the joy of natural belonging, when I am on my own in solitude, in nature or walking our dog. In fact, some of my happiest experiences are when I'm going on coastal walks, swimming alone in the ocean, riding my bike, exercising or writing. I love the practice of pouring a cup of tea and taking it to my desk as I work. I love the feeling of listening to my favourite music in the car. I now experience natural belonging through these simple rituals rather than through the eyes of other people.

Natural belonging is the foundation of every relationship we have. If we feel safe, content and inspired when we're on our own, then we will take this emotional tone to the rest of our connections. If we feel anxious, distracted and bored in our own company, then our connections with others will have a desperation or urgency to them. We will be unable to discern whether we are connecting with someone else because we want to be with them, or because we cannot be alone. This may also affect our capacity to work with others, as we can be tempted to ask our colleagues to work harder than necessary purely because we need distractions. Having a clear boundary between ourselves and others means that our sense of self doesn't rely on external value and approval.

Think of natural belonging as being like the backpack we might pack before we set out on a long journey. If we prepare well and stock up on useful items, we will feel more relaxed and confident about the journey. If our backpack is not filled with essential items, we will feel ill-equipped and unable to enjoy the ride.

The final point to make about natural belonging is that we don't have a lot of models for how to do it well. When we watch TV shows and movies, the scenes rarely portray a character alone and happy in their own company – there's not much drama in that! And when ordinary people do natural belonging well, it's rarely talked about or witnessed, because it's a private experience. What's more, the smart-phone age has meant that we now fill our natural connection time with mindless scrolling and browsing. We can now catch up with what someone has posted online without actually connecting with them. It's as though we've become addicted to being stimulated, so instead of spending nourishing time on our own, we're simply passing time with distractions. This has made us all deeply uncomfortable with being undistracted in the present moment. We have come to see such time as boring, or empty or stifling silence.

Research shows that the side effect of being constantly distracted is an inability to deeply focus when we want or need to. In fact, a 2017 study by the McCombs School of Business at the University of Texas at Austin found that the mere presence of our smartphone reduces our cognitive capacity.[16] In the study, participants were asked to complete a series of tests that required full concentration. The participants who had their phones in another room significantly outperformed those whose phones were face down and silent on the desk in front of them. Leaders therefore have the evidence base to encourage their people to work away from their phones. This also applies to school students who spend the school day with their phones in their pockets – even if they aren't allowed to use them. If we use our natural belonging time strategically, then this leads to greater creativity, productivity and overall wellbeing in other areas of our life. Other words for natural belonging include solitude, mind-fulness and conscious awareness.

Questions to ask about natural belonging

What feelings arise when I am on my own?
What experiences do I associate with being on my own?
When do I feel safe and content in my own company?
What do I like doing?
In what ways do I avoid my own company?
What are some negative practices or habits I engage in when I am on my own?
Do I feel nourished by my local area?

Take action

Natural belonging is most nourishing when it is intentional. The key is to become your own trusted adviser or friend. What's one thing you can do today or this week to nourish yourself during time alone? How can you connect with yourself in a way that reflects the person you have always wanted to be? And a good question to guide your daily actions: is this task taking me towards the person I want to be, or distracting me from it?

2. Belonging with others: close relationships

This second element of belonging refers to the one-on-one relationships we have with the people we love. Loved ones can be our intimate partners, our children, grandchildren, our parents, grandparents, brothers, sisters, family members like cousins, aunts or uncles, close friends and mentors. These are people we can be completely ourselves with, and are often characterised by close physical contact – such as cuddling your child or holding your partner's hand. Conversely, a negative experience of this type can feel painful – imagine having an argument with a loved one or feeling betrayed by someone you trust. The removal of one of our close relationships – for example through divorce or death – has a profound impact.

Frank's story of belonging

Frank is in his early seventies and his wife Joan died a year ago. He has been grief stricken and chronically lonely since Joan died, as his wife would typically make their social arrangements and initiate phone calls to family. Not only has he lost her love and companionship but he perceives that he has also lost his connection to his social network. Frank recently saw his doctor, who diagnosed him with depression. The doctor asked him if he had any other close family members. Frank replied that he had a son, John, but that he lived in another state. His doctor urged him to contact John. Feeling vulnerable, Frank called John that afternoon; John was overjoyed to hear from him. John showed him how to use FaceTime so they were able to see one another. Frank's two-year-old grandson, Hudson, was there too. Frank enjoyed seeing him and felt a bit better as he went to sleep that night.

The next day, John rang Frank and invited him to visit for an extended period. He said that they had a flat at the back of their house, set up with a bed, bathroom and kitchen.

Feeling like he had nothing to lose, Frank agreed to visit John and his family the following week. When Frank first arrived he took a few days to settle in as it was so shocking to be out of his comfort zone. John and his wife Kiara were kind but didn't realise how overwhelming it was for Frank to be away from home. It was like losing his wife all over again because he had never gone away without her.

After a couple of weeks, John said that Kiara was thinking about returning to work a couple of days a week. He asked Frank whether he would consider looking after Hudson on those days. Frank was anxious at the thought of it, since he certainly hadn't spent that long with John when he was Hudson's age! But again, he thought 'what do I have to lose?' He agreed, and started spending two days a week with Hudson. Frank started to enjoy the routine they developed together: go to the beach, go to the park, go to the shops, go home and rest.

During one of his days with Hudson, Frank ran into an old friend, Gus, who had moved to the city where John lived. Gus's wife had also recently died. Frank arranged to meet up with Gus and now they meet up each week to play cards or chess, or to go for a walk.

Frank is now thriving. John is thriving. Kiara is thriving. Hudson is thriving. While Frank can never replace Joan, he has chosen to focus on his other close relationships.

If we return to the image of us plugging into different sources of connection, losing someone we love feels like our plug has been yanked out from its source. Considering Frank's story, we can imagine his connection needs being mostly fulfilled by his wife – he had one giant plug connected to her heart. When Frank's wife died, it was as though his plug was cut off from connection entirely. While Frank can never replace his wife, he has restored his connection by plugging in to new sources: his son, his daughter-in-law, his grandson and his friend.

As per Dunbar's number, we generally have between five and fifteen family members and close friends with who we experience this type of belonging. When we are born we consciously experience attachment to others for the first time. These formative experiences of belonging to our primary caregivers create precedents for how we experience attachment *for the rest of our lives.*

When we have close relationships with people, we communicate with them regularly, by speaking, via text messages or in the exchange of emails. We might live with them or see them as often as we can. Their wellbeing is important to us and we care deeply about them.

When selecting people for close relationships, my research has shown that compatibility over time is less about chemistry or having things in common, and more about understanding and respecting someone's Connection Type, which is what I call our emotional habitat or emotional energy.

Our Connection Type refers to:

- How much time we need alone
- The social environments where we feel most comfortable, or most 'like ourselves'
- How often we want to go out
- How often we want to speak
- What we like to talk about
- How fast we speak
- How animated we are when we express ourselves
- How we bond

- How many different people and groups we want to socialise with on a regular basis
- How much time we want to spend with family
- How many friends we want to speak to, and see, each week

Understanding, respecting and honouring these aspects of a person is much more significant than a shared interest or hobby. This explains those relationships we have where, on the face of it, we have nothing in common (no shared interests, hobbies or habits) yet enjoy meaningful and rewarding affinity. When we find other people who are compatible with our Connection Type, this forms the basis of a close human connection.

Questions to ask about belonging with others

Can I be myself with this person or am I playing a role based on who they want me to be?

Is this relationship equal in power?

Is this relationship based on trust and respect?

Is this person's connection consistent, or does their connection fluctuate from hot to cold?

Are we both equally committed to each other?

Do we both feel appreciated in this relationship?

Is the relationship enjoyable?

Take action

Belonging in close relationships requires mutual trust and respect. The most successful friendships and intimate relationships are those where both individuals contribute an equal amount of effort to the relationship. This doesn't have to be the same type of effort: one person might initiate phone calls and meeting up, whereas the other person might be thoughtful in other ways, such as always remembering birthdays or actively listening. Consider these two questions to help guide your relationships: is this connection taking me towards the person I want to be, or away from it? Does this person bring me comfort and joy?

3. Belonging in social groups

Belonging in groups refers to the positive experience of being with others in various social contexts, such as our family of origin, extended family, our work colleagues and teams, our friendship groups, a committee at our child's school, a book or walking club, a choir or a religious community. This type of belonging can be positioned on a spectrum from peak experiences of celebration to positive acceptance to social exclusion. Think of belonging as gaining momentum from natural belonging through to one-on-one belonging, and on to social belonging and then to collective belonging. There should be an upward groundswell – as we become more at ease in solitude, our experiences of being with others in groups is amplified. The feeling of being accepted and participating in celebratory rituals in groups boosts our physical and mental health. This is why social isolation is so damaging, as we see in the next story.

Joe's story of belonging

A few years ago, I had just finished a university lecture on social change when I was approached by one of my students. He said, 'Hi, I'm Joe. I've just come out of jail, and I need some help with my business.'

At first, I was confused. Had this person escaped from the jail that was approximately 5 kilometres away? I responded by asking, 'Are you a student enrolled at this university?'

He laughed. 'Yes, of course I am! I finished my sentence a month ago and this is my first lecture on campus. I am starting a business to help ex-inmates and I was wondering if you could help me.'

Trying to sound casual, I asked, 'How long were you in jail for?'

'Ten years,' Joe replied.

In my head I was quickly going through the *Crimes Act*,

trying to work out which crime would lead to that kind of sentence. I was silently hoping it wasn't for anything violent.

He obviously read my expression and said, 'For commercial drug supply.'

I was struck by his confidence and by the fact that he had openly shared his past.

'What's your business?' I asked.

'I want to help ex-inmates find employment after they leave jail. People think that inmates reoffend because they have no chance of being rehabilitated. It's actually because they can't find a job, they can't find anywhere to rent and they can't meet people because no one wants to have anything to do with an ex-offender. You talked about the rate of recidivism in your lecture: jail obviously doesn't work. I want to make a difference. I want to start a social enterprise.'

As Joe was talking I was reminded about the power of belonging to social groups. In ancient history, people who committed offences were punished by being sent into exile. This was considered to be a punishment worse than death, because a person was banished from the town or city and deprived of their social identity. I was reflecting on how offenders in our society are still treated this way once they finish their sentence because they are excluded from participating in social groups. This reinforces their identity as being outside acceptable society.

I was inspired by the fact that Joe wanted to help the people he had left behind and that he was looking for a way to address a complex social problem.

I told him that I would do my best to support him. I went back to my boss at the time, Professor Leanne Piggott, and shared the conversation. She had a brilliant idea to give Joe's social enterprise plan to social impact MBA students as a project they could work on. This paired Joe with clever business minds who advised him on how to grow. Joe has never looked back. He now has both a business (Confit) and a not-for-profit (Confit Pathways). I am proud to be on the board of the not-for-profit organisation. Through Confit Pathways, Joe has been awarded funding to run programs in juvenile justice centres. With the help of Professor Piggott, Professor Eileen Baldry and others at UNSW Sydney, Confit Pathways has also organised a scholarship for people to move from juvenile justice into university. Joe and I are now working together on a wider project to reimagine jail in our society.

The experience of ex-inmates who can't find work or accommodation is one extreme of being excluded from social groups, but we have all experienced the pain of being left out of a group or conversation at some point in our lives. Feeling a positive sense of belonging in social groups is one of the most beneficial experiences we can have in terms of our mental and physical health. If we get natural belonging right, positive social connections flow from there.

Questions to ask about belonging in social groups

Do I have positive one-on-one connections with a majority of people in the group?

Can I be myself in this group, or am I playing a role to fit in?

Does it feel joyful and effortless for me to be in this group?

Can this group be together in comfortable day-to-day conversation and in celebration?

Do we support each other through life's ups and downs, or is my participation in this group contingent upon me acting in a certain way?

Take action

We gravitate towards social groups that either reinforce our personal values, or represent who we want to become.

In the first case, we might join a sports team because it reinforces our value of strength and physical health, while a work team reinforces our desire to fulfil certain professional objectives. When our values are reinforced, the group represents the best parts of who we are.

We are instinctively drawn to these people because of the way they make us feel and the elements of our personality that they evoke. Joining a group of this kind is usually straightforward because we have a values match. The group members recognise themselves in us and we recognise ourselves in them.

In the second case, we participate in social groups with people who are a model of who we want to become. We want to be like the people in these groups because they represent who we might become if we were the best versions of ourselves. This can make this type of group membership complex, because we are aspiring to be like others in the group rather than enjoying *who we already are* when we are in the group. In his book *The Culture Code*, Daniel Coyle calls this behaviour 'status management', whereby we fit in to go along with the group and maintain our status as a group member, rather than trying to lead the group, impact change or take the group in a new direction.[17] Some status management is typical, especially when we are new to a group or in a professional context. When we are *constantly* engaging in status management, we don't experience comfort or celebration in a group because we are worried about maintaining our position.

The key is to find a group that reinforces our values but doesn't ask us to constantly play a role. This explains why natural belonging is the foundation of all other belonging, because when we honour ourselves, we come to groups with a different emotional energy. We come to groups with positivity and upbeat energy rather than insecurity. Others will treat us as we treat ourselves.

4. Collective belonging in the world

This type of belonging gives us a strong sense of identity within our local area, our city and our country. It plays an important role in reinforcing our sense of who we are, as we make meaning from where we live, where we spend leisure time and what we do on a daily basis.

We experience collective belonging through the day-to-day connections we have out in the world. We can experience this type of belonging with social acquaintances such as our child's teacher or a local barista. We can also experience this type of belonging with people we don't actually know beyond a regular friendly smile, such as the person serving us at the local supermarket or the stranger we cross paths with when we are out for a walk.

Examples of clicks in the world	Examples of clashes in the world
Smiling at a stranger	Ignoring a stranger walking past us
Happy small talk in a shop	Being ignored or dismissed in a shop
Being given way into another lane in traffic – and waving to say thanks	Letting someone drive before us, or someone cutting in front of us in traffic, and they don't acknowledge the gesture or wave to say thanks
Opening a door for someone or offering our seat on public transport	When someone pushes in front of us in a line
Volunteering for a not-for-profit or being part of a community group or faith-based community	Walking past a homeless person asking for help
Going to a school fundraiser or participating in a fun run	Deciding not to participate in our community
Cheering for a sports team ☺	Our sports team losing ☹

Collective belonging might involve chatting to someone who works in a shop or at the reception of your gym, or it could come from your connections to a like-minded network online. A positive collective connection can be when a stranger opens a door for us and we feel pleasantly surprised. Sometimes these small gestures can renew our faith in humanity. Recently, I was waiting in a car park as another car was preparing to reverse. The driver stopped reversing and got out of the car. They approached me so I lowered my window, not knowing what to expect. This delightful stranger said, 'Here, you can take my paid ticket. It's got another two hours on it.' This act of thoughtfulness and generosity put me on a high for the rest of the day. Another example of collective belonging to me happened recently. I was leaving an office building and a woman in front of me had her phone drop out of her bag. Of course I let her know and picked up her phone, like you would have done. This is collective belonging – the feeling that we all need to look after each other.

According to a series of studies in various parts of the world, positive collective connections (or engaging with people we don't know) are correlated with improved mental health and wellbeing.[18] We all felt the absence of collective belonging during COVID-19 lockdowns. This sense of the world becoming smaller and only being exposed to the people we know highlighted the importance of collective connections in our day-to-day lives and the key role they play.

Nicholas Epley is the John Templeton Keller Professor of Behavioral Science at the University of Chicago Booth School of Business. He researches social cognition, which is how we think about other people. Part of this work relates to how we interact with strangers. He has identified what he calls an 'anti-social paradox' whereby we consistently underestimate how much we enjoy talking to strangers. It's fascinating how we aren't very good at predicting what will make us happy. One guarantee from the research is that belonging and (positive) connection always makes us feel better.

Our sense of collective belonging also shapes our social identity in the world: we express ourselves to others through where we live, where we spend our time and the teams we support. I can see this as a parent – my children are shaping their identities through the state and national sports teams they follow and the area we live in. When we go overseas, we are defined by our national identity and this is another important aspect of belonging.

Questions to ask about collective belonging

How do I interact with my community?

Am I kind and considerate towards strangers?

Do I make an effort to make connections with people in my local community?

Do I feel like I am part of something greater than myself?

Do I support businesses and sports teams from my local area, or from an area that feels like home to me?

Am I proud to be from my area, city, country etc.?

Take action

As the research suggests, *community is immunity*. When we feel happy to live in our local area and we actively participate in local initiatives, our health thrives. I know I have said this about each aspect of belonging – because it's true – but this is our village! You can start by making an effort with the people you encounter in your local area. Small talk with strangers makes us feel good. Follow a local sports team or volunteer for a community group. Start with small steps. There's a local ocean swim near where I live and it's my goal this summer to join in.

Create your belonging circle

Our experiences of the four elements of belonging give us our belonging circle:

© The Ality Belonging Circle

You can fill in each section of this circle based on how fulfilled you feel in that area of connection. For example, if you love your friends and see them often, then you would fill in the Friends segment entirely. But if you would like your friendships to be more enriching or you would like to see your friends more, then perhaps you could fill in that segment to 50 or 60 per cent. When it comes to the Partner segment, if you are happy with your intimate partner or are happy without having a partner, then you could fill in that segment entirely. If you are unhappy in a relationship or looking for love, then you could fill that in partially, depending on your situation. Completing this activity can indicate the areas we need to focus on to improve our experience of belonging. Ideally, all of the parts of the wheel would be full, but it's normal for our senses of belonging to ebb and flow depending on what's going on in our lives.

The Belonging Circle also shows that our intimate partner is only one-eighth of our belonging needs. We often (unconsciously – and unrealistically!) expect our romantic partners to fill up our entire belonging circle instead of diversifying our sources of belonging. When we have multiple sources of belonging, we don't place pressure on one or two individuals to make us feel nourished.

Three ways to be lonely

Just as I have identified four different types of belonging (natural, close, social and collective), researchers have identified three different types of loneliness: intimate, relational and collective.[19] **Intimate loneliness** is the longing we feel for an intimate partner. This explains why someone can have a supportive family, a wonderful network of friends and a great job yet still feel 'lonely'. They are not lonely in general; they are lonely for a particular type of connection with an intimate partner. It's important to understand the different types of loneliness because it helps us makes sense of (and avoid judgement of) our feelings.

The second type of loneliness is **relational loneliness**, or craving quality friendships. These are the friendships that support us throughout our lives. The Nurses' Health Study from Harvard Medical School demonstrates the importance of friendships, particularly as we age.

It shows that strong friendships have a protective effect on women throughout our lives. The study found that 'Strong predictors of high functioning among older women were having close friends and relatives and presence of a confidante.'[20] The researchers concluded that not having close friends or a confidante has the equivalent health effect of heavy smoking or obesity. When we see it in these terms, it makes me think that cultivating friendships should be prescribed by doctors!

Therefore we experience relational loneliness when we are missing close friends and confidantes. As this type of loneliness has a detrimental impact on our health, it makes sense to seek out and nurture close friendships with as much vigour and motivation as we seek out financial security.

The third type of loneliness is **collective loneliness**: the drive we feel to establish a broader social network.[21] This is correlated with the sense of belonging we feel in social groups and equates to the experience of social and collective belonging. When I had my first baby, I experienced an overload of close human connections (with our baby, my husband and my mum). On the surface, I had all the emotional support I needed. And yet I also felt a strange sense of loneliness at the time, which I can now see was a mix of relational and collective loneliness. I missed connecting with my friends in the way that we used to, and I missed the collective belonging with people out in the world because I was spending so much more time at home.

This is why change and transition can feel lonely (and why we tend to avoid change), because our connections are so disrupted. The different types of belonging – and different types of loneliness – also explain why we have different modes of connecting with different groups of people. The most common issue I hear is people struggling with the transition between work and home, when we move from social/collective belonging to the close, one-on-one belonging. When we understand it from the perspective of different forms of belonging, we can make sense of the adjustment. It requires a different part of us, as though we are changing gears in a car. In the following chapter you'll see that belonging and human connection have more dimensions than we realise.

chapter 3

Connection creates
new worlds

I remember an experience I had on the school playground when I was six years old. Back then, my friends and I would play *Rainbow Brite* at lunchtime, based on the 1980s cartoon. This game was my suggestion – I absolutely loved the show. Being ~~bossy and controlling~~ a 'leader,' I assumed the role of Rainbow Brite and everyone else alternated between the various other parts. That's what I thought leadership looked like when I was six.[*]

But here's how life teaches you lessons.

One day I ran down to the playground, beaming with excitement and ready to play the role of Rainbow Brite. As I arrived on the scene, I realised that my 'friends' had started playing the game without me. Someone else was already playing Rainbow Brite.

MUTINY!

In my six-year-old brain, I actually had a moment of wondering how they even knew how to play the game without me in the lead role. After taking a breath (or more likely a series of short breaths), I walked over to my friends and made the following emotionally mature statement to the girl who had taken my place: 'You can't be Rainbow Brite, I'm Rainbow Brite!'

---

[*] Author's note: yes, I am mortified that I acted like this. But I'm a high-intensity connector so I've decided to share this embarrassing display of behaviour with the world.

Rightfully so, my friend turned around and said, 'You're not the only one who can get a turn of being Rainbow Brite. You can be the horse this time!'

It was like a slap in the face.

Feeling outraged, I very briefly considered finding a new group of friends. Then I realised that it was more important to me to keep the connection with my friends than it was for me to get what I wanted.

The connection *was* what I wanted.

Of course I surrendered. I played the role of the horse. And do know what? I still loved the game! And I also learnt my lesson, realising that a democracy is better than a dictatorship, even on the school playground. I also learnt a key lesson that would eventually shape my work: that groups and teams work best when we all take turns to lead. After that, we rotated the parts so that everyone regularly played the part of Rainbow Brite.

Now this might seem like an inconsequential playground story, but such encounters form the basis of how we learn to exist in the world through our connections with others. Even though I was six years old, I was learning at that moment to work with others, to collaborate and to surrender my desires for the greater good of the group. We take all of these identities into every group dynamic we participate in and constantly adapt who we are. We all have the capacity to change the way we belong and connect, because it starts with our mindset. True belonging involves everyone's participation and therefore flourishes when we invite others to bring all of who they are to the space. We need to see ourselves as being forever moulded by connection.

> **Our personalities are clay, and human connection shapes the people we become.**

I'm so passionate about the Connection Type model and its associated research that I now spend the majority of my time consulting to organisations about team dynamics and wellbeing. There are many examples I have encountered in this work of human connection shaping our reality. The sparks of belonging and connection dominate every house, workplace, school, community group and sports team around the world as we all strive to meet this vital psychological need. Human connection affects our choices – from the minor (who will I call?) – to large-scale political decisions (do we want free trade with this country?). It's at the core of our life. Here are some examples of the far-reaching effects of human connection.

Example 1: the meeting

It's a rainy afternoon in winter. Twenty executives are filing into a boardroom for an advisory group meeting. It's held on the twentieth floor of a building in the centre of the city. The table is sparkling with polished oak veneer and water glasses. The attendees settle into their leather seats and arrange their belongings in front of them. Some make small talk as they come in, others throw their heads back as they laugh, and still others prefer to keep to themselves, fiddling with their bags or checking their phones. The dynamic of the meeting is set before the official business even begins.

If someone feels socially insecure before the meeting, this will affect their contribution; they will be more likely to engage in what social psychologists and behavioural economists call 'information cascades' and submit to groupthink in decision making. This means they will defer to others and go along with the rest of the group. If someone feels confident and connected before the meeting, they will be more likely to demonstrate positive leadership and communication. The way that companies are run can depend on our Connection Types and whether board members click or clash with others. This also happens in juries, where people overlook rational decision-making processes to go along with the group and avoid uncomfortable conversations.

Example 2: the graduation party

It's a Friday night and high school graduates start arriving at a house party, some in groups of two or four, some alone. One seventeen-year-old walks up the front path like he is looking for snipers in the front garden – his eyes dart around and he moves as quickly as possible, desperate to find a friend and make a connection, unable to deal with the social discomfort. A boy calls out to him as he walks towards the house. 'Hey man! I've been calling you!' The boy he is calling is seemingly oblivious and disappears into the house. The second boy feels rejected and humiliated, worried that other people saw him being ignored. This minor social rejection causes him to drink an excessive amount of alcohol at the party to numb his feelings. These micro experiences of disconnection can have a strong impact on our choices.

One girl smiles broadly as she walks up the front path, flanked by two of her friends. She greets everyone she sees with a radiant smile. One of her friends is shy and sheepish, unsure of where to look. The other looks straight ahead, and struts as though she is a model on a catwalk. In their adolescent social system, power is based on attractiveness, and they are the alphas. In any social system, the leader is always the alpha, as they have the highest rank in a hierarchy system. Therefore, the alpha is always the most representative of what the group values. Their embodiment of the group's highest value give them the highest rank. In this group of high school graduates, everyone values being desirable to others: belonging and acceptance are highly prized. These girls decide who is accepted and who is excluded. This gives them considerable power, even if it is toxic. This explains why some leaders wield toxic power, because they give themselves the power to decide who is in and who is out. They are arbiters of belonging.

Example 3: the kindergarten classroom

The kindergarten students are all giggling in the classroom. Their teacher is reading them a book with lots of jokes. They are delighted. When the teacher says the word 'bum,' some of the children cover their mouths while others let out their laugh like a balloon that has been released when it's full of air. One child stands up and does a silly dance, mimicking the character in the book. The teacher gives a wry smile and theatrically turns the page, relishing her audience. This teacher, with her playful and performance-based approach to teaching, doesn't realise the full impact she is having. She is teaching these children that learning is exciting and relational and offering them the gift of humour as a key to wellbeing. These children will absorb these lessons for life.

Example 4: the football game

The footballers huddle in the tunnel as they prepare to run out on to the field. Some are jogging on the spot, others have their eyes focused on the ground, and others are chatting and laughing nervously to while away the seconds. The voice on the loudspeaker announces their team. The captain starts clapping and rallying the troops. 'This is it. This is our game, our chance. Let's go!' The captain didn't need to speak here – he could have just lead his team out on to the field. But this is why he is the captain. He has just turned the team from a collection of individuals into a collective force. The team wins.

In every moment, in every part of the world, people are either harnessing or blocking the power of belonging and connection. And this power is what makes the world go around. Tiny gestures and micro communications like smiles, open body language and welcoming glances can have huge impacts.

Choices we make in relationships

Have you ever had a relationship that you just couldn't figure out?

Have you ever been on a relationship roller-coaster, or had a relationship that broke your heart, no matter how hard you tried to make it work?

Or have you ever felt the joy of love or friendship that you thought would never end, only to have it fade away with no explanation?

If you answered yes to any (or all) of these questions, then welcome to the human race! If you answered no to the questions above, then it's amazing that you can read this book under the age of two!

There are easy ways to improve our connection with other people, and there are also clear reasons why we are initially compatible with some people and not others. I deliberately say 'initially compatible' because it is my view that we can have fruitful experiences with most people over time, regardless of whether we click or clash at first.

Before I started my research in human connection and culture, I believed two key ideas about relationships:

> I believed that connection was a performance we did for other people to see whether we liked each other or not.
>
> AND
>
> I believed that our choices in connection - whether we tell the truth or not; whether we show who we are or keep ourselves hidden; or whether we say what's on our mind or stay silent - didn't really matter in the grand scheme of things. I thought whether we clicked with someone was a foregone conclusion based on our personalities.

Now I know that:

> Connection creates new worlds - when we connect with another person we create a new reality with them. It's not about whether we like them or whether they like us; it's about how it feels for us both to be in the connection.
>
> AND
>
> Our choices in connection matter: they can create a ripple effect throughout families, groups and organisations and change the world.

Through my research and experience, I came to realise that I did not understand the fundamentals of how connections work, even though I was making and using them every day. I wish I'd known everything I now know about Connection Types when I was younger and falling in love, choosing jobs and university courses and making friends for the first time. I would have saved so much time and energy if I had only known that flourishing in love or at work always comes down to our Connection Type. From a health perspective, we experience belonging when we click with people and we experience emotional stress when we clash with people. So, if clicking is so good for us and the key to our happiness and wellbeing, then the big question is: How do we click?

If you haven't already, take the assessment! You can access them by hovering your phone over the QR code on the inside cover of your book.

It's time to talk about who we click or clash with.

part two

Discover your Connection Type and connection environment

chapter 4

What's it like to connect with you?

What's it like to meet you, talk to you and love you? What's it like to work with you? Knowing the answers to these questions (and therefore understanding how other people see us) is called external self-awareness.[22] It's hard to achieve accurate external self-awareness because it's almost impossible to get a clear picture of how someone else really feels about us. Do our loved ones give us a realistic perspective, and if they do, is it just based on their mood on that day? Do likes and follows on social media offer any insight into what kind of people we are, or do they just reflect the image that we project? And if people don't like us, are they ever going to let us know?

To help with how complex we can all be, the Ality Connection Type model explains the roles we play and the emotional energy we carry when we're connecting in relationships and teams. Your Connection Type identifies the type of connection environment you need in order to experience belonging and avoid loneliness. Our connection environment relates to elements such as:

- How physically close we want to be in relation to others – for example, whether they are in the same room or in the same building.
- How many conversations we want to have on a daily basis.

- What we prefer to discuss during these conversations – whether it is impersonal topics such as the weather or deeply personal topics such as our life purpose.
- How long it takes for us to open up to someone or trust someone.
- How we respond when we feel vulnerable.
- Our greatest challenges.
- Whether we are likely to initiate discussions in a group.
- When we feel most supported in a group environment.
- The type of hand gestures we are comfortable using and how animated we are when we are communicating.

Understanding what we need from our environment allows us to make life decisions and plan activities that bring out our best. Once we know our optimal connection environment, we have our Connection Type.

The Ality Connection Type model offers insight into the circumstances we need in order to connect with other people and our preference for building belonging and relationships. The model reveals how we communicate and lead, and it gives us a shared language to explain our preferences. Identifying our preferred connection environment helps us draw conclusions about our emotional energy compared to other people, and make sense of the way people react to us. It allows us to read and lead the room (if we have the desire), so in this regard the model is an empathy tool. My vision is for people to use this model to understand work teams, sports teams, classrooms, families and relationships.

The Ality Connection Types

Somewhere on the model that's printed on the inside front cover is your Connection Type. It's one of my favourite things in the world to sit down with someone and talk through their Connection Type and what it means for their relationships and career. You can see that the model has four quadrants with two axes that measure our social environment in two ways:

1. *Frequency of human connection* on the vertical axis: how much human connection you need and want, and therefore the amount of connection that brings you comfort and fulfilment.
2. *Intensity of human connection* on the horizontal axis: the type of connection and bonding you need and want, and therefore the connection that brings you joy and makes you feel alive.

These measures are then combined to identify an individual's ideal role in different social contexts, such as relationships and teams, and as a leader.

I want you to visualise that every connection you have is like standing at a foosball table with your hands on two levers. The two levers that you move are:

- Frequency: how much you talk, how fast you talk, and how much connection you need in order to thrive; and
- Intensity: your preferred topics of conversation, the nature of your hand gestures, the time it takes for you to open up to another person, the nature of your disclosures, the tendency you have to absorb the emotions of others and the way you process all of this emotional information.

Our frequency represents our appetite for connection; we feel comfort when this hunger is satisfied. Our intensity represents the type and temperature of connection that brings us joy and lightness when at an ideal level. These two levers characterise the social environment we need in order to experience belonging in the world.

In the Ality Connection Type model there are 17 Connection Types in total and each type is compatible with certain other types. In the model you will see the four main types across the four quadrants (Light, Water, Green and Earth), as well as five Boundary Types: Dawn, Coral, Garden and Mountain, with the Shapeshifter at the centre of the model. You can take this assessment for free (accessible by scanning the QR code printed on the inside cover) to discover your Connection Type.

The types on the right-hand side of the model are all considered to be high intensity in the way they connect. This means that they seek out dynamic and outwardly expressive environments and, as such, I've given them names from parts of nature that are also dynamic and outwardly expressive, such as Spark, Sunlight and Ocean. These types rise and fall and have evident cycles, like the Dawn breaking and the Stars appearing at night. A Spark will flare and provide beauty like a candle and then fade until it is 'reignited' by a fulfilling connection.

In contrast, the types on the left-hand side of the model are low intensity. This means that they seek out more consistent, predictable and inward processing environments. For example Garden, Tree and Earth types are all alive but they thrive below the surface. To the naked eye their connection is hidden but predictable.

The following chapters explore the two core concepts of frequency and intensity so that you can understand the basis of your Connection Type.

chapter 5

Frequency: how often do you like to connect?

Our frequency score identifies whether we prefer environments that are low frequency, mid-frequency or high frequency in terms of human connection. It therefore describes how often we prefer to be near and talk to others – our connection frequency refers to how *often* we like to be in the company of other people (i.e. all the time, often, some of the time, rarely or never). It measures our appetite for human connection.

Frequency has the following components:

1. How often we want to be in **proximity** to other people – for example, in a house, office or café with people near us but not talking.
2. How often we want to be **in conversation** with other people.
3. How often we like to **contribute to conversations**.
4. How **quickly we speak** during conversations i.e. the pace of our speech.

A low-frequency result indicates a preference to be on our own (or in our own world) for more than twelve hours of the day. A low-frequency connector could be a piano player or a swimmer, happy to practise their craft for six or more hours each day. Or it could be a lawyer who finds fulfilment in working for a minimum of twelve hours a day on their own. The connection needs of a person with the lowest frequency score (close to minus 100) on the Ality Connection Type model will be met by non-human sources such as independent work, animals, nature, fishing, gardening, puzzles and crosswords, musical instruments, reflection, books, music, TV and tech devices.

A mid-frequency result means that you prefer a balance of time with others and time alone. Think of a primary school teacher who is on their feet and actively connecting for at least six to eight hours a day and then goes to the gym after work, and then comes home to quiet. A score close to the middle (around 0) means that you prefer to connect with other people 50 per cent of the time and retreat into solitude the remainder of the time.

High frequency means that you prefer to spend more than twelve hours a day with other people. Picture someone who works in sales who spends a lot of their day talking and then goes to a cocktail party in the evening, or an event planner who is social and animated for most of their day and into the night. A person with a very high frequency score (close to 100) will seek out human connection – face-to-face, over the phone or via email or text – in most of their waking moments. Of course, our connection frequency will not be the same every day. It will wax and wane with our energy levels, but there will be a consistent pattern over time of introversion or extraversion. Ask yourself: when do I feel most 'at home,' or most like myself? What do I look forward to: spending time alone or spending time socialising? Do I feel most like myself when I am on my own or with others, or does it vary? If I could design a perfect weekend, what would it involve: more than 50 per cent alone, or more than 50 per cent with others?

There is no wrong or right, or good or bad frequency. It is simply your preference. By a certain age, we are usually familiar with how much connection we want. This connection model gives insight into exactly where you are located on the introversion–extraversion scale.

In the following three sections I break down the major characteristics of high-frequency, mid-frequency and low-frequency individuals.

High-frequency connection

Take a look at the model printed on the inside cover of the book. All the types above the horizontal line are considered to thrive in high-frequency environments: that's Meeting Place, Foundation, Rock, Mountain, Spark, Star and Sunlight types. These types are re-fuelled by human connection and feel *most like themselves* when they are in the company of others. They thrive when they can move across a range of relationships and feel a strong sense of belonging when they are part of different groups. This can be a strength as not everybody can comfortably juggle multiple connections at once. People who seek out high-frequency environments are known as extraverts.

High-frequency types are most comfortable when more than 50 per cent of their time is devoted to positive human connection, which means that socialising, collaborative work and active family connections are more natural (and therefore easier) for them than for low-frequency connectors. The flipside of this is a point of vulnerability for the high-frequency type. If an individual isn't aware of the frequency preferences of people around them, they can feel hurt when a loved one, friend or colleague prefers less time together. In close relationships, it is particularly important that high-frequency types know to not take it personally when others need to retreat. It's not about you; it's about their comfort zone of connection.

Understanding this has the power to transform relationships between high- and lower-frequency connectors. Imagine if your closest friend only wanted to spend half the time together that you wanted, not because they don't love you, but because they're wired to seek out less connection than you. Imagine that they only wanted to share half the phone calls, texts, coffees, weekend trips or social events you wanted to. If you push these boundaries, your friend will feel overwhelmed and will need to retreat, even if you're completely oblivious and having the time of your life.

It is paramount for high-frequency connectors to respect the needs of people who have a smaller connection appetite. If they offer this respect, their low-frequency companion will return to the connection refreshed and renewed. They will feel grateful and understood, allowing the connection to thrive to new heights. On the other hand, forcing the connection will lead to the other person feeling resentful and defensive. Many high-frequency connectors have lost relationships or sabotaged opportunities for love only because they couldn't identify or understand the lower frequency needs of their loved ones and colleagues.

It is equally as important for the high-frequency connector to understand and acknowledge their own needs. Remember, high-frequency individuals are refuelled by human connection. They need to spend a lot of time with people to feel nourished. The best strategy to fulfil these needs (without overstepping others' boundaries) is to diversify their connections. High-frequency connectors should avoid investing all their time in just a few people. Instead, they should aim to have a friend on every corner! Then, when the low-frequency connectors in their lives need to withdraw, there are others to call on. By their nature, high-frequency people will usually have a large social network to tap into. If not, it won't take long to build up one as making new connections comes naturally. By contrast, low-frequency types like to keep their network more contained.

Mid-frequency connection

Flip to the inside cover of the book again and take a look at the model. With scores on the horizontal line, Garden, Shapeshifter and Dawn types are positioned at the middle of the frequency scale. In their ideal social environment, mid-frequency connectors spend around half of their time with people and the other half enjoying their own space. Mid-frequency connectors are also known as ambiverts because they have a balance of introversion and extraversion in their connection behaviour, which is usually a response to the demands of their environment rather than an active preference. Mid-frequency connectors need to set clear boundaries with others. Without boundaries, they risk falling off the tightrope between being refuelled by people and being drained by them.

A good starting point for mid-frequency connectors is to observe and note the signs when they feel out of balance. Understanding the emotional response associated with too much or too little connection is crucial for effectively managing time and communicating their needs to others. Some examples include:

- Feeling drained to the point that interacting with others is a major effort. This is a sign of too much connection.
- Feelings of restlessness, self-doubt and a sense of overthinking. These are signs of inadequate connection.

Mid-frequency connectors should practise, and get comfortable with, saying no. Being open and candid about our connection style and need to refuel will help to make saying no to people feel less personal. Finally, during those precious times in natural belonging, mid-frequency connectors must be intentional. They should take care to engage in pursuits that give them energy and avoid numbing behaviours, such as drinking too much, mindless scrolling or binge-watching TV. It is common for Garden, Shapeshifter and Dawn types to feel overwhelmed during unstructured time alone; the trap is to respond by doing things just to pass the time. Instead, mid-frequency connectors should take the time to understand exactly what they need to do in this time to feel re-energised. With clarity on this, they will find alone time becomes a fulfilling haven.

Low-frequency connection

When you look at the model on the inside front cover, you'll see low-frequency connectors or introverts located below the mid-line. They are Water (Elixir, Ripple Effect, Ocean), Green (Shades, Observer, Tree) and Coral types. With frequency scores below zero, these types primarily seek out social environments where they can be by themselves most of the time, only feeling the need to connect with others occasionally. At the beginning of this chapter I mentioned how low-frequency individuals feel most comfortable connecting with non-human sources. Note that this doesn't reflect a disinterest or lack of devotion to their loved ones; rather, it's just their way of refuelling and connecting with their emotional habitat.

Although low-frequency individuals shy away from large crowds and prefer a lighter social calendar, they can still be powerful per-formers and leaders. To perform well in these environments, however, relies on a diligent approach to downtime. Experiences that require high levels of confidence, or being outgoing or outspoken, must be matched with adequate downtime, away from other people. Low-frequency types use up a lot of their energy in these environments and so missing the personal time to recover is a sure path to burnout. Even when managing connections with only a few people, low-frequency connectors need the time and space to withdraw into their habitat (wherever that may be) to reflect and rejuvenate.

But let's be real: many connections in life cannot simply be turned off. Family, work, friends and our community may, at times, need constant effort and attention. Without open communication, this can be overwhelming for low-frequency types, especially if their loved ones are high frequency. Honest conversations about connection frequency help all parties understand that their differences are not personal; they are the result of having different appetites for connection. Be careful not to criticise those with higher frequency natures, for example by blurting out 'Do you ever stop talking?' or 'You are too much!' There is no 'correct' amount of frequency and we must respect everyone's preferences.

A small appetite for connection will also manifest itself in the size of a person's social network. Low-frequency connectors aren't interested in being friends with everybody. They are satisfied with a small and tight network. In their eyes, it's about quality over quantity.

chapter 6

Intensity: how do you bond?

The other day I was having a conversation with my sister and a friend. My sister and I were talking, and after a while my friend said, 'Okay, enough sharing.'

My sister and I laughed, immediately realising that our full disclosure and unfiltered conversation was making our friend uncomfortable.

It was too *intense*.

Intensity measures the style or nature of connection we like to experience in our social environment. It is the temperature of connection that we find most comfortable, and we turn the dial up or down depending on our preferences. On my first date with my husband, he asked if we could talk about 'Sunday night topics; something light and easy'. This request was a response to the intensity of the connection; it was his way of dialling down the intensity.

We might also try to dial up intensity when we ask questions of a person we've just met in order to find out more about them and go deeper. 'Where did you grow up?' 'What do you do?' These questions are designed to move from the impersonal into the personal. They are code for saying 'I want to know more about you. I want to understand you better. I want to know who you are.'

Intensity is a measure of our emotional transparency. It describes how openly we share our emotional energy with others, and also how readily we absorb the emotional energy of others. I compare low-intensity connectors to blockout curtains – they cannot be seen through and thus conceal what is inside. I compare high-intensity connectors to sheer curtains – they are transparent and reveal what is going on inside. It is my great hope that the language of low and high intensity can become as widely understood as the language of introversion and extraversion, in order to help people recognise and honour their emotional needs.

Low-intensity connectors	Mid-intensity connectors	High-intensity connectors
Reserved in communication; focus on consistency rather than intensity of connection; focus on actions over words	Chatty and friendly	Expressive and emotional
Prefer human connection to be based on shared, positive experiences over time rather than talking	Prefer human connection to be a combination of shared positive experience and entertaining, light-hearted conversation	Prefer human connection to be based on engaging and meaningful conversation
Closed body language, minimal hand gestures	Neutral, casual body language with hand gestures between the mid-line and the thighs	Demonstrative body language and hand gestures above the mid-line of the body
Slow to trust, build trust over years	Build trust over months	Build trust within weeks

We often give signals to others that their intensity is too high or too low for us. We might avert our gaze so we're not making eye contact or change the subject to move away from a high-intensity topic. Imagine a mother–daughter connection where the child is high intensity and wants to bond through deep conversations with their mother. A lower intensity mother might avoid, cut short or scroll through her phone during these conversations, thereby communicating to the child that her style of bonding creates discomfort and she should lower her intensity. This clash can be overcome by the mother understanding the needs of her daughter, and either allowing for more depth in conversations or, if this is too confronting for the mother, exposing the child to people on 'her wavelength' to enable these conversations to take place and honour the child's needs. The first step is always identifying our needs for belonging, and then being attuned to the needs of others.

When we measure the intensity of connection environments, we look at:

1. **Emotional energy, tone and topics of conversation.** Low-intensity connectors have closed body language and convey their emotions with less potency. High-intensity connectors are open in their communication and body language and convey their emotions vividly and potently. Low-, mid- and high-intensity connectors can communicate in a positive or negative tone, as per the table below.

Low-intensity connectors	Mid-intensity connectors	High-intensity connectors
Positive expression:	**Positive expression:**	**Positive expression:**
At ease	Friendly	Enthusiastic
Relaxed	Open	Excited
Peaceful	Smiling, chatty	Animated
Easygoing	Talkative	Very talkative
Good-humoured, smiling	Lighthearted	Grinning, laughing out loud
		Making jokes

Low-intensity connectors	Mid-intensity connectors	High-intensity connectors
Negative expression:	**Negative expression:**	**Negative expression:**
Withdrawn	Distracted	Aggressive or passive aggressive
Reserved	Disengaged	Hostile or sad
Downcast	Unfocused on the conversation	Antagonistic, cynical, sarcastic, negative
Aversive	Putting on a brave face	Abusive or self-doubting
Vulnerability as avoidance	Less talkative	Vulnerability as lashing out or blaming others
Apathetic: asking 'What's the point?'	Deflect questions or conversation	Provocative
Bored, disengaged		

Low-intensity connectors prefer social environments where they can bond through shared experience and develop trust gradually. As such, their conversations will usually be focused on public, less personal topics such as the weather, sport and day-to-day events. In contrast, high-intensity connectors bond through talking and sharing, so they prefer to discuss more personal topics such as emotional challenges, relationships, new ideas and vulnerability.

Remember: this comes down to preference. Mid-intensity connectors love having high-intensity conversations about low-intensity topics such as sport and politics, like a friend of mine who is an ex-professional athlete and a current professional coach. He said that when he was growing up, his family would engage in high-intensity conversations about sport. Of course, we can have high-intensity conversations about sport, politics and day-to-day events. It is the nature of the talking that determines the intensity of the connection.

Low-intensity types are reserved and unemotional in conversation, mid-intensity connectors are open and friendly in conversation, and high-intensity people value truth and connect by opening up about how they're feeling and hearing about how others are feeling. Low-intensity connectors consider these types of conversation to be overwhelming and potentially a violation of their emotional boundaries.

Questions to determine the intensity of a social environment include:

- Are you required to talk in order to fit in or act like everyone else?
- Do conversations have an emotional or personal tone?
- Are people talking about how they think and feel?
- Are people personally engaged with issues as they share their thoughts and feelings?
- Do you feel the connection in your body when you are in this environment i.e. is your heart rate elevated or are you pulsing with adrenaline?
- Are voices raised (in a negative connection) or animated (in a positive connection)?
- Are people using enthusiastic hand gestures?

If you answered yes to most of these questions, the social environment you are in is high intensity. If you answered no to most of these questions, the connection is low intensity. It's uncomfortable and leads to a clash when there is a mismatch in intensity: you might have one person with an animated voice, expressive language and hand gestures while the other person has a mild expression and their hands in their pockets. Neither person leaves that conversation feeling good about the connection.

2. **Bonding patterns.** Low-intensity types connect and bond by being together and sharing positive experiences over time. High-intensity types connect and bond by talking and sharing deep, emotional conversations. Mid-intensity connectors prefer a combination of talking and shared positive experience. A low-intensity connector might ask someone on a date that avoids conversation, for example, a movie or a concert, whereas a high-intensity connector will need to have conversations in order to bond. They will prefer dinner or a coffee.

3. **Disclosure:** how long it takes for you to open up. Low-intensity types are generally reserved and can take years to get to know (peeling back the layers of who they are and how they feel). High-intensity types are open books who can feel connected to others in under an hour of conversation. In the following three sections I break down the major characteristics of high-intensity, mid-intensity, and low-intensity individuals. In conversation, a high-intensity person will comfortably turn the dial up on enthusiastic conversation and hot topics and a low-intensity person will then respond by turning the dial down towards cooler, less confronting ones. Low-intensity types will often deflect high intensity with humour.

High-intensity connection

Do you ever feel like you're too much for people? Or that you feel more deeply than others you know? When you are a high-intensity connector, you have to do a lot of emotional work to filter your big emotions and make them acceptable to typical social interactions.

High-intensity people seek out deep and intense human connection. They will open up to others very quickly, ask big questions and be transparent about their mood and opinion – no matter the topic. For high-intensity types, their feelings fill them up to the point where they *need* to be expressed in some form. Without expression, their high-intensity thoughts and feelings start to feel like they are too much to handle, as though they might eventually cause an implosion.

High-intensity people can be high, mid- or low *frequency* (extroverts, ambiverts or introverts), and they're all located on the right-hand side of the Ality Connection Type model. Light and Dawn types seek out human connection to express their emotions in conversation and shared energy. Water types channel their emotions into time alone or with a few loved ones. High-intensity types feel deeply and channel these emotions into their relationships. They are highly attuned to their feelings and spend a lot of their time and energy thinking about other people; what they said, how they feel, why they behaved in a certain way, and what they might do next.

High-intensity people become frustrated when only mundane topics are being discussed and get impatient with too much small talk. A high-intensity type only begins to feel connected to people when there is a palpable and flowing discussion. This type of interaction energises those who seek out high-intensity emotion and makes them come alive.

In the same way that high-intensity types become immersed in a shared emotional experience, they also need to feel interested in the work they do. If high-intensity types do not enjoy their work or do not feel 'lit up' by a relationship, the lack of connection will affect them in a profound way. They won't just dislike a job; they will detest it. They won't just fall out of love with someone, they will find it unbearable to be with them. Certain moments affect them in a deep way, becoming all-consuming and life-defining.

Just as high-frequency types need to be aware of the needs of their low-frequency loved ones, so too do the high-intensity types need to appreciate that other personalities are less intense. The first step to honing this awareness is to learn the verbal and non-verbal cues of low-intensity connectors when they are engaged in a conversation:

Verbal cues	Non-verbal cues
Active contributions to the conversation	Smiling
	Nodding
Response words like 'yes' and 'oh really?' spoken in a genuine tone	Facial expressions
	Direct eye contact
Engaged sounds like 'mmm' and 'ah'	

The second step is to practise being adaptive. Instead of expecting others to connect deeply, high-intensity connectors should use their observation of verbal and non-verbal cues to dynamically dial down their intensity or pull in the reins completely if that's what the situation demands.

Mid-intensity connection

Mid-intensity connectors have excellent range and versatility in their interactions. They are found along the vertical line of the Ality Connection Type model, and lend themselves well to a variety of contexts, from busy workplaces to parties to one-on-ones. That said, mid-intensity types do have a threshold for highly intense emotional conversations. When crossed, the scales need to be rebalanced, often by a physical release such as exercise. Scores close to zero are mid-range for intensity, indicating the person is comfortable in most situations. They can move seamlessly from small talk to listening to deep thoughts and emotions all within one conversation. They can 'go there' and support another person with depth of emotion, but they usually don't initiate it.

The mid-intensity mode of connection blends the shared experience style of low-intensity types with the conversational and personal style of high-intensity types. This adaptability leads them to excel in team settings as they don't dwell on emotions but are perceptive and reflective on them when they arise. In turn, this builds resilience and the ability to separate one's self from the emotional intensity of others. They can happily chat to a stranger on a plane without feeling awkward or burdened. Equally, they can come home after an intense meeting, dinner, or party without over-analysing the dynamic. They enjoy human connection but don't get lost in it. That's a gift.

Low-intensity (consistency) connection

In contrast, a negative intensity score (between −1 and −100) indicates the person connects best simply by physically being in the company of others – conversation is not essential! Low-intensity types are located on the left-hand side of the model and they bond mostly through shared experience. If you prefer to focus on actions over words and value *consistency* rather than intensity of connection, then you are low intensity.

Less is more when it comes to conversations with low-intensity types. Preferring to bond through experience rather than interactions on a personal or emotional level, these people tend to engage with others and then move on, like a breeze blowing through a tree.

They are likely to experience discomfort in close interactions involving deeply personal or emotional topics. When feeling trapped in an overly intense interaction, they will signal their discomfort in obvious but subconscious ways: fidgeting, looking away, slouching, and curt and quiet dialogue. Or, if possible, they will physically move themselves away from the interaction. It's important for low-intensity connectors to be aware that people who are engaging with them in an intense way are usually just trying to connect, and are not trying to overwhelm, target or make them feel uncomfortable.

A common strategy for a low-intensity type to avoid discomfort is to steer the conversation back to more lighthearted topics such as current events or funny stories. However, it's important for low-intensity types to be mindful that, for someone who's being open and vulnerable, this behaviour can be perceived as cold, dismissive or impersonal. Such is the comfort trade-off between low-intensity and high-intensity types. Nevertheless, one strength of the low-intensity connector is that they don't dwell on social situations. They can go out and connect with people without wasting mental energy preparing for all possibilities beforehand and over-analysing their interactions after the fact. Even though low-intensity types don't tend to absorb the emotional energy of other people, there will come a time in their life when it is useful to have the tools and techniques to process their emotions. This emotional literacy – the capacity to read and understand one's own emotions and the emotions of others – is a valuable life skill.

chapter 7

Analysing your Connection Type result

Your current versus your preferred type

When you take the assessment, you will be given two dots on the model as your results. One dot is a red dot – this is how you are currently connecting. The other dot is a green dot – this is how you would prefer to be connecting. Your current and preferred type represent the types of connection that you move through in your current environment. I am often asked if we change our Connection Type throughout the day or week or when we are around different people. The answer is yes, but not always. Some people have their red and green dots in the same place, whereas some people have a significant gap between the two. The red dot (current connection) normally indicates the type of connection you bring to groups and out in the world, while the green dot (preferred connection) indicates the type of connection you bring to one-on-one trusted connections and natural belonging.

The distance between our current and preferred type indicates the extent of the change in how we connect as we move between our relationships. I call this distance between our current and preferred type our 'orbit'. So if you have your current type as a Foundation type and your preferred type is a Mountain type, this indicates that you move between Foundation and Mountain in your connections. This is your connection orbit. The gap between your red and green dots (between where you are currently connecting and how you would prefer to be connecting) indicates the extent to which you need to adapt to your environment. If your current and preferred types overlap then this means that your environment matches your needs for belonging, but if you have a large gap between your red and green dots, this means you are exerting a considerable amount of mental and emotional energy towards adapting to your environment. A gap between your current and preferred environments can create stress, because you are forcing yourself to connect in a way that doesn't feel natural, as per the examples below.

Click or clash at work

Case study 1: two company directors

I recently worked with two male company directors who completed the Ality Connection Type assessment. The results of the first director showed a large gap between his current type as an Earth (Rock type) connector (up in the top left of the model) and preferred Coral connector type (down on the bottom mid-line axis of the model). The second director's results gave a small gap between his current and preferred types – both as Star connector types.

When I was talking to the director with the large gap, he reflected that he 'has to be someone at work that isn't consistent with how I like to be outside of work. In my work arena, I'm not sure it's easy to change the way I act and remain successful. Maybe that's why I have high blood pressure.' This director experiences a clash and not a click with his work environment. Although he's highly successful, his needs for belonging are not met by his work environment: he has a clash with his work environment.

The other director has had a long career in the same industry and is in good health. He doesn't experience the same amount of stress. His preferences for connection are aligned with his day-to-day environment, so he is operating in his emotional habitat. This director experiences a click with his work environment. This is a clear reflection of how our belonging is linked to our physical and mental health.

Case study 2: a corporate team

When working with a corporate team, it is fascinating (and revealing!) for me to compare the position of everyone's current Connection Types to their preferred Connection Types.

In an assessment I conducted during the COVID-19 lockdowns, the team members were all working from home, which made it difficult to access their preferred high-frequency and high-intensity connection. Reviewing the results allowed managers to identify the individuals with the biggest gaps between current and preferred connections, and target their interventions in the culture to create more opportunities for team connection. One thing we've all learnt recently is that connecting online can never entirely replace face-to-face connection.

Where does our Connection Type come from?

Imagine that when we are born we are like a seed planted in the ground. This seed represents our core personality traits. It has been planted in particular environmental conditions that represent our family system and culture and influence how we grow. Over time it becomes impossible to separate the seed from the conditions it has been planted in, just like it becomes impossible to separate a person from the circumstances of their upbringing. How the seed grows and whether it flourishes is reliant on the ecosystem. The flower or tree it's grown into is no longer just a seed; it is a flourishing daffodil or a strong gum. Then the flower or the tree undergoes experiences in its ecosystem and environment: it might endure drought or flood, it might flourish in warm breezes and ample light. Just as we can never predict the conditions that a plant might live through, our personalities form over time in response to our family systems to the point where we cannot separate the person from their earliest environment.

This is what happens to us. We are all born with personality traits and raised in family systems (either genetic or adoptive) by primary caregivers who create a particular culture that further moulds our identity. We are then influenced additionally by our social environment as we grow up. Our raw personality traits are planted in our family system and then grown in our cultural environment. Just as a flower learns to grow towards the light or a tree might store water in its roots, we adapt to our family system.

Through the process of being a part of a family and cultural system, we don't necessarily learn our preferred Connection Type; we learn the optimal way to connect in order to receive positive feedback (i.e. love, respect, praise) from the people around us. We adapt our personalities to survive in our environment. We work out if our caregivers like to talk a lot about emotions or if they prefer us to process our feelings on our own. We learn if our caregivers like to connect by talking or by completing tasks together, such as cooking or swimming. We learn whether we get more love from being loud or quiet; opinionated or reserved; demonstrative or aloof. We develop preferences based on our environment and learn to manage our emotional energy. This is why it's critical to understand how you currently connect *and* how you would prefer to connect in an ideal world.

Assuming we were raised by more than one caregiver, my hypothesis is that our preferred Connection Type is found somewhere between where our primary caregivers are found on the Ality Connection Type model. Check it out with them!

Can we change our Connection Type?

Yes and no. Our Connection Type is set by the time we are approximately seven to ten years old and then adjusts gradually over time in response to different environments. For example, my research shows that our frequency declines as we age, which won't come as a surprise to anyone when you compare the amount of human connection you sought out as a child compared to the amount you seek as an adult. But it doesn't change as much as you'd think. We still stay within the same segment or type, we just move further down in frequency within that type. There are many people who are social butterflies in their eighties, just as there are some children who prefer ample time on their own. As a core part of our personality, our Connection Type is fixed through a combination of genetics and our earliest environment. To return to the seed analogy, a daffodil is never going to completely change into another type of plant, just as we never fundamentally change our nature.

Even though we don't radically change our Connection Type, I have worked with hundreds of people who have suffered an injury at work and as a result changed their approach to connection. This makes sense, as an unpredictable life event like an injury, illness or the death of a loved one can make us feel incredibly vulnerable and will change the type of social environment that we seek out. Just as a tree might lose its leaves or branches in a storm or a flower might be burnt in the sun, we adjust our connection to life experiences. However, my research shows that this change is temporary and that we can restore our Connection Type after a setback. On the surface it may seem that the person who was previously animated and social is now withdrawn and reserved; this is part of the healing process rather than a long-term change. I remember one particular session when I presented to a group of injured workers about their Connection Type. A beautiful lady came up to me at the end of the session and burst into tears, telling me, 'I used to be a Sunlight type and now I'm a Green Observer type. I used to go out all the time and be the life of the party. Now I can't even go to the shops without feeling uncomfortable.' This is a common story that I hear from people who have suffered an injury or debilitating illness, both massive life events that of course change the social environments we feel comfortable in. People who have experienced traumatic injuries or illnesses report this about connection:

- Not wanting to be a burden on their loved ones.
- Not wanting to 'bring anyone down' by talking about their pain.
- Not wanting to be identified with their injury.

To anyone currently feeling like you are 'not yourself' or not 'who you used to be,' please know that you will not feel this way forever. You have not changed irreversibly. I have worked with so many people who, through baby steps of belonging, connection and other steps to well-being, have healed their Connection Type back to where it was prior to their life event or adjusted it to a new preference. In some cases, they may not return to where they were because they get very clear on their preferred Connection Type through the process of healing.

The bottom line is: to a great extent our Connection Type, like our personality, is fixed through a combination of genetics and our early environment. But, also like our personality:

- It mellows over time.
- It is disrupted by major life events.
- It can be modified through a combination of conscious intention and action.

I have actively modified my high-intensity Connection Type to be closer to the middle since I developed the model. My family and I have moved to a different area that gives me a stronger con-nection to my environment and a greater sense of natural belonging. I have started working exclusively on my own business with a range of clients and I make conscious efforts to contribute to my commu-nity, particularly through my sons' school. This is all in the name of meeting my greatest psychological need: belonging. I want to help you discover and name your ultimate belonging and connection environ-ment because this can bring out the best version of your connection.

The comfort zone of connection: conclusions from the research

In the research study of 5000 people who completed the Ality Connection Type assessment between 2018 and 2021, my team identified the 'comfort zone' of human connection where a majority of people prefer to connect.

The majority of the red dots were concentrated close to the centre, with a skew towards the yellow zone. This indicates that most people prefer to connect in a mid-frequency, mid-intensity way with occasional bursts of high intensity, which was supported by the allocation of Connection Types, as the most common one was Shapeshifter, followed by Star and then Observer. Ocean and Earth were the least common.

If your type is close to the centre of the model, you have excellent range for connecting with others. If your type is on the periphery, you are an outlier when it comes to connecting with most people, but this gives you other strengths such as above-average visionary thinking, courage, empathy and grit.

There were some interesting findings about connection from the research study.

1. Males are statistically more likely to be Green, Earth and Garden types, while females are more likely to be Light, Water and Dawn types. People less than thirty-five-years old are more likely to be Water types. Older people (born before 1955) are more likely to be Green types. If you're between the ages of forty-five and fifty-five, you're more likely to be a Light type. These generational trends could be linked to the different experiences of education and parenting styles as they've changed over time. I go into this in more depth in the sections on each type.

2. In my work with teams across all industries, people consistently report that they prefer connecting in a small group of three to five people. This could represent another comfort zone of connection, whereby the group is small enough to manage the dynamic and create psychological safety, but large enough to provide some diversity of connection. There is compelling evidence to suggest that the most functional and highest performing teams are between three and five members strong. It could also help with family planning to know that an overwhelming majority of people prefer connecting in a small group.

I most prefer connecting:

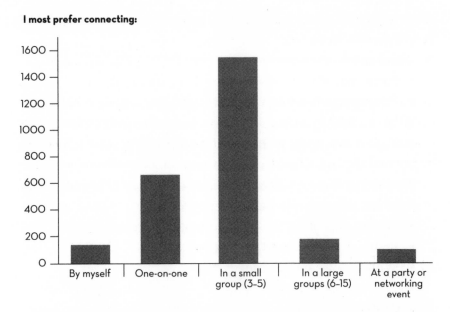

3. A majority of respondents prefer to talk to other people either some of the time or often, compared to those who are fulfilled by rare or occasional interactions. This finding can assist leaders to know that people want to be engaged in active connection at work for at least half the time. You can use this research to create a schedule for your team that involves half a day of meetings or face-to-face engagements, with the other half of the time dedicated to focused work.

4. Participants reported that they prefer to be around other people about half the time or often. This aligns with the research that a sense of belonging is linked to positive physical and mental health – being around people makes us stronger. Only a tiny minority reported that they like to be around other people as little as possible. This is interesting from the perspective of loneliness, because when we understand how often we like to be in the company of others (even without talking), we can create the social environments we need to experience belonging. This is a form of intimacy that we underestimate, the kind where simply having other people in the same house or apartment without feeling pressured to talk to them brings comfort. It is something that should

be built into policy making, with housing for students and older people. We thrive when we are close to others.

5. When people feel vulnerable or stressed, a majority reported:
   - Expressing their emotions to someone they trust.
   - Putting on a brave face and pretending everything is okay.

What is a healthy response to stress and vulnerability? We discovered from our research that we don't all have positive models for how to respond when we are on edge or experiencing pressure. Most respondents reported 'expressing emotions to someone they trust' but all other respondents reported:

- Putting on a brave face and pretending I am okay
- Distracting myself and finding an escape
- Withdrawing and shutting down
- Feeling flooded by emotion

A minority reported 'getting defensive and lashing out,' which indicates that there is a group of people who must feel very misunderstood when they are feeling vulnerable as their behaviour represents the opposite of what they are feeling. These antisocial responses to vulnerability may even lead to behaviours such as drug use and violence as a way to escape from emotional pain.

This section provided a background to the Ality Connection Types model and its associated research. I'm hoping you now feel comfortable with the concepts of frequency and intensity in shaping our sense of belonging and the connection environments we seek out. Now we're ready to dive in and learn all about the 17 Connection Types.

part three
The 17 Connection Types

It's now time to look closely at the 17 Ality Connection Types that form the model. As you read through this part of the book, you'll be able to recognise the behaviour of people you've loved, befriended, worked with and clashed with! And hopefully you'll be able to understand what makes them click.

You will now have the results of the Connection Type assessment you can access by hovering your phone over the QR code on the inside cover of the book. These results will tell you which Connection Type you are, but it's also worth learning about the others so you'll be best able to form meaningful relationships and communicate with the people around you.

This section covers the key characteristics, communication style, leadership styles and challenges for each Connection Type.

chapter 8

Light types:
Spark, Star and Sunlight

Characteristics	Tools to enhance relationships
High frequency: warm, social, extraverted	Learn to process your emotions before you seek out connection with others to avoid enmeshment and drama
High intensity: emotionally expressive; connect through talking	
Feel most like yourself when you are connecting with a wide range of other people and groups	Understand that natural belonging is the foundation of all other connections
Passionate and enthusiastic	Be curious and gentle with yourself instead of lashing out when you feel vulnerable: conflict doesn't have to be explosive and it's best to have some time to reflect before you engage in highly emotional communication
Light up, warm up or 'heat up' the room	
Changeable, dynamic and all-encompassing emotional energy	
Core values: truth and high energy	Collaborate; create opportunities for others to contribute
	Demonstrate active listening; don't just wait to talk or worry about how you are being perceived

Light types: characteristics

Light types have a preference for high-frequency and high-intensity human connection. You feel most comfortable when you are regularly connecting with other people and you want your connections with others to be based on meaningful and fulfilling conversations. You value honesty, authenticity, and high levels of energy in terms of verbal and body language when you're talking to people. You're looking for people to share who they are through talking, just as you are willing to share who you are.

Light types are named after bodies of light: sparks, stars and sunlight. This is because your emotional energy is warm and attention-grabbing. It also varies from day to day and over time, just as your Types do in real life: sparks flash before our eyes until they burn themselves out and need to be reignited; stars either light up the sky or are obscured by the clouds or the bright lights of cities; sunlight can be warm and inviting or overpowering and destructive. In the same way, Light types are extreme connectors who can both inspire and overpower.

Introducing the three Light types

1. Spark

When we see fireworks in the sky or a candle is lit, we are mesmerised for a moment as we admire the flickering light. Time is suspended as we lose ourselves in the colour and movement. In the same way, a Spark Connection Type brings warmth and delight to human connection. You lift others with your upbeat presence and you bring enthusiasm to a group. You are able to adapt your connection style to the people around you and have mastered the universal forms of connection: storytelling, good humour, laughter and humility. The Spark type is closest to the centre so the 'light' qualities are less pronounced than the Star and Sunlight types who are more extreme and further from the centre.

2. Star

For thousands of years, people have looked to the night sky for inspiration and navigation. In the same way, Star connectors provide inspiration and navigation for groups. Your Connection Type shows the way to others and you command influence wherever you go through your confident and seemingly effortless social nature. At your best, you are animated without being overbearing and you make others feel seen. You are a captivating performer, taking your X factor with you wherever you go.

3. Sunlight

Sunlight can light up, warm up or heat up, and Sunlight types have all of this potential as a powerful force in any group. You are a tone setter and a truth teller. At your best, you are a fearless leader of a group with the capacity for visionary thinking. Your Connection Type lends itself to being fired up or on fire. You light the way for others when you are able to convert your intensity into vision.

Light types: communication style

Light types are expressive and enthusiastic communicators. You are eager to talk and share your ideas. You can lose track of time and even lose track of the topic that started the conversation. Your conversation naturally takes many tangents and your energy grows as the connection continues. You enjoy talking with others and your hand gestures and facial expressions are animated. You are at ease in the company of other people.

Light types do not enjoy focusing on minor details in conversations. You prefer focusing on the big picture (the view from the sky). You will feel constrained by a co-worker or a partner who only wants to talk about precise details of quarterly reporting and project plans. You don't seek out activities like keeping records and collating data as it lacks human connection. Of course, you may be able to engage in such pursuits; it's just not your preferred mode of connection.

Light types: leadership style

Light types lead by focusing on vision and strategy. The Light type believes that people do their best work when they feel inspired and energised. You motivate people with your enthusiasm and passion.

You carve out a path and encourage people to join you. You prioritise forward momentum and 'shining a light' on the team and/or organisation. Your approach is characterised by lighting people up.

You are usually generous of spirit and will spend time building relationships with your family or team. You also identify with the collective and/or organisation, so the family's success will be your success and the team's success will be your success. While Light leaders are generally good at managing up and down, you do have to work on peer-to-peer collaboration because this will create a culture of leadership across the organisation. This means that you may need to sacrifice some of your vision or strategy to work more effectively with your equals (or managers of other teams) rather than defending your strategy.

Light types are commonly among the leaders of big organisations, because you are often the most confident or most enthusiastic in the room. You naturally seek out human connection so you are comfortable with assuming leadership positions. You are ideas-oriented and come up with creative solutions to problems. At your best, you are able to integrate the contributions of everyone in the room and turn them into a cohesive narrative. You are sparked by change and innovation.

The shadow side of this approach to leadership is that the Light type runs the risk of leaving people behind. Not everyone enjoys constant communication, change and innovation. Not everyone is inspired by big ideas. Some people may find your approach exhausting. People whose types clash with Light types may find this leadership style overbearing or interfering. Light leaders can occasionally lead people to burn out if the team is not motivated in the same way.

The Light type may also be inclined to shine a light and walk an inspired path without first consulting with the rest of the group. This can convey a sense of egotism but this isn't necessarily the case – it's generally that Light types are so excited about the plan that you can't wait to get started. Light types can enhance leadership by building consultation with everyone in the team into your planning, as well as prioritising one-on-one connections with everyone on the team, not just the other high-intensity types who you automatically click with. Make sure you use feedback as coaching opportunities – the interpersonal connections produced by your leadership are a more important metric than the short-term performance of your team.

Light types: challenges
Enmeshment and outward processing

Being high frequency and high intensity doesn't feel like a choice or preference for Light types, who seek out human connection as a form of emotional release. You are the labradors of human connection: social, animated and excitable. Extraversion is a necessity for you, a form of emotional oxygen. This is a blessing and a curse for Light types, because people are simultaneously your strength and your vulnerability. This can become problematic when you use other people to process your feelings, instead of taking the time to process emotions on your own before you connect with other people.

In her book *All About Love: New Visions*, author bell hooks writes:

> Many of us seek community solely to escape the fear of being alone. Knowing how to be solitary is central to the art of loving. When we can be alone, we can be with others without using them as a means of escape.[23]

When you use human connection as a substitute for your own emotional processing, you can blur the line between you and others. Your emotional experience becomes enmeshed with theirs and you can't differentiate between their story and yours. This contributes to burnout and co-dependent relationships because you accrue the residue from other peoples' emotions in your mind, and no doubt they accrue residue from your emotions as well. Over time this builds up and overloads the connection, like an electrical fuse that is being used by too many power points. The outcome is that you burn out relationships and feel the need to end them instead of taking time to process and returning to the connection in a sustainable way.

Enmeshment also leads to drama when you process your emotions through other people, because this can be volatile and unpredictable:

we tend to overshare and be overshared with. We don't know which emotions are going to arise during connection (for us or for other people) and the resulting roller-coaster of connection turns into a kind of thrill: 'What will happen? What mood will they be in? How will I feel after seeing them?' Connection hinges on the capacity of both parties to share their emotions in a raw and no-holds-barred way, and as such, connection that is low intensity becomes 'boring' for the Light type.

Emotional burnout

As enthusiastic human connectors, Light types often seek out opportunities to connect, even when you don't have the time or energy. As a result, emotional burnout is a cyclical issue for Lights. You will often choose human connection even when you are tired and overworked. This desire to connect needs to be balanced with self-care and Light types need a clear sense of their priorities each day i.e. do I need to go for a coffee or clean my house? Do I need to stay at this party even though I'm exhausted and have to work tomorrow? Do I need to say yes to a new project with a team I love even though I'm struggling to finish my existing projects? The answers to these questions will vary from day to day and week to week, but learning to say no will reap benefits for a Light type's energy levels and sense of accomplishment. It's important to remember that you will enjoy human connections so much more if they are curated, meaning that you are intentional about where and when you connect with others. Connecting for the sake of being with someone else when you are both tired and busy is often unfulfilling. Experience and trial and error will teach you to self-regulate and when to choose rest over connection. NB: I'm writing this from experience as a Light type because it has taken me years of choosing connection over rest to realise that it doesn't bring out the best in me! A useful question for Light types to ask themselves is: how would I love to feel at the end of the day? This shifts our focus so that we say yes to the right things.

Listening and inclusion

Light types must be careful to practise active listening when others are speaking. Interrupting is tempting when you are enthusiastic, with so much to say, but you will become a more adept human connector if you learn to listen without just waiting for a lull when you can speak next. Giving someone our unconditional and undivided presence is the greatest gift we can give.

Your confidence in your humour and your self-assured communication style can occasionally come across as being dominant to lower frequency connectors like Green or Water types. What you may think is amusing may actually offend others. When you are too comfortable in a group, you can become complacent with your leadership role and take advantage of it. This is a powerful lesson for Lights, who often play leadership roles in groups. For this reason, your core challenge is to model inclusion and compassion for all Connection Types, and to not leave anyone in the shadows. You need to respect that other people are different from you. Just because someone is not speaking doesn't mean they have nothing to say.

Conflict

As you are a high-intensity connector, your approach to conflict is also likely to be high intensity and highly verbal. You often say things or act in ways you don't mean and then regret it later. Some people might perceive your manner to be aggressive or argumentative when from your perspective you were just having an interesting, robust and engaging conversation. Light types feel emotions very intensely. This means that you are very sensitive to emotional conflict and can likely go from 1/10 to 15/10 on the emotional energy scale in a short period of time. The way to overcome this is counterintuitive: learn to spend time alone well. You will become less reactive to other people and better able to regulate your emotions when you are connecting with other people. Not every issue needs to be aired and processed: some conversations are better left alone!

You don't respond well to passive aggression or the silent treatment in conflict as this shuts down the connection and has the effect of dimming your spark or drawing a curtain on your sunlight. Rather than trying to 'win' in an argument, it's always helpful to investigate your role in the conflict and to use it as an opportunity for greater insight and closeness. It's useful to learn mantras for conflict because you are less likely to pause and reflect on your emotions before reacting to a conflict situation. Even if it feels inauthentic to say things such as 'I think we both need time to think about this' or 'I'm feeling frustrated now and I need some space' in the heat of the moment – especially when you are used to expressing yourself – I guarantee it will change the way you engage with those around you.

It's also useful to realise that all of us contribute 50 per cent to every conflict we're involved in. Ask yourself:

- How have I contributed to this, even through my omission or inability to act?
- Am I making a genuine effort to see this from the other person's perspective?
- What would be the best outcome of this disagreement?
- Are we both ready to talk calmly and constructively, or should we take a moment to reflect first?
- Am I recognising and honouring our differences in the way we communicate?

Conflicts can only be genuinely resolved once the emotional inflammation has been removed from the situation. If you are in a conflict with a low-intensity connector, it may be a positive opportunity to use the pause in the conflict to ask yourself: what do I want to achieve from this conflict? How can I use this conflict to create a healthier connection? Is this old or new anger? Old anger is suppressed from a past experience and new anger is a healthy and proximate response to a situation.

Vulnerability

For Light types, experiencing vulnerability, shame, sadness or depression will feel as though a cloud is dimming your light. You will feel dull, like the difference between a day of brilliant blue skies and an overcast one. Your frequency and intensity will jump around as your identity shifts away from your typical social self. You may lack the fuel for human connection because you don't 'feel like yourself' and withdraw from your active social life. Or you might continue to communicate with others, even in vulnerability, but you are likely to be irritable, distracted, aggressive and overly sensitive.

In these periods, you need to connect within. You may resist this and want to scroll through social media or distract yourself with TV, movies, the internet or partying, desperate for distraction. But these numbing behaviours are unlikely to bring back your spark. It's imperative that you learn to go within and develop positive coping mechanisms when you feel vulnerable. Imagine your vulnerability as a young child asking you for attention. Numbing behaviours are the equivalent of ignoring the child and pretending it's not there, whereas meditation and mindfulness are the equivalent of turning to the child and engaging with them. Develop a daily practice of contemplation and mindfulness to establish connection within. Even though you are nourished by human connection, you will find your interactions even more rewarding if you have the capacity to go within.

Light types in particular need to engage in nourishing habits during time alone, otherwise you risk imploding. If you are a Light type and you can relate to this experience, make a list right now (on your phone, which I know is nearby in case anyone contacts you) of all the things you can enjoy doing when you're on your own. This could be, for example:

- Reading a book: with a list of books you want to read
- Cooking a favourite meal
- Listening to or playing music
- Shopping or going to a market
- Walking along the beach or somewhere in nature
- Something creative like writing or painting
- Going to the gym or to an exercise class.

Without this list of potential activities to hand, Light types can panic and shut down when on one's own and automatically look for something to fill the void.

Let's now explore the three Light types in more detail: Spark, Star and Sunlight.

Spark

Sparks are close to the centre of the model, in the low range for both high intensity and high frequency. Sparks are universal communicators. This type:

- Is a bright spark in a group, with a verbal and gregarious connection style
- Is an engaging and enthusiastic connector
- Has an extensive social network
- Is sociable and personable
- Prefers to be in the company of others rather than being alone
- Has a warm and versatile way of relating
- Is comfortable being the centre of attention and enjoys storytelling
- Thrives on human connection
- Leads by creating a plan and inspiring others to come with them.

Characteristics

Sparks are high-frequency connectors, with a score between 0 and 100. This means that you prefer the company of other people *most* of the time (55–60 per cent). This still means that you enjoy your own company for 40–45 per cent of the time, which is a considerable amount of time alone. Sparks are also high-intensity connectors, with a score between 0 and 100. Being close to the centre of the model means that this type is confident to communicate in a range of contexts to a variety of people.

Spark types are refuelled by human connection and you feel most like yourself when you are in the company of others. You enjoy the communication and interaction that relationships bring. While you may take this for granted, this is one of your strengths, as not everyone thrives on relationships as much as high-frequency types. It is natural for Sparks to be in the company of others: this makes socialising, busy workplaces, and engaged family time easier for you than for low-frequency connectors. On the flipside, as a high-frequency type, you need to make sure that you don't take it personally when someone requires less connection with you than you would like with them. It's

LIGHT

not a reflection of you or the relationship if someone needs to retreat into their inner world; it's about their connection needs.

As a Spark connector, you light up a room and people are drawn to your warmth. You're like a human candle in a group of people. There's a sense of relief if you are in the group, as people know that you will carry the conversation and keep the mood positive and upbeat. Like a candle, you're also able to be mellow and simply set a positive mood through your soft warmth. Establishing connection with others comes easily to you and it is enjoyable for you. The universal forms of human connection (humour, storytelling, celebration, fun and authenticity) are a natural extension of your personality. Human connection is therefore a part of who you are. For this reason, you can come across as being 'lucky' and 'popular,' as though relationships are effortless for you, whether they are or not. You often seem to be where the fun is, telling a story, concocting a plan or laughing with others. You bond with others through animated conversation and are comfortable connecting in a variety of ways: face-to-face, over the phone, via text and online (depending on your preference). You are a warm and engaging connector. Your natural affinity for connection means that people like having you around.

Being a Light type means that you are a confident verbal connector and enjoy being in the spotlight, even if in some cases the spotlight is merely the undivided attention of your partner or a couple of friends when you're telling a story. You are an asset to any group and often seek out (or take on) leadership roles, whether it's in your family, sports or work team or a group of friends. You will thrive in leadership positions as you are comfortable communicating with a crowd and you have the perspective to see the bigger picture and understand the people you are leading. You also have the courage to introduce new ideas. Spark types lead with vision and enthusiasm; you use your charm and charisma to persuade others that your way is the best way to go.

Where to from here?

You have the insight and the social skills to promote inclusion in any group or team. You can read the room and know what people need in order to feel a sense of belonging. You are refuelled by socialising

Fareed's story

Fareed is a Spark who I interviewed. He had the following to say: 'If I'm with a group of friends I'm like a kid in a toyshop. No-one gives me the shits. When they're on the same par as you – story-telling, having a laugh – I find this is one of the best parts of being in a group environment. You feel like everyone is in the same boat as you and you feel more positive about things.' His Spark nature was evident when he told me:

'I have eight friends from kindergarten – we meet every year and I'm the main organiser. I like organising things for people to get together. I keep up close contact with people, like ringing them on the phone and having a yak. Close contact allows you to share emotions, and not bottle them up. A lot of people don't have that outlet to divert emotions or stress. I like expressing how I feel and my emotions. I'm a big bloke but a softie.'

with friends and family, so you need to make this a priority each day or each week. You embody light and your company is illuminating for others. Not everyone has your capacity for bringing people together and meeting their needs. You will feel fulfilled if you curate opportunities for people to come together. You enjoy generating conversation and fun for others. A full social calendar is your comfort zone. You can change the lives of others by asking: How can I make someone else feel like they belong today? Even though you are warm and social when in the company of others, you can extend your generosity to making sure that everyone is in the room.

Develop a daily practice of contemplation and mindfulness to establish connection within. Even though you are nourished by human connection, you will find your interactions even more rewarding if you also have the capacity to go within.

Sparks learn and grow through mentoring, challenges and leadership positions. If you want to develop, find a mentor or coach in your field who you respect and have that mentor set goals and challenges for you. You need to be pushed out of your comfort zone, constantly going higher and higher. You also thrive on opportunities to inspire others. If you are able to integrate the inspiration of others into your routine, this will allow you to channel your intensity in a positive way. Make sure you stay inspired to reach your highest potential and keep your inner spark alive.

Star

Star types are high-intensity and high-frequency connectors. This type:

- Lights up when connecting with others
- Has a verbal and gregarious style
- Radiates warmth and brings an X-factor to a room, stage or table
- Shines wherever they go, as though there's a spotlight on them
- Influences people with their opinion, with people wanting to follow their lead and spend time with them simply because of their compelling and confident style
- Nudges people towards high-intensity conversations rather than just engaging in small talk
- Prefers to be in the company of others rather than being alone
- Is popular, with an extensive social network
- Usually finds themselves at the centre of the action or 'in the right place at the right time': this isn't luck – it's a result of their compelling connection style, so they create the action
- Is well suited to leadership roles, leading through vision, charisma and inspiration.

Characteristics

As a Star connector, you are likely to be influential in your professional field or social circle and accustomed to being the centre of attention. Connection seems to be effortless for you, and people marvel at your warmth.

Stars in the sky are held together by their own gravity. Similarly, you are self-assured and self-possessed, ruled by your own desires rather than the impulses of the crowd. However, this trait can also come across as being untouchable, unrelatable or intimidating. Strictly speaking, this isn't because of anything you do. People have a complicated connection with you; on the one hand they want to observe you from afar and be captivated by you. On the other hand, they want to connect closely with you. It's hard to do both at the same time, so you may feel that you are often managing this tension.

This explains your core challenge: to be as interested in others as they are in you. You will continually seek out an audience or a group to lead in some form throughout your life, otherwise you will feel lacking in purpose. This is not a flaw in you or a sign of narcissism, it's simply a fact of being a Star type. While you have a magnetic presence and draw people towards you, you generally don't need other people in the same way as they need you.

This is best explained by the difference between the performer and the audience. The performer is immersed in their performance, giving their all, while the audience simply watches, eyes transfixed on the stage. Once the performance has finished, the audience wants some of the performer's magic, but there is not enough to go around. This is a snapshot of your connection style. You usually leave other people wanting more.

You are high intensity, which means that you bond through deep and stimulating conversations. You feel close to others when you can openly share your emotions, but there are only a select few with whom you will honestly share yourself.

Being a Star type means that you are a confident verbal connector and enjoy being in the spotlight. You are also able to confidently facilitate conversations in groups. You are an asset to any group you are part of and often seek out (or take on) leadership roles, whether it's in your family, sports or work team or a group of friends. You will thrive in leadership positions as you are comfortable communicating with a crowd and you have the 'star' perspective to see the bigger picture and understand the people you are leading. You also have the courage to introduce new ideas. Star types lead from the sky; they use vision and charisma to persuade others that their way is the best way to go.

Where to from here?

Your confident Connection Type makes you magnetic to others, however there will come a time in your life when you will need to establish a sense of yourself without the crowd, group, company or team to endorse you and give you the feedback you seek. The most powerful Star types are the ones who become their own point of reference, who don't need external validation and lead from a place of purpose rather than from a need for approval. The most fulfilled and powerful Star types will lead according to their values rather than popularity.

When you are a confident performer, it's easy to get lost in the persona that other people see. Don't fall into the trap of losing your connection to yourself just to please the crowd. Stay connected to your authenticity. The group is drawn to you because you have a strong sense of who you are and where you're going. What's more, you have the desire to take other people with you because you thrive on connection. Just make sure you don't lose yourself along the way.

You are a born leader. Star types learn and grow through mentoring, challenges and leadership positions. You will thrive when you find opportunities to inspire others and become the person to show the way for a group or team. You are happiest when you are working on behalf of a team, in an area you care about. This could mean planning exciting events like holidays or parties, creating a strategic plan for your work team, or brightening up someone's day with your positive energy. You love new projects and positive connections.

The mix of being drawn to people, plus being a born leader, plus being high intensity and feeling emotions deeply can cause Star types to feel overwhelmed by connection. The signs of overwhelm are over-thinking and over-analysing your relationships. The antidote to this is to reconnect within and stay inspired in order to keep your inner star shining. Be guided by the answers to these questions:

- What (person, project, idea) is calling me next?
- Is this joyful to me?

- What do I currently value in my life?
- When do I most feel like myself?
- Which of my own qualities keep me inspired?

You also thrive on opportunities to inspire others. If you are able to integrate inspiring others into your routine, this will allow you to channel your intensity in a positive way.

Sunlight

Sunlights are in the extreme ranges of high intensity and high frequency. These types generally:

- Have different modes of connection that can be either illuminating, warming or overheating, depending on their mood
- Have the vision and insight to inspire others
- Let truth guide them, even when it is uncomfortable for people to hear; they are often the truth-teller in a group
- Light the path and show people the way forward; their leadership style is powerful, and they often become the group, team or relationship compass but they must lead from afar because your connection style is too overwhelming to lead close up
- Need to manage their intensity as it can become overpowering; their challenge is to convert the intensity of their mind and heart into a light for others.

Characteristics

You are human sunlight. This is a superpower and like all superpowers it brings the potential for both great power and great challenges. Just as the sun itself has three key functions (to light, heat and provide energy), Sunlight types do the same. Therefore, as a Sunlight type you are always providing energy to others. This energy can either *light up, warm up* or *heat up* human connection.

Sunlight is a positive natural force when: we channel it for power and it lights up the world; we use it as a measure of time and space in order to understand direction, growth, momentum and perspective; it signals a new day and enables us to see where we're going; it keeps humans, animals and plants alive as we follow its cycles; we're prepared for it with protection such as a T-shirt, hat, sunglasses and sunscreen; we're under an umbrella or in the shade of a tree; we're relieved from the heat by swimming in a pool or in the ocean.

Yet sunlight can also: increase the temperature to uncomfortable levels; burn our eyes and skin; make us sweat and overheat; dry the moisture out of living things; create drought when there is too much heat and not enough rain – causing an imbalance in the ecosystem.

From a human connection perspective, Sunlight types are a positive force when:

- They channel their light and intensity into insight, vision and power.
- They offer a new perspective and way of seeing.
- They light the way for others, acting as a human compass.
- They are in relationships with others who are resilient to the power of sunlight, or even bask in it.
- They are in a group situation where their intensity is complemented by lower intensity types who can deflect their intensity with humour and lightness.

However, Sunlight types have also been known to:

- Shock or even offend others with their willingness to share their raw emotions and unfiltered moods.
- Make confronting statements without concern for how others will respond.
- Heat up a conversation or relationship to uncomfortable levels of intensity and volatility.
- Make others feel intimidated or uneasy.
- Cause unnecessary conflict or drama.

If, as a Sunlight type, you channel your emotional energy positively, it can provide the vision and insight to inspire others. In this mode, you can be *fired up* and *on fire*. However, if the intensity of your sunlight has no outlet, it can overheat and implode. In this mode, you can start emotional fires and blow emotional fuses. When you're like this, connecting with you can be similar to eating hot chilli peppers. Some people want chilli on everything they eat. When other people taste chilli, their eyes water and they take a while to recover. This is your emotional impact when your energy is not given a positive outlet. More than other Connection Types, Sunlight types need to channel their intensity into a constructive pursuit, lest the powerful energy form a mental pressure cooker and spill over into your connections with others. Your challenge is therefore to avoid being overcome by the power of your mind so you can convert your intensity into light for others.

You often set the mood of a room. This is a great delight for everyone if you are feeling positive, but a huge weight to bear if you are feeling low and your overpowering energy brings everyone down. This can feel like pressure if you are surrounded by people who rely on your leadership or inspiration.

Sunlight types open up to others very quickly, with 'full disclosure' being your rule of thumb. You use your mood and opinion to establish connection with others and if people ask how you're feeling, they shouldn't expect, 'I'm well, thanks' in response. They should expect an honest answer communicated through voice, facial expression and body language.

The intensity that you can handle in a connection with someone else may actually cause the other person to feel overwhelmed, controlled or dismissed. Not everyone wants to have a deep and meaningful conversation or even constant spoken communication. This is a powerful lesson for Sunlight types, who often set the tone and mood in group dynamics. For this reason, a challenge for you is to allow the dynamic to lead itself. You do not need to be speaking when you are in the company of other people. You do not have to be in control of a relationship for it to work. You need to respect that other people have different needs for connection. Addressing this challenge may be as simple as inviting others to make decisions about where you will go, what you will do and what you will talk about. It could also be as complex as learning to self-regulate your need to control the dynamic and practising restraint in this area.

LIGHT

When you feel vulnerable, ashamed, sad or depressed, you are likely to feel as though a cloud is obscuring your sunlight. Sunlight types usually experience vulnerability when they are alone because they are faced with the intensity of their thoughts and feelings. As you are a high-frequency and high-intensity connector, being alone can feel like the noise in your head is increased to an unbearable volume.

When most other types experience vulnerability, they decrease their frequency because they lack the energy for human connection – so they withdraw from their social life. Not you! Your frequency will likely increase and your intensity will also increase.

It's hard to spot vulnerability in a Sunlight type because it often looks like acting out and lashing out. When a Sunlight type is feeling vulnerable or anxious, they will often stay out later, drink more and party harder or lash out at loved ones with provocative and aggressive statements. You will continue to communicate with others when you feel vulnerable, but you are more likely to be irritable and overly sensitive. Sunlight types will leap into an intense, emotional discussion with people you love, and with people you hardly know. You will dive deep into your own thoughts and emotions and you are eager for the same to be shared back to you.

While you can occasionally . . . ahem . . . regularly be guilty of interrupting, you usually want to listen as much as you want to be heard. The interruptions aren't meant to be offensive; they are reflective of the enthusiasm the Sunlight connector feels in the conversation – you are jumping out of your skin to communicate. You want to soak up all that human connection has to offer. That's how emotions feel to high-intensity people: like they are overpowering energy that needs to be exchanged.

In fact, a Sunlight will often get carried away by the momentum of an emotionally charged conversation and spiral into a heightened emotional state. It's only after the conversation has ended that a Sunlight will realise that most of what they said in that state is an exaggeration of what they actually think and feel. If you are a Sunlight and you find yourself in this situation, potentially arguing with another about something you don't even feel particularly strongly about, you need to remove yourself from the situation until you return to yourself.

It's in this state that other types wilt or wither in the connection of a Sunlight type. The energy is just too overpowering and intimidating, like walking into a fire.

Where to from here?

Sunlight types learn and grow through larger-than-life challenges and visionary leadership positions. You would respond well to a partner, mentor, coach or team who can inspire you to reach your highest potential and keep your inner sunlight shining. Better yet, learn to inspire yourself!

To channel your intensity and vision, you need to constantly create new things and then share them to inspire and connect other people. You need a variety of social groups where you feel safe to be yourself and speak your (highly intense) truth. A creative outlet is key, as it will allow you to express all of the intensity in your mind on the page or canvas or in music. Try starting your own podcast, making any kind of art, taking dance or music classes with others, or giving talks on your area of passion. You would love working for yourself or working in an organisation where you have a lot of autonomy.

You feel a sense of belonging (and earn your connection money) by being in the company of others, so this is often the most natural habitat for you. However, if you can learn to be alone and tame the intensity of your mind through contemplative practise such as meditation and mindfulness, this will be the defining triumph of your life. It will also bring you greater emotional regulation and richness to your connections.

Here's the bottom line: your connection is a bit like a wild horse. You can choose to stay wild forever and connect with others however you like, based on how you're feeling at the time. You can also choose to regulate your emotions and learn to read others and channel your power and energy into pursuits that give you a positive return. You can also choose a bit of both. Ultimately, you want to be surrounded by people because it makes you feel safe and happy, and the key to maintaining healthy relationships is strong communication and mutual respect. You can keep a bit of your wildness and still have harmonious relationships. You will need to find people who like a challenge!

chapter 9

Water types:
Elixir, Ripple Effect and Ocean

Characteristics	Tools to enhance relationships
Low frequency: feel most relaxed in your own company, one on one, or in small groups	Human connection doesn't have to feel like hard work. Relationships don't require you to heal others. Even though you have this capacity, it's not your responsibility. You can have fun and light connections, too. Start by directing the same love and energy that you give to other people to yourself.
High intensity: feel emotions deeply, emotionally expressive; bond through talking when you feel psychologically safe	
Core values: awareness and empathy	
Genuinely caring and intuitive	Emotional boundaries will set you free. Your challenge is experiencing meaningful connection and maintaining your sense of self at the same time.
Excellent problem-solvers	

Water types: characteristics

Water types have a preference for low-frequency and high-intensity human connection. You feel most comfortable when you are connecting:

- on your own
- one on one or
- in small groups.

You bloom when connection is based on meaningful and fulfilling conversations. You value psychologically safe, genuine connection and nourishing emotional energy. A Water type could be just as happy (or even happier) on your own as you are in the company of others. It's as though you live underwater, in your own inner world of emotional processing. When you do come to the surface to connect with people, you want it to be enriching connection with a few select individuals; you prefer quality over quantity.

WATER

Water types are named after bodies of water. This is because your emotional energy is absorbing and all-encompassing. It also varies from day to day and over time, like the ocean. Human connection for a Water type feels like someone has just entered a pool with you; your 'emotional water' is impacted by the interaction and you have to adapt. If we visualise what it's like when we sink into a body of water, we see the water accommodate us and it resettle around us. This is how a Water type adapts to human connection with others. Unlike solid Connection Types like Earth and Trees that always stay fixed in place, water will change its course and envelop anything it comes into contact with. This constant sensing and adapting that Water types undertake when connecting with others can be draining, which is why you recover through low frequency. Like the tide, Water types connect and then withdraw to restore your energy and your flow.

Introducing the three Water types

1. Elixir

An elixir is a healing liquid that in mythology cures illness and grants eternal life. Elixir Connection Types transform the emotional experience of other people with their presence. The Elixir type is closest to the centre so their typical 'blue, water' qualities are less pronounced than the Water types who are further from the centre and more extreme.

2. Ripple Effect

A ripple effect occurs when one initial act or event flows outwards to impact on people and situations outside that initial interaction. Similarly, Ripple Effect connectors have such a powerful impact through their creations and their relationships that they build influence even though they aren't as visible, overt or loud as others in the way that they communicate.

3. Ocean

The Ocean can be the most restorative, inviting and rejuvenating force. It can also be lethal and merciless, leaving humans powerless to conquer its force. In the same way, Ocean types are extreme connectors who can either heal or overwhelm. Even though humans live on land, the ocean actually covers approximately 70 per cent of the Earth. This speaks to the power of Water types because even though the Ocean may not seem to shape our day-to-day lives as powerfully as the Earth, it is the most prevalent force in nature. It has an understated form of power that these Water types also possess.

Water types: communication style

Water types come across to others as warm, genuine and friendly. You are content when everyone in the connection feels psychologically safe and happy. As a result, you spend your time observing the dynamic and ensuring that everyone feels comfortable. If you sense that someone isn't contributing enough or is lacking confidence in the conversation, you will ask that person a question to bring them into the conversation. In this way you act as a check on the dominance of any Light types in the group.

Alternatively, a Water type will deflect an uncomfortable topic of conversation to prevent conflict. You tend to be very perceptive and even enigmatic because you read human behaviour well but don't feel the need to participate in the dynamic. The Water type is the person who everyone wants in the room, but at the end of the conversation people will leave and realise that the Water type hardly spoke, causing everyone to reflect on what they were thinking. In this way, Water types are humble and are happy to give other people airtime. This is the power of this type. You communicate by steering and guiding the conversation. You create inclusion by bringing everyone (except perhaps yourselves!) into the conversation.

Water types take on the feelings of everyone in the room. This is why connection can be overwhelming for you. You want everyone else to get along and be happy, which can be a lot of pressure when your enjoyment of human connection depends upon the experience of every other person in the room.

Water types: leadership style

Water types are powerful leaders but not in the typical sense. These types lead as executive producers, meaning that you use your wise counsel with a chosen few to distribute your ideas more widely. An executive producer is the voice in the ear of hosts talking on a television program. At all times the hosts have an earpiece connecting them to the studio and the executive producer is the person prompting and guiding them (obviously unheard by the audience). Similarly, you are the voice in people's heads that they listen to, respect and internalise. You make suggestions and speak quietly into the ears of the people you lead. This builds trust and ultimately leads your followers to internalise your ideas and implement your approach.

You are not a loud or overpowering leader and actually prefer to be out of the spotlight, but you do make a formidable impact on the outcomes you create. You realise that people usually wield more power behind the scenes and have no desire to be the centre of attention while you are orchestrating your strategy. While the higher frequency Light types or Earth types might be the people on television in the spotlight, you are the one deciding what stories people are listening to, and which opinions are being shared. This approach to leadership is reminiscent of the Lao Tzu quote: 'A leader is best when people barely know they exist, and when his work is done, his aim fulfilled, they will say: we did it ourselves.'

Water types intuitively understand that people do their best work (i.e. are more productive, focused and efficient) if they feel a sense of

WATER

belonging and feel respected in the group. As such, Water types need to ensure that everyone feels comfortable before the actual work can begin. You do this by cultivating meaningful one-on-one relationships with everyone in your team. This is a strong basis for your leadership because you create a foundation of trust, loyalty and belonging – you make people feel like they are part of a family. Your strengths are in building relationships and communicating your ideas throughout your organisation with the help of your team. You don't leave anyone out, whether it's a stakeholder or a direct report.

A downside of your leadership style is that you tend to only hire and surround yourself with high-frequency connectors like Light and Earth types. You do this to compensate for your low frequency and you set up your team to convey your message on your behalf (just as the executive producer uses the TV hosts to convey the message of the show).

You therefore need to ensure that your high-frequency team is getting enough connection from you – your once-a-week meeting with them might be enough for you, but it might not be enough for them. Also, if you have low-intensity team members, your approach of cultivating one-on-one relationships could be too confronting and intense for them because they prefer a team environment. To address these challenges:

1. Try organising more opportunities for your team to connect as a whole or with each other. They need to build relationships with each other, not just with you.
2. Be proactive about hiring all Connection Types, not just high-frequency types who will deliver your message. This will build diversity of connection on your team.

Finally, your kryptonite is overcommitting – you can see all the things that need to be done and it's typical for you to do most of them. Avoid the 'Today I should have' narrative and replace it with 'Tomorrow I will . . . '

As you are a high-intensity leader, you need an intense way to restore your energy. Schedule daily movement and weekly pampering so you know your physical and mental health will be looked after. As you're always giving externally, you need a source of energy that regenerates you.

Water types: challenges
Boundaries

As Water types absorb others in connection, there is often no clear separation between you and the people you're connecting with. If you haven't learnt ways to manage this, you may feel emotionally tossed around on a regular basis, as though human connection feels like swimming in a rough ocean.

The golden rule for establishing healthy boundaries is to work out how you feel before connecting with someone and then how you feel afterwards. Every emotional exchange involves giving and taking and Water types are naturally giving and generous connectors. You give out healing and empathetic energy, and you receive whatever someone is giving back. If the other person is emanating positive and animated energy, then you will receive this and feel a boost in your sense of belonging.

If you constantly feel drained after connecting with others, you have two options: either organise more time for you, or have a robust system of sorting through emotions that belong to you and emotions that belong to other people – or both.

After connecting with someone, ask yourself:

- Does this emotion belong to me? If yes, I need to process and heal it.
- If this emotion does not belong to me, do I want to hold on to it or do I want to release it? If you want to release it, you can visualise a magnet over your body extracting all of the emotional residue you have collected, or use a yogic lion's breath where you exhale deeply with your tongue out as far as it can go.

Implementing emotional boundaries is a key challenge for Water types and this will largely determine your experience of human connection.

WATER

Overthinking and overfeeling

Another challenge for high-intensity connectors is overthinking. Having a high intensity score means that relationships and group dynamics have a strong impact on you. High-intensity connectors tend to put their emotions under a magnifying glass and to process emotions deeply. It can take more time for a high-intensity connector to process and recover from an emotional experience than a low-intensity connector. This can present as insomnia or symptoms of anxiety where you feel 'stuck in your head'.

Research has shown that identifying emotions as they arise can help us to process them more efficiently. If you notice yourself in a loop of negative thinking, simply say to yourself 'I am overthinking' or 'I am worrying about something that may not happen'. This act of conscious awareness takes the power away from the negative pattern and gives you more control over your thoughts.

My best friend in high school once casually left her mobile phone in the car overnight when we were in our late teens. I couldn't believe it: 'What if someone wants to contact you?' I said. She laughed at me and replied, 'You always think the sky will fall in if you can't instantly talk to someone. Most things can be figured out tomorrow.'

This has become my practice. As a typical Light type who is used to processing my emotions in the company of others, I've worked on dialling down the intensity of my connections. And now I realise that not every emotion needs to be processed or discussed or talked about right then and there. Most emotions are like clouds that float through the sky. We don't need to lasso the cloud and bring it up close in order to feel every single one. Most can just float on by. This has been an emotional revolution for me.

My friend of many years is a Water type. She has taught me that you can experience and maintain connection without seeing or speaking to someone. This is intuitive connection: when closeness is felt even in the absence of physical proximity. If someone you love doesn't need to spend as much time with you as you would prefer, their frequency is lower than yours. They may feel a higher intuitive connection with you and need less physical time together.

Conflict

As you are a high-intensity connector, your approach to conflict is also likely to be high intensity. A Water type in conflict is likely to be passive aggressive or use the silent treatment – you process disagreements with others deeply and it takes time for your response to rise to the surface. In conflict, the clear waters of your connection become choppy and rough as they do when there is a storm over the ocean. Your gentle lapping waves transform into pounding whitewash breakers. You express this through your body language when you turn away from others, your facial expression where you either avert your gaze or glare, and through your capacity to walk away from a conflict until you resolve how you are going to react. You can take a considerable amount of time to re-surface after a fight.

WATER

Vulnerability

When you feel vulnerable, ashamed, sad or depressed, you are likely to feel 'flooded' by emotion and feel as though you could drown in your feelings. It's no accident that I use these terms, unique to Water types, to describe the experience of Elixir, Ripple Effect and Ocean types.

In vulnerability, your frequency will decrease and your intensity will increase. You will lack the fuel for human connection because you don't 'feel like yourself' and you will withdraw from your social life. You will avoid contact and communication with others, and if forced into connection you are likely to be irritable, distracted and overly sensitive. If you can find a healing practice or a place that brings you back to yourself during these times, you will transform your relationship with yourself, and as a result, with others.

Let's explore the three Water types in more detail: Elixir, Ripple Effect and Ocean.

Elixir

Connecting with an Elixir is like walking along the ocean shore or wading through a clear pool of water. Elixir types are close to the centre of the model, in the low ranges of high intensity and low frequency. They generally:

- Energise and calm people at the same time, just like a swim in balmy water
- Thrive on intimacy with a select few people and prefer to spend time one on one or in smaller groups
- Enjoy connecting with others but are overwhelmed by constant social activity; they need time to reflect and withdraw into your inner world
- Follow a rhythm of connecting and withdrawing like the ocean tide
- Feel comfortable in deep emotional conversations; Elixirs can relate to most people but prefer to avoid small talk
- Tend to have challenges with emotional boundaries, not knowing where their emotions end and someone else's begin
- Worry and internalise their fears.

Characteristics

Your connection feels like the point where the gentle waves meet the sand, creating an energising and yet calming impact all at once.

The ocean shore has the capacity to simultaneously energise, calm, renew and heal us. The hypnotic rhythm of the waves is so powerful that it can transform our mindset and modify our outlook on life. This is what it feels like to connect with an Elixir. People come away from you feeling transformed and refreshed, with a clear head and a fresh perspective. Your connection doesn't make demands of the other; like a walk along the beach, a person is free to place their feet in the water or stay on the sand.

When you connect with someone else, you simply invite them to bathe in your connection. This translates as your acceptance of others' vulnerability and your tendency to be non-judgemental. Your primary imperative in connection is to calm, energise and heal. You create a safe space for others to connect.

The strength of your connection is also your challenge. You are expressive and want to make sure that everyone is feeling comfortable. You tend to feel emotions deeply and absorb emotions readily, so you may find it tough to work out whether the emotions you feel belong to you or to someone you have just connected with. Understanding this boundary in every emotional exchange becomes the superpower of a Water connector.

As you are closer to the centre of the model, you probably have many of the qualities of a Shapeshifter type and may often find yourself accommodating others. Your return to your own preferences and emotions may give you an expansive feeling of freedom. As your connection mirrors the cycles of water, you may benefit from therapeutic healing rituals relating to water, whether it's your daily shower or bath, a swim in a pool, lake or ocean, or just simply washing your face. The feeling you have when you immerse yourself in water is the same feeling you give others when you connect with them.

People see you as a genuine and empathetic listener. You are perceptive and adopt a warm and caring tone when you are talking to others. You are inclusive and very aware of how other people are feeling in your presence, whether you are at home or at work. This could translate as a self-consciousness of what to say and how to act; because you always want to make others feel welcome you are more focused on them rather than your own comfort. It reminds me of the difference between the host and the guest at a party. The host is always wondering if the guest is comfortable and has enough to eat and drink. The host is there to welcome the guest. You are often the 'emotional host' of connections – you may not always verbalise it, but you are consistently checking in on the people around you. This explains your need to periodically withdraw and reconnect with yourself and your own needs.

You will need to communicate to your loved ones that you need time on your own to regroup and recalibrate; to return to yourself and your own feelings. You will find open-plan offices and constant online communication like group chats and social media overwhelming and will need regular, scheduled downtime. You can't help absorbing other people's emotional energy, whether you are conscious of it or

WATER

not, whether you are at work or at home, and whether you are in a relationship with the other person or not.

People are drawn to you – you are like an emotional magnet – and you need to protect your emotional energy so that you are at your best. If you only focus on making other people happy and meeting their needs, you will burn out and shut down, requiring forced time on your own to recuperate. This might be a feeling that you have always had but never been able to identify, because you take it upon yourself to accommodate other people and adapt to the social situation you are in.

Where to from here?

You are naturally drawn to nurturing and energising others as this is your primary mode of connection. You take other people's feelings to heart and this can become a heavy weight. The key is to also nurture yourself, which is best done through rejuvenation. Any sort of healing therapy will restore you: for example, massage or hydrotherapy. Always have a holiday booked and treat yourself to daily exercise to clear out any mental residue. If you are feeling overloaded on human connection, you will be able to restore your emotional energy if you are intentional about your time alone. Don't just succumb to the numb feeling and lie in bed, watch TV or scroll through your phone. Actively nourish yourself: what energises you? Pets, cooking, gardening, music, self-care?

It's important for you to communicate your human connection needs to those closest to you. At home and at work, it may help you to articulate how you operate to others. This will allow you to manage your human connections without causing offence to others. Elixir types I have worked with in the past will typically make a joke of it along the lines of, 'I've hit my limit and need to hit the eject button'. This expresses your need to withdraw without offending or insulting anyone. Elixir types who are parents will need to actively make time for themselves because the pull to nurture will be strong. Alternatively, Elixir parents may find that they parent in waves of engaging and withdrawing, perhaps to focus on work or self-care.

Elixir types learn and grow through developing deep and rewarding relationships. You find meaning in nurturing others. In a leadership position it is important for you to develop emotional relationships with the people you lead and these relationships need to be based on trust, loyalty and honesty.

You will thrive if you structure your time around a rhythm of connection and withdrawal into your haven. Make sure you stay connected to your inner rhythms and understand the inner flow that sustains you. If you are connected to this flow, you are better able to absorb others in your nourishing and deep connection.

WATER

Ripple Effect

Ripple Effect types are high-intensity and low-frequency connectors.

- They leave others feeling renewed and transformed, like a refreshing ocean swim.
- They produce a powerful ripple effect and generally carry considerable influence in their relationships and/or professional field.
- They have close and passionate relationships but can happily tolerate extended absences from loved ones.
- They thrive on intimacy with a select few people and only occasionally like to spend time in large groups.
- They follow a rhythm of connecting and withdrawing like the ocean tide.
- They like to connect through deep emotional conversations.
- They tend to have challenges with emotional boundaries; not knowing where their own emotions end and someone else's begin.
- They worry and internalise your fears.

Characteristics

You are a connection paradox. You are people-oriented but at the same time you are introverted. You are warm, genuine and interested in others and at the same time you crave the peace and quiet of time to yourself. You love people but you don't need people. This is a fascinating and alluring combination. You appreciate time with others but there is no desperation to your connection. You always leave people wanting more. This paradox is potentially not picked up by other personality profiles because your mix of introversion and people orientation is seemingly opposed.

One Ripple Effect type I've worked with described her Ality Connection Type as 'refreshing'. She said that other personality profiles couldn't explain why she is capable of having – and enjoys having – high-intensity experiences some of the time (for example when she teaches and gives public speeches), but then feels drained after these activities and needs to restore her energy. She loves people but can only stand connection for small, intense periods and then she needs to withdraw. Typically, personality profiles categorise people-oriented introverts as compliant, pleasing and eager for approval. In contrast, Ripple Effects are multifaceted. Like the ocean, your impression to others or 'shoreline' is beckoning and approachable, but your offshore waves are intimidating in their depth.

Alongside your desire for time alone in your inner world is a deep need for security and acceptance. Your self-sufficiency actually hides your fear of the uncomfortable aspects of connection: conflict and disagreement. But this isn't evident to other people. They just see you as aloof and independent.

When you do 'come to the shore' to connect with others, the experience for them is like diving into the ocean at its perfect temperature. They feel renewed and nourished. They don't want it to end. They delight in travelling over the waves of your conversation and following your current as you ebb and flow. They feel different when they resurface. Like the ocean, your connection is all-consuming and energising, but incapable of being possessed or harnessed. You command respect from the people you connect with.

As a Ripple Effect type, your influence extends beyond your immediate connections with others. You have the capacity to produce a far-reaching impact on others through the nature of the connection you provide. People think about what you have said and done long after you have left the connection with them. They adopt your views and perspectives not because you asked them to but because you express yourself with quiet clarity and conviction. You convey to others that you have given deep consideration to the issues you care about. You speak thoughtfully and gently, taking the time to make eye contact. You are engaged but not overly animated so it doesn't feel as though you dominate the connection. You are a good mirror of connection because you are adept at reading the needs of other people. It's as though you meet people where they are, and then gently encourage them to go deeper, to meet you where you are.

Where to from here?

As a Ripple Effect connector, you need to realise that you do not need to be a high-frequency connector to have the impact you were born to have. You aren't solely responsible for communicating your message; you can rely on the people in your inner circle to broadcast your message for you. Just be who you are and have the patience to see how far-reaching your influence can be.

You will thrive if you structure your time around a rhythm of connection and withdrawal into your haven. Make sure you stay connected to your inner rhythms and understand the inner flow that sustains you. If you are connected to this flow, you are better able to absorb others in your nourishing and deep connection. Protect your emotional energy so that when you are connecting with others, you can be fully present.

You will reach your highest potential if you work out how to rise from your depths. You can feel lost in the strong undertow of the overthinking and overfeeling that can challenge Ripple Effect types. You need a daily ritual that allows you to rise to the surface, such as exercise, meditation, dance or a movement practice such as yoga. The key is to get out of your head and into your body so that your emotions can be processed and released.

Even though you are capable of reading the emotions of other people, it is not your responsibility to solve their problems or even make them feel better. This pattern can set you up for co-dependent relationships where you become the rescuer. As a human being, you are entitled to rewarding and enjoyable connections with other

WATER

people. It won't bring you joy if you feel like you constantly have to work at relationships. Healthy relationships are based on two people connecting on an equal footing that brings pleasure to both. If you are consistently cast as the empathetic rescuer in every relationship or group, this will bring heaviness to human connection for you.

When I was first writing this section on Ripple Effect types, I suggested that the way to heal this rescuing pattern was for you to develop new beliefs about relationships; to approach connection in a new way. I now realise that this is unhelpful advice because it encourages Ripple Effect types to go against their fundamental nature. Instead, I think it's more powerful to see the wounds of other people as being collective rather than individual. Collective wounds have arisen because they are shared by many people living in the same culture. Examples include a lack of self-worth, covering up inadequacy with egotistical achievements, anxiety owing to over-stimulation, approval-seeking, fear of abandonment, and an inability to trust. These wounds show up in different ways but are shared by many people.

If you sense discomfort or tension in another person, it may help you to view it as a collective wound to be healed rather than their individual pain to be alleviated. From this perspective you can see yourself as a healer of collective pain, like the power the ocean has to heal. The questions that follow may be useful for you to ask yourself after you have left the person:

- What pain does this person trigger in me?
- Where do I feel this in my body?
- How does it feel?
- What does it need?

This call to see pain as collective is not intended to be overwhelming; ironically, it's actually quite freeing to acknowledge that we are not responsible for healing others: that is their job. This is simply a way to process any pain or negativity you absorb from others so that you do not identify with it.

You have so much potential to lead people, organisations and cultures that we need you to rise above the patterns that keep you stuck in rescuing people. We need you to lead us, not save us.

Ocean

Ocean types are at the extremes of high intensity and low frequency. You are a rare type, with only a minority of people showing up as Oceans in the Ality Connection Type assessment. In addition to the main features of a Ripple Effect, Ocean types generally:

WATER

- Have the courage and the passion to explore uncharted emotional waters
- Find infrequent yet deep and intense human connections very rewarding
- Draw people in and make them feel seen
- Portray an other-worldly quality
- Have a healing and soothing connection
- Are fiercely independent and self-possessed
- Enjoy working alone or in small teams
- Are very sensitive to connection with others
- Like to process thoughts and emotions before sharing with others
- Bring renewed perspectives to groups after spending time 'under-water' emotionally
- Lead as the group's moral conscience: people will turn to Oceans to ask: 'What would you do?' or 'What do you think?'

Characteristics

As an Ocean type, you are one of the rarest Connection Types. On the extremes of high intensity, you are attracted to profound and powerful emotional experiences. You are unafraid of raw emotion and in fact seek it out; you would prefer the truth over insincere politeness any day. Your capacity to feel deeply combined with your fierce independence makes you an intimidating force and commands the deep respect of other people, just like the ocean.

The ocean can deliver large and uniform swells, crystal clear and gentle waves or pounding and crashing waves, and rips with a strong undertow. It's not as though the ocean makes a conscious decision about the type of waves there will be each day. It is the result of many variables: the tides, the currents, the wind, the weather and the season. As an Ocean connector, you also feel the full spectrum of emotions, with no filter. Your heart is untamed. It may be that you never know how you are going to feel in the morning, just as we never know what tomorrow's swell will bring, though we can try to predict it.

I invite you to love yourself for this, despite occasionally longing for a simpler life where your emotional experience is less complex. Love the fact that you are just like the ocean and can change your form depending on the social context. In a stormy connection, you may use powerful and crashing waves (strong, decisive language and commanding body language) to connect, whereas in a sunny connection you may use gentle waves that rise and fall (lighthearted conversation and relaxed body language). As with any power, this connection could be inviting or threatening to others. People need to be able to read the ocean and swim or sail confidently before they connect deeply with you.

In terms of human connection, your habitat is the deep ocean water, out at sea. This means that you find meaning in exploring the far reaches of human thought and emotion. Occasionally you may feel that you have lost sight of the shore by spending too much time in your inner world but then you will surface and get your bearings by entering the public world of relationships and community.

By now you will have realised that you do not seek out human connection on any terms. You like your connection to be highly curated and meaningful. Otherwise you would prefer to flow on your own. You therefore relate to others by inviting them to 'swim' in your rich inner world.

As a result of your emotional intensity, your relationships with others are often complicated. You will relate best with people who can understand, appreciate (or even admire) the depths of your emotional experience. There will be some people who you will clash with because they cannot meet you in your intensity. They are not your people. Your people are ocean lovers who go out to the water each day wondering what it will deliver, ready for whatever mood the ocean might be in. These people use the ocean to wake themselves up, to exercise or as their recreation and enjoyment.

You are happy to explore your own emotions or to navigate others through their emotional territory. You are undaunted by raw emotion. Your connection is healing and passionate. You have deep insight into people and intuitively understand what they need. For this reason, connecting with you as an Ocean type is like being out at sea. People are transformed after connecting with you.

In order to connect with others, you either take them to the depths with you, or you come to the surface to connect with them. You prefer to take others to connect in your high-intensity habitat, so you bond with them when they enter your dimension. It may just be easier for you to connect with those few who match your high level of intensity (Star, Sunlight or Dawn types), or at least to connect with people in a high-intensity context, for example, in the creative arts or in the healing professions. When you connect with others, you invite them to swim in your connection. This translates as your acceptance of others' vulnerability and your gentleness.

There is power and challenge in being an Ocean connector. While people love to be absorbed by your connection and it is in your nature to connect in this way, you must consciously retreat after the connection in order to replenish. In this way, you mirror the ocean tides, connecting, absorbing and retreating. I don't need to remind you of this, because it will start to feel as if you can't breathe emotionally if you have been bombarded with too much human connection.

You are a masterful connector because you have the sensitivity, awareness and insight to know what other people need. On the other hand, there aren't many connectors in your habitat so it may be difficult for you to meet those you can connect with easily: after all, it's not crowded out in the deep ocean. For this reason you may find that you eventually make compromises in intimate connection, simply to experience the company of others. Your partner may find you intoxicating without realising that you are working hard behind the scenes to present a unified identity to them.

WATER

Where to from here?

You will thrive in relationships where you have unlimited freedom. You seek out other people who can meet your intensity without trying to control or change you.

You lead as the conscience of any group you are in. You have a strong moral compass and people look to you for guidance about the right way forward. You don't rely on the good opinions of other people to define you and you are respected for this.

As an Ocean, you need to acknowledge that you do not need to be a frequent connector to have an impact. Just be who you are and have the patience to see how far-reaching your influence can be. You will thrive if you structure your time around a rhythm of connection and withdrawal into your haven. Make sure you stay connected to your inner rhythms and understand the inner flow that sustains you. If you are connected to this flow, you are better able to absorb others in your nourishing and deep connection.

You spend most of your psychological energy in the depths of the ocean. When you find people who can meet you there it's a welcome relief, but you've become accustomed to inhabiting uncharted waters on your own. While it's not your natural way to seek out constant opportunities to socialise, knowing that you can rely on some predictable human connection will be calming and uplifting. You are an innate nurturer so you will enjoy tending to your loved ones. In fact, you will devote your life to them. Find creative outlets to release your intensity: art, writing, poetry, cooking, sculpture, gardening or music will be nurturing for you.

chapter 10

Green types:
Shades, Observer and Tree

Characteristics	Tools to enhance relationships
Low frequency: you are most comfortable connecting on your own, engaged in activities that interest or relax you. You are happy to connect with people you care about, but for you it's about quality over quantity.	Be clear about what you need from connection with others. You are likely to be a lower frequency connector than a lot of people you connect with, so you will benefit from explaining to your loved ones and colleagues how often you want to spend time with them.
Low intensity: you bond with others through positive shared experiences over time, for example, 'We went to university together' or 'We served in the police together'. You prefer to avoid conversations about how you feel.	Make it clear that, although you might not need as much time with your loved ones as they do with you, you value their connection and you care about them. Many people measure love in terms of quality time together, so they may take your preferences for alone time personally.
You are a patient and reserved connector. You value comfort and respect in connection and groups.	

You appreciate 'to the point' communication. You are detail-oriented and logic-driven, so like to understand the basis for decisions from this perspective.

You represent stability and consistency in any group you are in.

When you are feeling vulnerable, you like to be left alone.

Ask questions to convey interest in the person you are talking to.

You may not enjoy talking about your emotions, but the people you care about might need you to do this. Showing vulnerability can bring you closer to others and may make you feel emotionally lighter.

Green types: characteristics

Once I was giving a workshop to a group of Green types. I was focusing exclusively on these types to make the workshop relevant for them. At one point I paused, and asked one of the participants, 'What's it actually like to be a Green type? It's the opposite of my type.'

He smiled and said, 'It's very peaceful. You should try it.'

For Green types, connecting with other people is a considered choice rather than a compulsion. This is an incredibly powerful way to enter connection because you don't need anything from your relationships with other people. When you are in the company of others you're happy to just observe, and you participate if you feel like it. You don't have anything to prove. Your connection cup is already full. What freedom! You don't have expectations of human connection because that's not your greatest source of connection.

Your connection needs are mostly met by non-human sources. This means that you feel a sense of connection (and most alive) when you are in your connection habitat, whether that is creativity, music, cooking, nature, puzzles, technology devices or something else entirely. Many Green types are happy to spend long periods of time on their own. For this reason, you often come across as an observer of human connection rather than an active participant in it. You are happy to 'keep to yourself' and 'get on with it.' As you are low intensity and low frequency, you don't ask a lot of the people you are connecting with.

When you do participate in human connection, there is still a part of you that mentally remains in your habitat. The musician is still playing music, the chef is still cooking, the software developer is still writing code, the entrepreneur is still going over the strategy, the investor is still watching the market, the tinkerer is still tinkering, and the TV watcher is still dreaming about being on the couch.

This is why you can appear to have a natural reserve when connecting with others. People may perceive you to be a reserved, aloof or non-verbal communicator. You usually only talk when you feel it is necessary. Alternatively, you may be able to have animated interactions with others, and then you need to withdraw into your own world. Your tolerance for animated conversation has a limit.

You may feel challenged, annoyed, bored or overwhelmed when you are connecting with other types. High-intensity (Light, Dawn and Water) types bond through talking and connecting on an emotional level. They may want more from you than you are able or inclined to give. They may also find your connection unpredictable ('But you were so lively yesterday?'). High-frequency (Earth, Garden, Shapeshifter, Light, Dawn and Mountain) types will generally want to connect more often than you prefer to connect. So you may frequently feel that you don't have enough energy to give others when it comes to human connection. Or, you could feel that other people are often demanding more from you than you want to give.

As I explained in Part One, we all have to earn $100 of connection money every day in order to feel nourished and avoid loneliness. It doesn't accrue and it must therefore be earned in each twenty-four-hour period. Whereas other types will earned their connection money from people – through being together or talking – you will want to earn your connection from non-human sources, through natural belonging (peace in solitude). This difference in preferences will cause other types to feel that you don't care about their connection as much as they care about yours, so you may often feel that you are letting others down. Green types normally respond to this by surrounding themselves with a small, select group of people who are:

GREEN

- also Green types
- low-intensity Earth or Garden types, or
- mid- to low-frequency Water, Dawn or Coral types.

These are the people you click with. These types of connectors will not have high expectations of you in terms of time or intensity. Your challenge is meeting others in the middle and taking risks in connection: for example, to build trust in a conversation or in a relationship. While you are less effusive and energetic in human connection, you are also more likely to be reliable, loyal and steady in your connection. You demonstrate your love and affection for others through generous actions and providing for them. You will go out to work or do the dishes with no fanfare or complaint. When it comes to relationships, you value action rather than conversation.

You may be low intensity, but you are high consistency

When you connect with others, it is like they are sitting under the shade of a tree. It is consistently peaceful, cooling and serene. Your connection feels like a momentary escape from the outside world. Trees cool the air through transpiration. Your connection produces a similar effect, with your emotional energy 'cooling' the group dynamic. It calms high-intensity connectors and brings a sense of relief to other participants in your presence.

The coolness of shade can also produce shivers in the group if your directness or silence creates awkwardness. You tend to be a keen observer and you also have a witty and dry sense of humour. You are able to sit and listen to a long conversation and then you can occasionally deliver one line that sums up the entire discussion, often leaving people in shock at the depth of your perception.

Introducing the three Green types
1. Shades
Shades are strategic connectors. In any given situation, they might decide to wear their 'glasses' and slink away from connecting, or to

step into the light and engage. Shades can be animated or withdrawn, depending on their energy for connection.

2. Observer
Observers generally connect with others by first observing and then deciding whether to interact. They have a reserved and strategic style. They are enigmatic and keep people guessing.

3. Tree
Tree types are the lowest frequency and the lowest intensity of all the Connection Types. They are the most independent and self-sufficient of all the human connectors. The few Tree types I have met were happy to live alone and work alone.

Green types: communication style

The dominant aspect of Green communication is your choice of whether to communicate or not. You are experienced in remaining reserved and non-verbal in a conversation. You listen and occasionally nod and smile to indicate your participation.

GREEN

If you do decide to engage in verbal communication, you are 'to the point'. Your conversation stays on track and you are economical in word choice. Your voice and energy are measured and well-regulated as the conversation continues. You say what you need to say in order to communicate your point. Your speech is not rushed and the strength, tone and pitch of your voice does not vary. You may occasionally make eye contact but prefer not to look others directly in the eyes for too long as you consider this to be confrontational. You tend not to use hand gestures or you use gestures below your waist. You may have your hands behind your back, in your pockets or across your chest.

Green types enjoy getting the details right in conversations. You are methodical and rely on the way things have successfully been done in the past. You feel overwhelmed and irritated by co-workers or partners who want to tell stories about the big picture and emotions. You don't base your decisions on emotions. You prefer to use facts and figures – this ensures that decisions are evidence-based.

Green types: leadership style

You may not think of yourself as a leader because you aren't as verbal or social as traditional leaders in popular culture. Our conventional idea of leadership has someone energising, influencing and inspiring others through rousing speeches and motivational activities. This is not your style. Nevertheless, your leadership style is very powerful because you lead by example. You work alongside others and your approach is, 'I will not tell you what to do; I will show you how to do it and we will do it together'. This is actually a masterful form of coaching and talent development, whereby you engage in support-ive error correction as you work with someone. You demonstrate to others how you want them to be.

The other interesting aspect you have as a Green leader is that you are usually a technical expert – think of someone like the person leading a space exploration program. Green types are task-focused and you will not respond well to leaders who do not share your tech-nical expertise. For this reason, you Green types will rarely seek out a leadership position unless you have the most developed technical capability in the team. This is what Green types look to leadership for: problem-solving and training. Therefore, this is what a Green type leader will provide. Initially the people you lead may struggle because they might want more direction or feedback, but over time they will come to respect and trust your steady, reliable and diligent approach to work.

Leadership is also contextual. In my work with a military organisa-tion, it became apparent that the Green approach to leadership would be sought in contexts such as being on a submarine or on a tour of duty for long periods. A representative commented: 'No one wants a Light, talkative leader on a submarine. You want someone who knows what they're doing, who knows how to operate a submarine, and who will get out of your way.'

The key to a successful Green leader is:

- Technical competence: you can do the job as well as anyone else on the team so you can provide direction and guidance to others

- Lead by example: you give clear instructions and then offer error correction as your co-worker engages in the task

Green leaders believe that people do their best work when you give them clear instructions and then allow them to get on with the job. As you are so task oriented, you may need to call in a team of people-oriented professionals to provide the relational side of team building.

Green types: challenges
Self-expression and vulnerability

As we have established, human connection is not your preferred comfort zone. As such, the vulnerable aspects of human relationships and intimacy are not going to feel natural for you. For example, a Water woman is married to a Green type. She went away for a week for work. On her return her Green husband was reserved and did not appear to be affected either way by her being home. When they were eating dinner that night he said, 'It's good to have you back.' Until that point, she reported feeling that he did not care either way about whether they were together or not. There was no demonstration of feeling or emotion.

Similarly, a daughter once asked her father to complete the Ality Connection Type assessment. His result was a Green Observer type. In reading the description of her father, the daughter reported to me that she was brought to tears. She had always thought that her father didn't love her in a way that she recognised because he didn't want to talk to her or spend time with her as much as she wanted to spend time with him. In reading about Green types, she realised that human connection wasn't his comfort zone and that the time he was spending with her was quality time for him, and a sign of his love for her. Green types tend to show their love through generous acts and providing for their loved ones.

While Green types rely more on non-verbal communication than speaking, there are clear ways to tell the difference between happy and vulnerable Green types.

GREEN

Happy Green types	Green types in vulnerability
Peaceful in connection with others	Resist most if not all connection with other people
Content in own company	Feel uneasy even in own company
Happy to observe and listen in a group	Will avoid being in social groups
Use non-verbal communication such as nodding and smiling to convey interest	Non-verbal communication is closed off: for example, folded arms, no eye contact, no smiling or nodding
Demonstrate love and care through generous acts and providing for loved ones	Appear distant and uninterested in conversation. Do not engage in generous acts for loved ones as often as other types

Interestingly, my research shows that males are statistically more likely to be low intensity (Green, Earth and Garden types) and women are statistically more likely to be high intensity. Additionally, people aged over sixty-five are more likely to be Green types. This correlates Green type connection with males who were born before 1955–57. This data led me to consider the style of parenting and family dynamics in these generations, which is the source of our Connection Types. We are given positive attention for behaviours that our primary carers want to grow, and we are given negative or no attention for behaviours that our primary carers want to discourage.

It is only recently that we have invited and encouraged males of all ages to share their feelings and to be aware of their emotional experience. For much of history, the emotions of men were suppressed and they were tasked with keeping women and children safe. Young boys were raised to always be strong and ignore or numb any vulnerability, with messages like 'boys don't cry, children should be seen and not heard, and men are providers while women stay at home.' As a result of this environment, the stereotype of the connection style of older males is more 'to the point' and less emotional, hence we may have more Green connectors who are older males.

This further indicates that individuals may present as a certain type because of their conditioning and socialisation, but perhaps this type doesn't truly reflect their preferred connection environment. This is why the nature of the Ality Connection Type assessment is critical, because every question asks how you currently are, and then follows up by asking how you would prefer to be. The gap between your current and preferred types represents the gap between who you are and who your environment wants or wanted you to be.

I am a firm believer that people can adapt to new environments. I am still in the process of learning to adapt and regulate my own Connection Type. We need to make space for people to connect in the way that they are most comfortable and to respect their Connection Type. Having said that, if you are a Green connector, your relationships will thrive more if you open up and express your emotions. This could mean hugging your family and friends when you see them or asking one more question in a conversation to show that you are interested in what the other person is saying. You could organise a bike ride with a friend, or a trip to the movies, since rewarding connection doesn't have to involve speaking. You can slowly increase your time with others where no demands are placed on you to contribute. You may also find that connecting with an online community works for you.

Green types are fixed and steady like the trunk of a tall tree. While this is a powerful contribution to a group or family, other Connection Types may need more tenderness and expression from you. Metaphorically speaking, your emotional energy isn't only characterised by the trunk of a tree; you also have access to the branches as well. Allow your 'branches' to yield and sway towards others.

When you are feeling emotionally exposed, this will feel more challenging. You may feel like your branches are falling to the ground and that your roots are incapable of providing the nourishment you need. Your instinct will be to go further underground. Your frequency will decrease. You will lack any fuel for human connection because you don't 'feel like yourself' and you will withdraw from your social

GREEN

life. You will avoid contact and communication with others and you will be hard to reach. If you can, share the more sensitive side of you with your loved ones – it is just as much a part of you as the other sides. While the trunk of the tree is fixed, its branches can bend. You can be strong and tender at the same time. Don't withdraw so far underground that you miss the light of human connection on your face. In my interviews with Green types, some have shared regrets about not telling their loved ones how they felt. If you're reading this, you still have that chance to let them know.

Conflict

You prefer to avoid emotional conflicts and your reserved communication style supports this. As you are a non-aggressive communicator, you rarely arouse aggression in others, unless someone close to you is passionately asking for you to speak more, show up more and share your feelings more. If you are forced into an argument, you will become passive aggressive for a time and then you will withdraw. You are capable of using 'the silent treatment' for as long as you feel is necessary.

If you are absolutely required to have a difficult conversation you will state your position bluntly, then you will allow the other person to have their turn, and then you will want to move on and never discuss the matter again. If you do have the courage to show up for difficult and uncomfortable conversations, they can ultimately be a source of connection and can bring you closer to your loved ones.

Let's explore the three Green types in more detail: Shades, Observer and Tree.

Shades

Shades are strategic connectors. In any given situation, you might decide to wear your 'glasses' and retreat from connecting, or to remove them, step into the light and engage. Shades are in the lower ranges of low intensity and low frequency. In general, Shades types:

• Are warm and personable when the glasses are off and they are engaged

- Become reserved and aloof when the glasses are on: they can become emotionally invisible
- Feel uncomfortable in deep emotional conversations
- Are very perceptive observers of human behaviour
- Experience their strongest connections with non-human sources of connection: these can include music and instruments, cooking and food, animals, activities in nature (surfing, bushwalking, fishing), TV, movies, tech devices, the stock market, contemplation, reading, puzzles, tinkering and creativity of all forms
- Speak economically; they prefer to say only what needs to be said and may occasionally come across as being abrupt or even insensitive
- Thrive on close relationships with a select few; they bond with people through shared experiences over time and, when it comes to intimacy, their approach is, 'Don't tell me, show me' – they express affection through actions, not words
- Lead by example
- Are most comfortable in their own company; a big challenge for Shades is to share who they are with others as, if they do not, they risk missing the full richness of connection.

Characteristics

As a Shades type, you are a strategic connector. You can either leave your glasses on and withdraw into your own world or you can remove them and interact with others. Your proximity to the centre of the model means that you have a choice of whether to interact or withdraw. Other Green types (Observer and Tree) do not make this conscious choice to either participate or withdraw as their clear preference is to withdraw.

When you do open up to human connection, you can be animated and witty, an active participant in the group. This is why your connection can be hard to read for others because they find it tricky to predict when you will open up and when you will retreat. Your enthusiasm for human connection has a time limit, so the people who know you well will be able to anticipate when you have reached your tolerance and will need to exit (the party, the conversation or the meeting).

This is why you should be strategic, because you need to work out how to 'invest' your time and energy for human connection. People who don't know you well may take it personally that you don't want to sustain a connection with them or that you have gone from hot to cold. Of course this isn't personal to them; it's just the nature of your emotional energy. I once had a romantic relationship with a Shades type when we were at university. As a Light, I wanted to talk to him every day and see him every couple of days; as a Shades type, he was happy to talk to me a few times a week. I perceived his lack of motivation to connect with me as a lack of interest in the relationship. On many occasions, I suggested we end the relationship as he clearly wasn't as keen on me (I felt like I was giving him a way out). He would insist that he cared about me, and that he was giving all that he was capable of giving. And he insisted that he wasn't connecting with anyone else, either.

How I wish I'd had this model back then!

Needless to say, the relationship didn't work out, but looking back on it I realise I was taking his connection style personally. His appetite for connection was less than mine then and is always going to be less than mine. Interestingly, shortly after we broke up, I ran into his best friend on a night out and we had an enlightening conversation. His friend informed me, 'You were never going to work out with him. He's happy to stay at home watching TV for hours and you're a social butterfly. He wants someone who's not going to ask too much from him.'

This is why Green types often prefer to be with others who are also low frequency or at least mid-frequency. Their understanding of what you need gives you the freedom to pursue your comfort zone of connection without feeling like you're unable to meet their needs. You develop closeness with people based on consistency and shared positive experiences over time. You don't like to connect through highly intense conversations or through sharing emotional truth.

When your shades are off, the energy you bring to a group is good humoured and perceptive. When your shades are on, you are reserved and distracted, perhaps looking at your phone or fiddling with an object instead of talking.

At work, you are task-focused and prefer to work alone for the majority of the time. You are happy to collaborate with others to the extent that you need to share technical details, and then you want the freedom to allocate your time and be autonomous. Being actively engaged in conversations takes a lot of energy for you, so you learn to conserve your energy by withdrawing, delegating or outsourcing. For example, if you are feeling drained in a meeting, you will withdraw your eye contact and body language, check your phone or computer more frequently, or simply announce that you need to leave. You earn the respect of your colleagues because you are committed to getting the job done and will keep working until all tasks are complete. You are happy to engage in work for as long as it is required to finish your tasks. It is just human connection that you place a limit on.

You have a natural ability to diffuse and defuse energy in groups. You are non-aggressive and don't use other people to process your emotions, like many high-intensity people do. As such, you are a 'cool' and relieving addition to any group. You are considered to possess a level head and are often the voice of reason.

GREEN

Where to from here?

In terms of your ingredients for connection, you will thrive when you have ample time to withdraw into your own world. This is your haven and where you feel most like yourself. You will also be nourished by a small group of people who understand and respect the way you want to connect.

You don't need to feel guilty about the fact that you can only sustain human connection for so long. This is the way you maintain your logical and level-headed approach to life. This is also your natural appetite for frequency in relationships, though you will benefit from clearly explaining your connection needs to others. The most functional relationships and teams do not contain the same types of connectors, but they *are* aware of everyone's needs in connection. They may even gently joke about the fact that the Shades type has reached their conversation limit, or that the Shades type will want to leave the party early. The point is, they don't take it personally.

All of us have different ways of opening up to others and connecting. Learn to identify high-frequency connectors and high-intensity connectors (the opposites of your style) in your life and try to meet them in the middle, or at least understand where they are coming from. They are not trying to overwhelm you with their openness and sharing; they are trying to bond with you.

If you soften and become more open to human connection, you will find that your intimate relationships also soften in response. Try to adapt your response to vulnerability. The world won't fall apart if you share your emotions with loved ones!

To move towards the centre of human connection, you could try to stay a bit longer in each conversation. Say what's on your mind. Tell someone how you feel. You'll be surprised by how good it feels to connect this way!

You will enjoy low-intensity and fun activities, such as playing and watching sport, playing cards and board games, going to movies and concerts – basically participating in activities where there's no pressure for you to engage if you're not up for it.

Observer

Observer types are low-intensity and low-frequency connectors and as a result you feel most like yourself when you are engaged in an enjoyable pursuit on your own. Observers generally:

- Connect with others by first observing and then deciding whether to interact
- Have binoculars as their icon as they watch human connection from a distance – this is emotional distance rather than physical distance
- Have a reserved, practical and strategic style of connecting – they are enigmatic and keep people guessing
- Are closed in their body language
- Don't ask a lot of the people they are connecting with – they don't have expectations of human connection because that's not their greatest source of connection.

Characteristics

As an Observer type, you are more likely to feel connected when you are away from other people and in your connection habitat, whether that is creativity, music, cooking, nature, puzzles, tech devices or being with animals. This is why you can appear to have a natural reserve when connecting with others. People might perceive you to be shy or a non-verbal communicator.

Many Observer types are happy to spend long periods of time on your own or in your own world. For this reason, you are often more of an observer of human connection than an active participant in it. You like to keep to yourself. I have met many Observers who prefer to live alone, or, if not alone, in a regional or rural area. If you are happy to be surrounded by people, your Observer nature may simply come through in the fact that you are happy to listen rather than being an active contributor to conversation. You generally prefer a slower pace of human connection, whether that is verbal or reflected in the place you live.

This doesn't mean you want or need a slow pace in your work. In fact, many Observer types are so task-focused that you work in industries that are high intensity and very demanding. I know Observers who work as judges, soldiers, firefighters, police officers, and corrective services officers. Though these professions are highly demanding, none of them involves lengthy emotional conversations with other people. As an Observer type, you can handle high-intensity situations but you prefer to avoid high-intensity relationships.

You approach your work in a methodical and logical way. You break down the job into a series of tasks and then you efficiently work through each task until the job is complete. You are the sort of person who I would want as my surgeon. I would trust that you would be able to focus on the operation for as long as required without being distracted by your emotions or by other people. You have a laser-like task focus, which makes you extremely well placed for positions that require complete immersion: for example, aeroplane pilots, engineers and operators of complex machinery. This task focus serves you well in your career but may cause some challenges in your relationships.

GREEN

You are not instinctively comfortable in the world of people, emotions and conversations. You prefer to engage with others on your own terms. You are a person of few words but, when you share, people listen. I once spoke to a Light Star type who was married to a Green Observer. She said that they often go out to dinner with friends and she talks more because her husband is very reserved. After she has been contributing to the conversation for more than two hours, he will close the night with a short story or statement, and in her words, 'That will be everyone's takeaway from the whole night! He'll say one thing and everyone will go "ooh" and "aah" because he has spoken!'

The first reason that people listen intently when you speak is because they're very interested in what you have to say. Your approach to verbal communication is quality over quantity, so when you speak it is because you have something substantial and meaningful to contribute. The second reason is that your tendency to observe rather than speak often gives you an acute perception of situations. This is why you are so effective in high-intensity situations. When everyone around you is being whipped up into a frenzy of drama and chaos, you have the ability to stay grounded and methodical.

You are patient and strategic with your verbal communication, which also makes you suitable for jobs in intelligence or even as a professional poker player. Every truck driver I have ever profiled is a Green type, and usually an Observer: able to endure days on the road with limited human connection. Your mindset is always situated in the practical implications of decisions.

For someone in a romantic relationship with you, your self-reliance and independence may become frustrating if they ever question your love and affection for them, because there's not a lot of evidence in terms of regular quality time or verbal outpourings that they can rely on. You will need to reassure them that you demonstrate your love through actions, not words. An Observer type I know gets his wife a coffee and the newspaper each morning before she gets out of bed. He may be a man of few words but he is a devoted husband. Make sure your loved ones know how much you care.

Where to from here?

You instinctively enjoy low-intensity activities that you can engage in on your own. For example, taking your dog for a walk, going fishing, playing music or a musical instrument, cooking, working, pottering in a shed, listening to an audiobook or podcast, watching the stock market, reading, and exercising in nature (running, surfing, walking etc.). If you're up for it, you might like to play a low-intensity sport such as golf, bowls or tennis, or you might like to go to a movie or concert.

You make friends and develop romantic connections by sharing positive experiences over time. You may meet someone through a friend who you see regularly and this develops into a mutual respect. You might work with someone for many years and over time your friendship will grow. People appreciate that you don't ask a lot of them, that you accept them as they are and are patient with them. You don't demand a lot of other people in relationships. If you are a parent, your children will appreciate the emotional boundaries and freedom you give them, but they may need a bit more verbal affirmation from you if they are higher frequency and intensity connectors. I have also met many women who are Observer types. They are adored wives and mothers because they are always there for the people they love, but they are 'no fuss' and practical about how they approach their relationships.

Observing human connection is more relaxing for you than engaging in it. You might be part of a family, friendship group or a sports team where you like to go along to social events but you are happy to be on the periphery – you don't need to be an active participant in the conversation. In my work I have encountered several female Green types who like to be a part of groups but are happy to listen – to observe – rather than speak.

To move towards the centre of human connection, you could try to slowly increase this kind of social time around others where no demands are placed on you to contribute.

To improve your connection with others, work on being curious and asking questions of others, and acknowledging and thanking

GREEN

others for being there for you: for example, 'I feel connected just knowing you are there for me when I need you.'

Tree

Tree types are in the extreme ranges of low intensity and low frequency, preferring to limit time with other people. In addition to the main features of an Observer, Tree types:

- Are the most self-sufficient of all human connectors
- Have their connection habitat as their inner world; they derive your greatest experience of connection from non-human sources: for example, they might connect with music, musical instruments, work tasks, animals, nature (surfing, bushwalking, fishing), creativity in any form (art, dance, writing), TV, movies, tech devices, contemplation, meditation, yoga, coding, reading, puzzles or just pottering and tinkering
- Don't feel the need to connect with a wide variety of people because their needs are largely met by their non-human sources of connection
- Are reserved and aloof in their connection style: they keep people wondering what you're thinking
- Are comfortable in their own company and so their challenge is to communicate with the people they care about and relate to their loved ones on their terms; in a constant state of reserve, they may miss out on the rich potential of human connection
- Are uncomfortable with deep emotional conversations
- Lead and parent by example.

Characteristics

The connection of a Tree type is a lot like the root system of a tree, existing below the surface of the earth and nestled in the soil. In human connection terms, the preferred habitat of a Tree type is 'underground' or 'on your own'. This makes relating to a Tree type quite difficult because they prefer their own company and do not actively seek out connection with other people.

Connecting with a Tree type is therefore like sitting up against the trunk of a tree. As a Tree type, your presence is powerful and even majestic, yet your communication is largely non-verbal. Much of your connection with other people will always remain out of sight and sound, just like a tree with a deep and complex root system.

As a Tree type, you are content to live on your own. You bond very gradually with people through shared experiences over time. Of course you have people in your life who you love and appreciate, but for you it's about quality over quantity. For example, you are content to have your family and a few friends and acquaintances to connect with.

Many Tree types are happy to spend extended periods of time on their own or in their own world. For this reason, you are often more of an observer or an avoider of human connection than an active participant in it. You like to keep to yourself.

Through my work, I have met many Tree types who will say that they are much happier when they're living on their own. This isn't always the case. One lovely Tree type I met during a workshop was a farmer and proudly shared with me that his nearest neighbour was 60 kilometres away from his house. He had his daily tasks associated with running the farm and he was very content with his life. When this man's wife died, he spent a couple of years grieving on his own and then met another woman through an old friend. He had brought his new partner along to the workshop.

She approached me at the end of my workshop and said, 'Okay, so you know what he's like. He's a beautiful and kind man and I'm in love with him. But he's a Tree type. I'm pretty independent and I have my own life. But I still want to talk to the person I'm in a relationship with. What do I do?'

My advice was that she should have an understanding with him that in order for the relationship to thrive, they will need to spend one good hour together each day where they are both intentionally interacting. This can involve talking or being physical with each other, but he needed to know that this hour can't be passive connection like watching TV or eating dinner in silence. The whole point about

GREEN

understanding someone else's Connection Type is not to change them; it's to create a bridge between people so that we can bring out the best in each other.

Tree types are so self-sufficient that, in times gone by, such types would have had the courage to be an explorer, to set sail for new lands or to enter the great unknown. At this point in history, you may have the courage to be an astronaut or at least an understanding of what it would take to go to Mars. You don't have a compulsive need to connect with other people in a predictable and comfortable way. This separates you from most other human beings and makes you extraordinary.

As a Tree type, you may enjoy minimal low-intensity human connections and then withdraw into your habitat (wherever that may be) to reflect and rejuvenate. A Tree type can still be a leader; you just need to be clear with your boundaries and manage your downtime in such a way that you can have space from other people. You may have times where you need to be confident, outgoing or outspoken. You are capable of being whatever the moment requires; it's just that these types of experiences take a lot of your energy and you will need to recover on your own afterwards. For this reason, the regular connections required by family, work, friends and community may often feel overwhelming for you.

Where to from here?

You will feel content if your life is filled with a series of low-intensity activities that you can engage in on your own terms. You might be a farmer, an astronaut, a soldier, a full-time parent on a property, a fisherman, a radiologist analysing reports, a computer coder or a truck driver – your preference is for your work to be low frequency and low intensity. You might happily live or work on your own and spend your days in your own world, getting practical things done and only engaging in human connection if necessary. You like knowing people are there if you need them, but you don't need a lot of human connection to get by.

Your self-sufficiency makes you extraordinary. You have the power to explore the far reaches of the universe without needing constant human connection. This almost makes you immune to connection with other people. There are many contexts and careers where it is an asset to not need people. The guidance for you is to find your comfort zone and settle into your daily routine.

GREEN

chapter 11

Earth types

Characteristics	Tools to enhance relationships
High frequency: welcoming, friendly, feel relaxed in groups and belong to multiple groups. You choose and curate particular groups of people and then you like to see them often.	Acknowledge that you are a leader: actively taking the lead and displaying power in a group can feel like the opposite of connection for you. Your capacity to bring people together is the foundation of good leadership. You will serve the group well if you embrace your leadership qualities.
Low intensity: bond through positive shared experiences over time and good humour. Prefer to avoid conversations about how you feel.	You may not enjoy talking about your emotions, but the people you care about might need to do this. Showing vulnerability can bring you closer to others, and make you feel emotionally lighter.
Backbone of groups, good at bringing and keeping people together. Your core values are enjoyment and acceptance.	Give new people a chance to join your groups.
Practical and down-to-earth, solid and dependable emotional energy.	
Like to be left alone when vulnerable.	

Earth types: characteristics

Earth types (Meeting Place, Foundation and Rock) have a preference for high-frequency and low-intensity human connection. This means that you like a lot of connection with others but that you want that connection to be light and easy. You feel most comfortable when you are connecting in groups of your choosing, engaging in good-humoured and relaxed conversation. Even though you enjoy regular human connection, you are quite selective about who you are connecting with. You don't want to connect with just anyone. You have your groups of 'chosen' people and you like to be in their company. In fact, when you are meeting people for the first time, you may even come across as superficially friendly but impenetrable and hard to crack.

You thrive when you are in groups of like-minded people, such as sports teams, friendship groups or work teams. You might have a group of people you play sport with once a week, or a group of people you play cards with. Once you're in a group of people, you might not think that you do anything special or out of the ordinary to establish connection with others. You just are who you are and you're happy in the company of your chosen groups. But there's actually something special about that. As explained earlier in the book, belonging to social groups can significantly improve our mental and physical health. Social groups can be our family, the neighbours on our street, old friends, our work colleagues, or a community group. This research is a great sign for Earth connectors, because you are the masters of curating social groups!

The experience of being in groups, families and teams comes naturally to you. You can't take this for granted as many people find group dynamics to be challenging or anxiety-inducing. Other Connection Types might overcompensate in a group and try to dominate or respond to the group dynamic by totally withdrawing.

For you, it feels instinctive to be in a group – it doesn't make you anxious and you are skilled at creating positive connections between others. You don't have a compulsive need to be liked or to be the

EARTH

centre of attention. For this reason you end up being liked and people are happy to listen to you. For many people, connection is a challenge or an effort, but you make it look effortless and easy. That's the paradox of your approach to connection.

As with all the connection quadrants, there are three levels of connection for Earth types.

Introducing the three Earth types

1. Meeting Place

A meeting place is common ground that people are comfortable to connect on: for example a park, cafe or a beach. Your accepting and inviting nature brings this emotional energy to a group.

2. Foundation

You are the foundation and backbone of any group to which you choose to belong. You have authority and a strong sense of right and wrong, and you always put the group first. This commands respect from others.

3. Rock

Your emotional energy is like the cliffs near the ocean. You make people feel safe to trust you and they know that you are strong enough to support them.

Earth types: communication style

An Earth type is friendly and personable on first meeting. You are happy to chat and make others feel comfortable but you don't give a lot away in terms of your facial expressions. Your non-verbal communication (body language) is quite hard to read, which means you probably have a good poker face, until you smile; this is when your personality breaks through. Your voice is steady and calm. You make eye contact with people you are communicating with and use regular nodding to convey your interest and respect for other people. You use hand gestures when you feel connected to the person you are talking to. If you don't want to connect or you're not interested in what's being spoken about, you will cut active eye contact and all active forms of signalling engagement.

You give others an impression of stability, even if you are feeling nervous, emotional or uncertain. This is a strength and a challenge for you, because it is your default position to wear an emotional shield and not let anyone in. In one interview with an Earth type, I was told:

> My poker face is sometimes too good and that was how I managed to pretend I had the perfect home life for so long as I grew up and even when I got older. Only people who knew me very, very well would be able to get things out of me or know when I was just pretending. It's the same now. It's part of how I'm able to act so calm at work when, really, I'm sweating and freaking out.

Once you get to know someone, you are a gifted storyteller and can capture anyone's attention with your humility and good humour. This often makes you the life of the party.

Earth types: leadership style

The Earth style of leadership is the captain coach – you are able to be part of the team and at the same time strive to get the best out of the team. An Earth leader doesn't give orders: they ask others to join in with the task. You have the unique ability to be both actively involved in the group's activities and also maintain a big-picture view to see what the team needs next.

You are out on the field with the other players and will only take a step forward once you are confident that the entire team is ready to step forward with you. You don't feel compelled to prove that you are the top performer in the team, but you do feel responsible for the team coming together to deliver a good result. If someone looks on, it's often unclear who the leader is until something goes wrong or there is a crisis.

EARTH

One Earth leader I spoke to said, 'I will always assign a task to the person who is best at that task, even if that means I end up having to do a crappy job. For example, if there is an opportunity for me as the leader to participate in a perk of the job, I will still allocate it to the person who is normally responsible for that section. I always assess decisions from an objective point of view, and from the perspective of fairness. The leader shouldn't get special treatment.' As an Earth leader you would never ask someone to do something that you wouldn't expect to do yourself.

An Earth leader is also very collaborative. You will present a problem for the group to consider and solve. You will put forward a solution but ensure that the group is supportive of the way forward. This is a very effective approach to leadership, built on a foundation of trust and respect.

Earth types: challenges
Claiming leadership

Although the Earth approach to leadership is highly effective in terms of achieving results, your instinct is often to avoid official leadership positions and instead embrace informal leadership roles. This is because you are humble and it is uncomfortable for you to assume positions that may give you authority over anyone else. As I was told by an Earth leader, 'I don't like all the pomp and ceremony of leadership. I like to be in the trenches, getting it done together, encouraging others, and leading by example.' This Earth leader used to take on deputy roles, which enabled them to lead from within the team and to focus on getting the best out of the team: 'When I played rugby, I was much more comfortable being a vice captain or being the senior member of the team who was responsible for everyone. My preferred method was to pick out the problem players and work with them for the betterment of the group. This method was a more discreet form of leadership. I like being a discreet leader. If the person who is captain is a dickhead, I'll hate that as well. I prefer the team captain to be nicer and more encouraging. I was always the vice captain role or the sergeant at arms where I could dictate what was going on behind the scenes instead of being the face of it.' Earth leaders, you eventually realise that you need to formally claim leadership and learn how to delegate.

Your skill in bringing people together automatically gives you leadership qualities. If you resist formal leadership positions you risk being frustrated by the people who take them on and make different decisions to those you would make. If you can combine your accepting, dependable nature with a strategy to move the group forward, you will be an unstoppable leader.

Emotional expression and vulnerability

Another key challenge of Earth types is your discomfort with expressing emotion. In speaking with Earth types, I am informed that you will only express their authentic emotions to your trusted partners. To everyone else, you are easygoing and laid-back, always deflecting uncomfortable situations with a joke and seemingly unaffected by day-to-day issues. This serves you because you can stay in control of your emotions and therefore your environment. This also serves the people around you well, as they feel psychologically safe in your presence because you are steady and dependable. But, over time, the people close to you may question your reluctance to share anything emotional or personal with them. In an interview with an Earth type, I was told:

> In the past I was always holding back, only ever pulling a curtain slightly apart to let people in. If I showed vulnerability to other people, I would regret it afterwards. Now I am with my first partner where I have ever shown complete vulnerability with nothing held back. That's taken a lot of growing up and a lot of different relationships.

EARTH

This Earth type observed that she definitely prefers having someone to open up to.

I invite you Earth types to experiment with sharing small aspects of how you feel with a trusted friend or partner. In evaluating what you would like to share, ask yourself: is this going to matter to me in ten years? If yes, then it is worthwhile to share it with someone you trust. In overcoming any discomfort, we all need to start with awareness. Having a witness to our emotions helps to process them. We can dwell on certain feelings and inner stories for a long time if we don't have the courage to share them and bring them into the light.

Impenetrable and hard to crack until . . .

I was told by an Earth type, 'When I meet people for the first time I will be surface-level friendly but I can be really stand-offish. I only open up with my close circle.' You can come across as being impenetrable and hard to crack until someone becomes part of your chosen circle. For this reason, it may help you to be a bit more open to newcomers at work or in your community. They could become a lifelong friend.

Let's explore the three Earth types in more detail.

Meeting Place

Meeting Place types are close to the centre of the model, in the low ranges of low intensity and high frequency. The centre of the model represents a score of zero for both frequency and intensity, so your type is above zero for frequency and below zero for intensity. Your emotional energy conveys good humour and ease. You have a comfortable presence and invite people to come as they are. You generally:

- Are steady, easygoing, and draw people in with your friendly and chatty manner
- Have an extensive social network, most likely belonging to several different social groups
- Prefer to be in the company of others rather than being alone, but still enjoy time on your own to relax
- Thrive on human connection
- Don't consider yourself as a typical leader, yet you have a powerful leadership style as the team captain–coach

Characteristics

You are usually the backbone of any group you are in, and your presence creates an inviting space for people to come together. Your Connection Type represents home, community and a 'come as you are' space that invites people to congregate. Your connection is focused on bringing people together and you tend to do whatever is best for the group. This reflects your laid-back and accepting nature. However, this is only what's happening on the surface, where each interaction with you is light and easy, like sand running through the fingers. Below the surface is different. Over time with the same person or the same group, this sand solidifies and becomes as hard as rock. You build unbreakable bonds with your consistency and loyalty. You value the wellbeing of the group over everything else, so there is a focus on stability and cohesion. As you are a low-intensity connector, you prefer to focus on the lighter side of life and avoid topics that are emotionally intense or heavy. You don't dwell on your emotions or become consumed with worry because this clashes with your connection values of ease and good humour. If there is someone who threatens these values in the group, you will prefer for them to leave or to be sidelined.

The universal forms of human connection (humour, storytelling, celebration, fun and authenticity) are wrapped up in who you are and what you expect from a social experience. Human connection is therefore a part of your personality. You are a natural and engaging connector. Your affinity for connection means that people like to have you around. You have a level head and you like to have fun, so you're often surrounded by others. You have a positive communication style that manifests itself in open body language and the use of humour to deflect or connect. You are often looking for opportunities to connect with your friends through fun and celebration. You love a party!

Given your agreeable nature, it is uncomfortable for you to recognise yourself as a leader of the group. For a Meeting Place type, actively taking the lead and displaying power in a group can feel like the opposite of connection. While you are happy to share your

EARTH

opinions with others, you don't like to tell anyone else what to do. You have no interest in controlling others. You believe that people will unfold in their own time. You believe that everyone plays an important role in the team, and that the team is more important than any individual. Your challenge is therefore how to convert your popularity and agreeableness into a humble form of leadership. You might think, *I'm not a leader – I just like being involved and a part of the team*, but in fact people will go wherever a Meeting Place leader takes them. The Meeting Place leader is the one who will step in and lead the group as a steady hand guiding the ship, so make sure you acknowledge the power of your leadership as you maintain your humility.

In fact, the latest research in leadership shows that we have moved away from the heroic myth of leadership, away from the impressive, dominating leader and towards the leader who can connect with others. The humble form of leadership that a Meeting Place models is in fact a very sophisticated form of influencing and inspiring others. I have met two classic Meeting Place leaders: one was the head of a fire department for twenty-five years and the other was head of a police area command for thirty years. They were both committed, driven, humble and highly respected.

You are steady, fixed and immovable. You're tough and stoic, qualities that are an asset in most contexts. However, this tenacity can come also across as stubbornness or inflexibility. Some of the more sensitive or intense connectors in your life may take this personally ('Do you even care about me?' 'You don't seem affected . . . '). Your capacity to power forward and 'toughen up' could be interpreted as lacking in tenderness to other types of high-intensity connectors. The upside of your approach is that you have considerable energy for human connection because you don't carry the emotional energy of others with you. You don't absorb the feelings of others and are able to use great perspective when you are evaluating the behaviour of another person.

The downside is that you can tend to see vulnerability as a sign of weakness when in actual fact it is a sign of humanity and strength. Your challenge is to learn how to yield and soften in your relationships. It is positive to let your guard down and share your emotions with those you trust. You may find that your need to numb your emotions lessens when you share them with others.

You could benefit from finding deeper ways to connect with your more sensitive or intense loved ones. Don't be afraid to share your emotions with those you trust. This can create a deeper connection and bring you relief. Admitting that you carry a heavy load will not undermine your strength. Talking about your feelings with others can be a positive source of connection.

As a Meeting Place type, you will experience vulnerability as though the earth beneath you is unstable or coming apart. You feel the need to dig your feet deeper into the earth, to regain control. When you are feeling like this you often put on a brave face for the world as you dig in and sweep your emotions under a rug. To others this can come across as stubbornness.

This strategy works in the short term, but over time your suppressed emotions can become heavier and heavier. You are likely to use some form of numbing to escape from your challenging emotions, such as overeating, excess drinking or watching too much TV. You may be smiling on the outside but inside you are desperate to distract yourself from your emotions.

At your most vulnerable, you will feel like you are crumbling and unstable. Your frequency preference for human connection will decrease. You will lack the fuel for human connection because you don't 'feel like yourself' and you will take a step back from your social life. You will put on a brave face when you see others and if you are forced into connection you are likely to be distracted or you will numb yourself: the lights might be on but there's no one home.

Get to know yourself during these times. Share your sensitive side with your loved ones, since it is just as much a part of you as the other sides. While the earth is solid, it is also changeable. It can soften and move. You can be strong and vulnerable. Don't let your armour become your skin.

You are motivated by the group's best interests, so you will only engage in conflict if it enables the group to grow. You prefer to avoid conflict and will become passive aggressive in anger. If you are required

EARTH

to have a difficult conversation you calmly and firmly make your views known and then you will give the other person a chance to do the same, but their point of view is unlikely to sway you. If you have the courage to show up for difficult and uncomfortable conversations, they can ultimately be a source of connection and can bring people closer together.

Where to from here?

You are gifted with an ability to bring people together to have fun. Think of ways to socialise with your social network: the more, the merrier! You will also benefit from being a member of a club or community group with regular meetings or social engagements. You are the backbone of any group you're in, so they'll be lucky to have you.

- You learn and develop through group leadership positions as a captain or coach, so start to recognise yourself as the kind of leader who each team needs.
- Understand that all of us have different ways of opening up to others and connecting. Learn to identify low-frequency connectors and high-intensity connectors (the opposites of your style) and try to meet them in the middle.
- You don't need any lessons in building belonging, but you do need to think about being a bit kinder and gentler to yourself. If you soften, you will find that your intimate relationships also soften in response. Try to adapt your response to vulnerability – the world won't fall apart if you share your emotions with loved ones!
- Meeting Place connectors can connect with anyone, anytime. That's the key to belonging, and belonging is the key to happiness! You will thrive if you belong to a variety of social groups. You like to have a new group for each day of the week, so set your life up like this and fill your calendar with a range of social activities, as this will switch you on.

Foundation

Foundation connectors carry emotional energy in relationships and groups that is strong, reliable and steadfast. You are, as the name suggests, emotional foundations for others. Foundation types are high-frequency and low-intensity connectors. In addition to the main features of Meeting Place types, Foundations generally:

- Make people feel safe, as though they have it covered and ensure situations are under control
- Are skilled at reading other people by being trustworthy and quietly hyper-vigilant
- Enjoy working with rules and systems and have a strong sense of right and wrong
- Believe that there is usually a 'best way' to get things done; usually it's their way
- Can occasionally be stubborn and outspoken; they have strong views on most topics and are unafraid to express these views to others
- Are a good judge of character; people like to know where they stand with a Foundation type, and this characteristic drives them to high popularity.
- Express their views in strong and assertive ways: 'this is how it is'.
- Use humour to divert high-intensity connectors from conflict and drama.

Characteristics

I started my career as a criminal lawyer. I wish I'd had my model back then, so it could identify for me why I was so affected by the high intensity and trauma of the courtroom and why absorbed the trauma of victims so readily. One of the first trials I participated in involved an accused person who would scream at everyone in the courtroom, and yell targeted abuse at the top of his lungs. He started out by screaming out a death threat to the police officer sitting next to me. I subtly turned my head to see whether the officer was at all affected by what the accused was screaming out. The officer leant into me and said, 'I think he's talking to you,' then started chuckling. I couldn't believe that he was able to laugh off a situation that was so serious.

EARTH

Later on, as the team had coffee, I asked him why he wasn't affected by the screaming or the death threat. 'Oh, it's water under the bridge,' he said. 'You get used to it in this line of work.'

'Yes, I can see that,' I agreed, 'but surely you must also be a tough and resilient type of person.'

'Sure, I'll take that,' he said, laughing.

In my assessment, this illustrates the behaviour of a typical Foundation type: a first responder able to take life-and-death situations in his stride. I was so relieved to have his tough and unfazed presence in that courtroom.

As a Foundation type, you represent solid ground to others. When people connect with you they feel supported and safe. They are able to trust your connection because you are very stable and steadfast – you're emotionally predictable. You tell the truth and you don't get emotional when you communicate. Even in conflict situations, you are able to be assertive but not aggressive. You can maintain humour in situations of high pressure or emotion. You show up and you are unwavering in your values and attitudes. You have fixed views on most topics and you share these views with others in a way that is clear and measured. In connection with others, you value honesty and reliability. Low-intensity connection equals high-consistency connection.

You don't become overwhelmed by group dynamics and you stay grounded and down-to-earth even in a crisis or emergency. For this reason, you are suited to high-pressure jobs such as first-response work (police, paramedic, emergency doctors, nurses or firefighters) or work involving tight deadlines and intense environments. This is the key: your low intensity connection with others allows you to stay clear-headed in high-intensity situations. This is your superpower.

Connecting with you is like pouring concrete to create a foundation for a building. Each interaction represents the pouring of wet concrete and yet over time the concrete dries into a resolute and protective foundation to be built on. You build unbreakable foundations with your consistency and loyalty.

Foundation types: Sanda's story

I conducted an extremely informative and eye-opening interview with a Foundation type, Sanda, who works in counter-terrorism protection. Here are some insights into Foundation type connectors based on that interview.

Foundation type connectors like to carefully select who they spend time with and they appreciate being near people without having to talk: Sanda tells me: 'My favourite people are all people I can sit in silence with. No one has to fill the silence. I like a lot of human connection but I like to dictate who I spend time with.'

Foundation types enjoy being in groups if everyone is comfortable. According to Sanda, 'If I am in a group of people, I am conscious of the dynamic of the group. I try to get like-minded people together and make people feel comfortable. The comfort and enjoyment of other people is as important as mine.'

Foundation types take responsibility for how people feel in a group, which is reflected in Sanda's experience: 'I feel responsible for everybody's time. If I feel like someone is being a jerk or makes a rude comment, I'll take it on myself to take them down a peg. I will sometimes avoid social interaction because it will take so much energy for me to make sure everyone has a good time.'

Foundation types can appear calm on the surface but be panicking underneath: Sanda says, 'At work we wear suits and I'll be sweating underneath my suit jacket. My armpits could be drenched, but I am cool as a cucumber on the surface.'

The challenge of a Foundation type can be an inability to change or respond to new conditions. Sanda sees that the downside of a Foundation type attitude is: 'this is the system, this is the rule, this is the process, this is what goes. And that's the way it's always been done.'

EARTH

Where to from here?

Whether you lead from the back or behind the scenes, acknowledging your powerful leadership role is key. Informal leaders can shape the team's dynamic and success, occasionally more than formal leaders or leaders by rank.

- Experiment with softness. In your conversations, instead of forming a view of someone instantly, try experimenting with some questions like 'What are your views on that?' and 'How did you come to form that view?' Or, you could soften your opinions by saying, 'My sense of what's going on is . . .', 'What I understand to be the case is . . .' and 'My reaction to that was . . .' Sometimes it's these softening phrases that are the difference between opening up connection with others or shutting it down. If you start a conversation with someone by saying 'What we need to do is . . .' or 'Clearly what's going on is . . .' you are basically communicating to them that their view or their role is irrelevant. Your challenge is to balance your clarity about how to get things done with your desire to get on with others. This can happen by softening the way you communicate.
- You need to have solid groups of friends in your social network and you will enjoy seeing them regularly. You will need a regular exercise schedule as being strong is empowering for you. You enjoy low intensity activities in a group setting, such as sports, art and music. Participating in teams is the key to your connection. If you are a Foundation type and you are experiencing loneliness, it's likely because you don't belong to enough groups. You can join a group by doing Pilates or water aerobics; bike riding or bowling. You can volunteer for a community organisation or not-for-profit. You can go to the same cafe, restaurant or community centre so regularly that you form strong social connections through that. Build group participation into your schedule and make it non-negotiable.

Rock

According to my research, Rock types are the rarest form of connectors with only eight out of 5,000 respondents matching this type

(0.16 per cent). It's still statistically significant and its own type – just unusual. If you are a Rock type, you can be proud of your uniqueness! These Connection Types are in the extreme ranges of low intensity and high frequency, which may explain why your type is so rare. It is an unusual combination to be both social and non-verbal. The desire for human connection in Rock types manifests itself in the need to be near others, but not necessarily talking.

In addition to the main features of a Foundation, Rock types generally have the following characteristics:

- They protect and uphold what is important to the group they are the self-appointed protector of the group's values.
- They are extremely task-based: they always know what needs to be done, and they get on with doing it. They like to have a series of tasks to complete as this makes them feel useful.
- People can count on Rock types to be consistent and strong every hour of the day, every day of the week. In this way, their reliability and tenacity provide the continuity for people to persevere, for groups to continue and for strong cultures to form.
- Rock types are the guardians of tradition, systems and laws. Whatever they care about, whether it is their family, their work, their country or all of these combined, they connect by upholding and advocating for what that person/organisation/nation stands for. They do not deviate from the central tenets of the group they align themselves with.
- In some ways, they are tough to crack. They are high frequency, which means that they are energised by the company of other people. However, they are extremely low intensity, so they like their connection with others to be non-verbal; they prefer to share positive experiences over time than to have intense conversations with people. They are more likely to bond with someone over a shared interest or passion, such as sport or service in the army. This means that it may be challenging for someone to connect with a Rock type if they don't share their interests. Rock types are more likely to click with someone who rolls up their sleeves and

EARTH

shares an experience alongside them than they are with someone who tries to connect to them through conversation.

- They have strong beliefs on most topics and it takes a lot to change their mind. They have unwavering views.
- People rely on Rock types for their consistency – they know that a Rock will always do what they say they are going to do. People come to them for their advice.
- They are as strong as an ox, and they have the courage of their convictions.
- They like working with rules and systems – they have a strong sense of right and wrong, of black and white.
- They make people feel safe, as though they 'have it covered' and as though situations are under control.

Characteristics

Congratulations on being the rarest form of connector! You are the most extreme version of an Earth type. Your connection represents the stability and safety of the most solid form of earth; rock faces and cliffs. You are stronger than solid ground. Your type of strength takes years to form.

As a Rock type you represent armour to others. If you are their ally (such as a family member, friend or colleague) they will experience your strength as protective and comforting. But if you are connecting with a stranger or you are opposing someone in conflict, your armour may be intimidating and impenetrable. For this reason, people want to be on your side. You have clear opinions about how things should be, and you understand the best way forward.

You are low intensity, and this means you are able to deal with high-intensity situations without losing control of your emotions. You would be well suited to high-pressure environments such as first-response work (police, firefighting, emergency doctors, nurses, paramedic work or the military). Think of Arnold Schwarzenegger's character in *The Terminator*, designed to feel no pain and no fear. We want a person like this in a high-intensity situation. We want this person to protect us. You are also suited to work involving tight deadlines and intense environments such as professional sport or professional coaching. This is your superpower, as your low-intensity connection with others allows you to stay clear-headed in high-intensity situations.

In a group setting, you represent armour to other people, for better and for worse. This armour is protective against external elements. This is why you are comfortable aligning yourself with groups that need support and protection, for example in security work or dignitary protection. The armour makes the group feel invincible, like we are ready for anything the world might throw at us. You create this sense of safety and protection in others through your stability and loyalty.

Having said that, hopefully you get to participate in groups that don't require external protection. Feeling compelled to protect others is linked to hyper-vigilance, which is a mindset where you constantly scan your environment for potential threats. As a natural protector, it will be necessary for you to spend time in environments that do not contain threats. You are a low-intensity connector, which means that you prefer to avoid discussing topics that are emotionally intense or heavy. Relaxation for you will involve low-intensity but social pursuits such as team sports, marathons and ocean swims.

You enjoy low-intensity activities in an organised setting. You might be a member of a club or organisation and you enjoy participating in the activities of that institution. You are drawn to organised groups, for example a sports team, a religious group, the military, a motorbike group, a close work team or strong family. You like knowing that you can trust the people around you and you enjoy seeing the people within your tight-knit group as often as possible.

EARTH

Where to from here?

Rock connectors form the armour of any group. Participating in loyal groups with strong values is the key to your connection.

- You are happy to play a leadership role in a strong and well-defined organisational structure, and you will fulfil your responsibilities without fear or favour. You are the guardian of your team – you will defend your team members to the death.

- As a leader you will create clear objectives and expectations for people to follow. There will be consequences for people who do not follow these guidelines. People feel secure with a Rock leader because the expectation framework and the boundaries are so clear. They know where they stand with you, and what you want from them.
- You can evolve your connection style by working on flexibility and empathy. Of all the types, Rocks are the most likely to dig their heels in on an issue. This could have a destructive effect on your connection with others because they may perceive that your views are set in stone and will never budge. More sensitive or intense connectors may feel that your connection style is uncaring or too harsh. One wife described her Rock husband as 'grumpy,' because he would have a gruff manner when his wife tried to talk about her emotions. A Rock mother used to say 'Pull yourself together' when her daughter was crying.

Make sure you have the courage to show up for difficult and uncomfortable conversations. They can ultimately be a source of connection and can bring people closer together. Don't let your Rock nature turn to concrete in conflict, because this is a barrier to connection.

chapter 12

Boundary types: Shapeshifter, Dawn, Mountain, Garden and Coral

When you look at the Ality Connection Type model, at the edges of the four quadrants and in the centre you'll see five additional types: Shapeshifter, Dawn, Mountain, Garden and Coral. These boundary types are combinations of the main quadrant types and are more likely to adapt their connection to the environment they are in. This chapter describes these boundary types and how they can work on compatibility with people who have other preferences for the frequency and intensity of connection.

Shapeshifter: the centre of connection

Shapeshifters are universal human connectors, able to adapt to the dynamics of any group or relationship. Being mid-intensity and mid-frequency connectors, they lie at the central meeting point of all quadrants. Shapeshifters are the only type that is compatible with every other type in the model. Shapeshifters generally:

- Are highly adaptive and comfortable meeting new people and travelling to new environments
- Are insightful and responsive in relationships
- Are highly empathetic and able to bring harmony to groups

- Tend to avoid conflict and will always seek to accommodate others first
- Lead by collaborating with others.

Characteristics

The definition of a Shapeshifter is someone or something that can change their form or nature at will, in order to adapt to their environment. Another word for a shapeshifter is a chameleon. As a Shapeshifter connector, you can change your form or nature depending on the group you're in. When you enter a group setting, you read the dynamic and work out what that group needs in order to achieve harmony. Then you become that – you express the emotional energy that the group needs.

The Shapeshifter is at the centre of the Ality Connection Type Model. This means that you are a universal human connector as you have the ability to adapt your connection to any person or group you are with. You are a human version of a universal power adaptor that can be taken to another country to provide power and connection in that new context. This, by the way, makes you a great traveller. You meet people easily, adapt to new environments and create rapport quickly.

It takes great insight into human behaviour to be a Shapeshifter. You are constantly observing and assessing group dynamics to determine what is required from you in order to create balance and harmony. All other Connection Types tend to impose their connection styles on a group in order to form a group dynamic. In contrast, you wait to observe the dynamic before adding what it needs. You can read a dynamic and then connect the people within that dynamic.

You easily sense the type of connection desired by the person or people in front of you, intuitively understanding their preference for connection. You then decide whether to become a mirror or a complement to that person's connection style. People may often comment that you are similar to them; this isn't necessarily the case, it's just that you are skilled at mirroring and complementing. Your superpower is that you are a human mirror and chameleon all in one.

While this may seem to be reactive, it actually requires great power and strength to be a Shapeshifter. Rather than having a Connection Type that you can't adapt, you allow the context to dictate the Connection Type you will use. This allows you to experience the full range of human Connection Types, flowing effortlessly between all quadrants of Light, Water, Earth and Green. Often when I am giving a presentation and I finish talking about the four quadrants, a Shapeshifter will raise their hands and say, 'I relate to all of them!' This is before I have given the Shapeshifter description. It always brings a moment of recognition when I tell them about the Shapeshifter.

Shapeshifters also say, 'But I am one person at home and another person at work and another person with my friends.' There is less consistency across the Shapeshifter's connection because each group asks them to become something new. In contrast, a Light or Green type won't vary their connection as much – their emotional energy is quite consistent when they are with their family, friends and co-workers. We know that Light types will be expressive and we know that Green types will be reserved, regardless of whether they are at home or at work. The consistent aspects of the Shapeshifter are good humour, a willingness to accommodate the group and agreeableness.

Establishing connection with others therefore comes naturally to you as a Shapeshifter. You are warm, friendly and tactful. Your natural gift for reading connection means that people like to have you around. If you think about what groups typically need in order to create harmony, it's empathy, good humour, lightness and thoughtfulness. These are all aspects of your emotional repertoire. You generally go with the flow and are happy to accommodate the consensus of the group you are in.

The Shapeshifter: nature or nurture?

While it is an asset to be a Shapeshifter, you need to determine whether this connection style was born (innate in your personality) or made (as an adaptation to your personality in response to your environment).

If you are an original or innate Shapeshifter, then you were adaptable, agreeable and easy to connect with from a young age. This makes

BOUNDARY

you an empowered Shapeshifter, meaning that it is natural for you to connect in this way and you are likely to be easygoing as an adult.

The adapted Shapeshifter

However, the Shapeshifter Connection Type can also be the result of adapting to a stressful or traumatic home environment in your early years. This environment may have constantly forced you to read the room for your physical or emotional survival. Basically, you needed to understand human behaviour early in order to navigate the turmoil in your early environment. You therefore adapted your connection style to respond to a caregiver.

We all adapt our connection style to a point, but Shapeshifters are the most accommodating of all the connection styles. If you connect as an adapted Shapeshifter, then you are adept at observing and responding to others, but as an adult you potentially feel anxious about or exhausted by connection. You probably make a point of avoiding conflict and feel relieved when you are finished connecting with others, as though you can finally relax. I recently met a man in his fifties after one of my workshops. As he approached me he burst into tears because he had realised that he was an adapted Shapeshifter. He said that he had become a people-pleaser because it was the only way to deal with the complex childhood he had. If you relate to this, then I invite you to use the Ality Connection Type model as a source of healing. The healing comes from finding your genuine preferences for connection.

Who were you before your environment made you change shape?

Like this man, if you are an adapted Shapeshifter, then you may benefit from discovering your preferred Connection Type. The first step towards understanding your preferred connection is to check the frequency and intensity scores in your results. Although you landed at the centre of the model, your scores for frequency and intensity will be located just inside one of the four quadrants: Light, Water, Green or Earth. If you check your scores, this will indicate your actual preferences for connecting. The score of 0 represents the centre, the score of 100 represents the highest frequency or intensity and the score of –100 represents the lowest frequency or intensity. On your assessment result, your preference is indicated by a green dot.

When you take the assessment, it gives you a red and green dot as your results. The red dot indicates where you are connecting now, but the green dot indicates where you would prefer to be connecting. It is one of the most satisfying moments when I'm working with others using the Ality Connection Type model and it can help an adapted Shapeshifter work out how they would prefer to be connecting.

Challenges
Making life decisions and being decisive

Q: What do you feel like for dinner?

Shapeshifter: I'm easy, I don't mind.

Q: Where do you want to go on holiday?

Shapeshifter: I like different places for different reasons. Where do you want to go?

Q: What colour tiles do you like best?

Shapeshifter: They're all great. I like this one, but I also like that one.

Although day-to-day connections come easily to you, you need to ensure that your life choices reflect what you really desire, and not just what the people around you suggest or prefer. You're very good at smiling, nodding and going along with the group while your real thoughts are hidden behind your expression (or perhaps your thoughts are occasionally a mystery to you entirely!). For example, as you are usually a mirror/complement to others in connection, some people might mistake this for a deeper connection. They could say, 'We just get each other,' and 'It's so easy for us to be together.' They don't realise how much work you're doing below the surface to bring equilibrium to the connection.

Therefore, making big life decisions can be a challenge for Shapeshifters, because when it comes to choosing work and love, you need to ensure that you're not just going along with what someone

BOUNDARY

else wants. Be on the look-out for controlling people who want to have someone easygoing to partner up with, whether at work or in a romantic relationship. Make sure you have a boundary that people can't cross. This boundary should protect your core values. That said, the most successful Shapeshifters tend to collaborate with decisive and driven connectors in their life and/or work, who the Shapeshifter feels confident to make firm decisions with. Shapeshifters need to partner up with naturally giving and generous people – just not other Shapeshifters! That could lead to a lot of indecision.

I was coaching an executive recently who is a Shapeshifter. He told me, 'I swore to myself I'd never be in my current position. But then it came up and it was what the organisation really needed. And now I actually love it.' This is typical from a Shapeshifter; you are so skilled at accommodating your environment that you end up internalising what the group or organisation needs. Then you can't differentiate between what you want and what the group wants. It's not necessarily something you need to change – if this executive loves his work and it serves the organisation well, then there's no harm. If your needs and the needs of the group are aligned, this is ideal. You just need to ensure that you keep checking the pulse of what you want.

The other challenge for an adapted Shapeshifter is emotional burnout. Being a chameleon can be exhausting as you are constantly tuning into the needs of others and then adapting who you are for them. As each context changes, so do you. Having an easygoing reputation is great until it prevents you from feeling strongly about anything. Your challenge is to honour your emotional needs and identity, at the same time as you adapt yourself to various situations. You might respond to this by saying, 'What if my emotional needs are satisfied by accommodating others?' If that's the case, then great. You just need to ensure that you feel loved, honoured and respected in the process.

You will prefer to avoid conflict than to face it head on. This is because your default connection style is to create harmony and balance. Conflict is the opposite of your natural inclination. Make sure you have the courage to show up for difficult and uncomfortable conversations. Without them, you will find that you become resentful and disempowered when the people around you are constantly getting their way.

When you feel vulnerable, ashamed, sad or depressed, you are likely to feel like a cardboard cut-out of a person, physically present but not mentally engaged. You will put on a brave face and do what the situation requires to accommodate connection but your heart won't be in it.

You will feel shy, anxious and muted, unable to change with your usual seamlessness. Your frequency and your intensity will likely decrease. You will lack the energy for human connection because you don't 'feel like yourself' and you will withdraw from your social life.

Reconnect by accepting invitations to one-on-one and group activities with trusted connections, balanced with time spent on your own interests. Ensure you are taking time out for yourself. You can't be all things to all people all the time!

Where to from here?

You are an excellent team player and derive power from the cooperative and collaborative relationships you build. You create connections between people and you are the common link. Shapeshifters learn and grow through collaboration. If you want to develop in any area, find someone in your field who you respect and team up with them. You thrive as part of a team when you are working alongside decisive and driven people. You love bouncing off the energy of others. If you are going to start a business, find a partner.

Your leadership style is characterised by collaboration and co-design. For example, instead of creating a strategy and then delivering it to your team, you would facilitate the team to design the strategy with you. This approach to leadership was introduced by the first technology companies that required the technical input of everyone in the team and is now sought after in many organisations. You could also benefit from finding a mentor or coach in your field who you respect and have that mentor set goals and challenges for you.

BOUNDARY

You need to be pushed out of being agreeable and into setting firm goals for your development.

You are most suited to positions that require flexibility, dynamic change, ongoing teamwork and new ideas. You will stagnate in positions where you are working alone, or where you are surrounded by people who take advantage of your accommodating nature. If you are able to bring others on a journey with you, this will allow you to channel your Shapeshifter nature in a positive way. Shapeshifters have the sweet life – you can connect with anyone, anytime. That's the key to belonging and belonging is the key to happiness!

You are the universal accommodator, so you are suited to all kinds of activities, essentially whatever everyone else wants to do! You are the only type that is genuinely compatible with all other types. Your adaptability makes you well suited to practical, hands-on activities. You don't have time for over-analysing when there's so much shapeshifting to do. You value spending time on activities that are universally useful or sought after for other people, such as eating and cooking, building houses, making clothes, playing sport, generating electricity or water etc. You like meeting people's needs, so learning a life skill will switch you on.

Dawn: Light x Water

Dawn types lie on the boundary between the Light and Water quadrants. Connecting with a Dawn is like watching the sun rise over the ocean. You are a high-intensity and mid-frequency connector. This means you are an ambivert who bonds with others through meaningful conversation and who also benefits from nourishing time alone. Dawn types generally:

- Make others feel that anything is possible for them; that there are infinite opportunities on the horizon
- Have the perspective and insight of Light types, combined with the nurturing and understanding of Water types. In this way, they embody the soft sunlight and the calm ocean: a powerful combination

- Connect with others by shining light on their highest potential; they do this by seeing the best in others
- Are accepting and non-judgemental of vulnerability
- Enjoy being with others half of the time, and then retreating to their own inner world
- Don't feel the need to set the tone with others like a typical Light type but they do enjoy interacting and connecting more than a typical Water type
- Are refuelled by connection
- Prefer to connect with others through conversation.

Characteristics

Your connection style is on the mid-line between the Light and Water quadrants. Your connection style brings a human version of the dawn, heralding the rising sun. You have great insight into the highest potential of others. You have the perspective and warmth of sunlight combined with the nurturing energy of the ocean. What does the dawn bring? Hope, optimism, inspiration and a new outlook. As the human dawn, this is what you bring to a connection. You make others feel that everything is going to work out for the best.

As you possess elements of both Water and Light types, your environment will dictate which part of you will prevail in any given context. If you are in a group with a lot of expressive Light types, you will relax into your Water nature and seek out meaningful connection by finding a one-on-one conversation. If you are in a group with a lot of thoughtful Water types, you will be more vocal and expressive. You are guided by the roles in a situation – if you are giving a presentation, you will draw on your Light charisma but if you are having a conversation with one or two other people you will bring out your Water empathy. This capacity to draw on two very different connection styles may cause Dawn types to feel torn in their identity, but I invite you to see this as your superpower: you have relational flexibility.

You are gifted in creating connections among others and in bringing positive energy to a room. You can read a dynamic and then connect the people within that dynamic. While a Shapeshifter type works out

BOUNDARY

what a group needs and then becomes that energy to create harmony, a Dawn type works out what a group needs and then coaches people in the group so that they can achieve that energy themselves.

You are content when everyone in the room feels connected and engaged; many others wouldn't be acutely aware of this dynamic but you are. Your connection style invites the person or people in front of you to share their desires with you and to be who they truly are. People feel comfortable being both strong and vulnerable in front of you. You shine light on their potential and remind them of who they are. This defines your leadership style. You lead by bringing out the best in people. Instead of saying, 'Come with me,' as a Light type would, you say to others: 'I see where you can go.'

Your natural gift for inspiring connection means that people like to have you around. However, these gifts that you bring to connection can also become your challenge. Your core challenge is to meet your own needs at the same time as you are a champion for others. Your approach to connection ('I am happy if everyone else is happy') can set you up for your emotions to be dependent on other people. I have a revelation for you: you are not responsible for the way other people feel. I'm going to repeat that: you are not responsible for the way other people feel. I want to give you a new approach to relationships and groups: you are only responsible for managing your own emotions and what you contribute to the group. As you often provide a holding environment for others to become who they are and live a life most true to them, you need to consciously give yourself permission to be who you are and to live a life most true to who you are.

Your awareness of the way that other people want to feel can prevent you from relaxing in a group setting. You are wired to tune in to other people, so when people are experiencing pain or discomfort, you share this pain and discomfort. In this way, you share the challenges of a Light type in overthinking and enmeshment. Overthinking is a key challenge for high-intensity connectors because relationships and group dynamics have a powerful impact on you. Like other Light types, you define yourself through the strength of your relationships and you tend to process emotions deeply.

You also share the challenges of a Water type in blurring boundaries and you need to be aware of the limits of your empathy. Research by social neuroscientists Eres and Molenberghs identifies three levels of empathy.[24] The first level is affective empathy, which occurs when we emotionally absorb the feelings of other people. An example might be when our hearts race as we watch someone else who is nervous on stage, or when we cry as someone else is moved to tears. Affective empathy is what Dawn types are intuitively programmed to do. It is a beautiful gift until you feel drowned by other peoples' feelings, so it is important to be aware of how we experience empathy.

The second level of empathy is cognitive empathy. This occurs when we can understand the feelings of others without experiencing the feelings ourselves. An example of this could be when a doctor listens to their patient as they provide an overview of their depression symptoms. It would not be appropriate or useful for the doctor to engage in affective empathy here as they will not serve the patient best by experiencing their emotional pain. The patient does not want their doctor to say, 'Oh, me too. Sometimes I can't get out of bed in the morning either.' The patient wants the doctor to understand their symptoms, make a diagnosis and provide treatment.

Cognitive empathy isn't just useful for doctors. Imagine you are sharing a problem with a friend. Do you want your friend to feel your emotions as you tell the story, or do you want your friend to understand your emotions and just listen to you? Generally, we want others to understand us and listen to us. We don't want them to walk away burdened by our emotions.

This awareness can be life-changing for Dawn types. There is a way of empathising with others that doesn't require you to absorb their emotions. You can even use 'cognitive empathy' as a mantra. The key is to understand the feelings of other people, and not to take them on as your own.

Once you have mastered cognitive empathy, the third level of empathy is emotional self-regulation. This dictates our behavioural reaction to the person. As Eres and Molenberghs write,

BOUNDARY

'Without an emotion regulative network, shared emotional states may inhibit our ability to perform tasks that require emotional distance (e.g., a surgeon operating on a child or a defence lawyer supporting a psychopath) or it may interfere with our ability to hide automatic biases (e.g., a parent being derogative to a teacher of a different racial background).'[25]

You can inhibit your reaction to someone else by asking yourself, 'How can I behave or react in a way that will serve this person?' For example, I want you to imagine that my ten-year-old son has to write a speech for his homework. I don't need to imagine this because it is happening in my house today. If I use affective empathy to react to him, then I will absorb his feelings of helplessness when he says, 'I don't know how to write a speech. I need help!' If I leave my empathy here, of course I will rush to help him because he is my child and I love him and I want to relieve him of his discomfort. In relieving him of discomfort entirely though, I may make the mistake of doing the task for him.

If I use cognitive empathy and self-regulation, then I will follow a different mental process: *He doesn't want to write the speech because it's hard. But he has done this before. He knows how to do it. It's just uncomfortable for him. He will be better served by following a process on his own.* Based on this reasoning, I will give him an outline of the process he can follow to write a speech and then support him if he has any questions. This sounds wonderful in theory but as any parent, relative, caregiver or teacher knows, it's not as easy in practice. He will of course keep trying to get me to feel his feelings and write the speech for him, so I need to use my cognitive empathy and emotional self-regulation to get him through, and keep reminding myself of the question: 'How can I behave or react in a way that will serve this person?' He will be best served if I don't write his speech for him.

As Dawn types champion others in their connection, there is often no clear separation between you and the people you're connecting with. If you haven't learnt ways to manage this, you may feel emotionally tossed around on a regular basis, as though you live in a pinball machine. You will feel like your peace of mind depends upon the people around you. Learning to master the different types of empathy will be the difference between you loving connection and resenting connection.

In conflict, you are likely to withdraw for a period of time and then return to confront the situation, displaying both your Light and Water tendencies. You will take time to retreat and analyse the situation, and then you are likely to be assertive once you return. You have the ability to reflect on conflict before reacting, and the ability to assertively confront a situation.

When you feel vulnerable, ashamed, sad or depressed, you are likely to feel like a robot: you are able to continue going through the motions because you don't want to let anybody down, but you won't feel animated or excited by life. You will put on a brave face and do what the situation requires to accommodate connection with others but your heart won't be in it. You will find it challenging to connect with others as their champion when you don't feel energised and positive. You are likely to feel more like a Water type in vulnerability and you will withdraw underwater to heal.

A Dawn type: Mat's story

Mat is a police sergeant in his twenty-eighth year of service and is a Dawn type connector. Mat generously agreed to write the following testimonial for the book:

> In hindsight, although serving in various functions of policing, each posting naturally graduated towards facilitating the betterment of others. This ranged from coaching small children in various sporting teams, to organising community events that highlighted each of their strengths, instructing recruits through to elite

BOUNDARY

> tactical police, to the education and development of all ranks. When forced out of operational policing due to major back surgeries, I dialled-up what I could do rather than focusing on what I couldn't. As a champion for my colleagues, it often involved questioning organisational policy, procedures, superiors and mentors. This precipitated emotional burnout, further complicating existing PTSD and depression that had arisen from my back injury. Together, these injuries prematurely ended my career and caused me to be under significant medical care. The story isn't over yet, though.

Where to from here?

As demonstrated in Mat's story, a key challenge for a Dawn type is emotional burnout. Being a champion for others can be exhausting as you are constantly tuning into their vision and then building them up. People come to you with vulnerability and may rely on you to elevate their energy. Your challenge is to maintain a strong sense of who you are and honour your emotional needs at the same time as you hold a space for others to thrive.

Dawn types learn and grow by creating spaces for others to learn and grow. As you have the qualities of both Light (enthusiasm, animation) and Water (one-on-one active listening and sensitivity) types, you need to identify the environments where you are more likely to demonstrate Light qualities and those where you are more likely to be a Water connector. On any given day, you may find that you oscillate between the two. There may be periods in your life or people in your life that bring out one type or the other. This is something you need to understand and manage. Make sure you remain your own champion, allowing yourself to be vulnerable and powerful at the same time.

You are well suited to any opportunity to offer insight into others and to help them achieve their potential. This makes you an extraordinary parent, educator, coach, psychologist, nurse, doctor or leader. You will thrive in positions that enable you to bring out the best in others.

Your comfort zone of connection involves pacing yourself and scheduling a balance of connection with others followed by regenerative time to yourself. Maintaining this balance is crucial for you, otherwise you will feel like you're on a seesaw of loneliness and being overwhelmed. Be proactive about structuring your week around this balance and be guided by the answers to these questions:

- When are you going for a walk on the beach?
- When are you relaxing?
- When are you exercising?
- When are you watching the sunrise or sunset?
- What lights you up when you spend time on your own?
- What genuinely restores you?

To improve connection with others, work on accepting help from others. You deserve as much nurturing as anyone else. Time in nature will rejuvenate you after time in the company of others.

Mountain: Light x Earth

Mountain types lie on the boundary between the Light and Earth quadrants. In connection, Mountain types are a beacon for others and a bridge between the earth and the sky. You are sought-after leaders in all organisational contexts. You are a mid-intensity and a high-frequency connector. Mountains generally:

- Absorb the insight and perspective of the sky and convert it into practical, grounded and down-to-earth strategies
- Have a powerful presence and are widely respected
- Are avid learners, preferring knowledge that can be readily applied in daily life
- Use constant learning as fuel for leadership, always wanting to implement their insights so that others will benefit
- Are resilient and tenacious: this is a strength, but it can intimidate more sensitive or intense connectors, so learning how to yield and soften with these people is an important challenge for Mountains

BOUNDARY

- Enjoy offering advice but at times, it would be better to step back and allow others to carve out their own path: with a little trust and encouragement, others can achieve great things in unpredictable ways
- Have great versatility in connection – they are relatable to all Connection Types.

Characteristics

When others meet you for the first time, it is as though they are standing at the base of a Mountain. There is a sense of 'looking up' and beholding your imposing presence. This is about your emotional energy, not your physical height! You have a unique Connection Type in that you combine the insight of the sky (perspective) and the groundedness of the earth (pragmatism). No other Connection Type has this combination. This makes you a powerful leader as you are able to balance vision and action.

You are an asset to any group you are in and often seek out (or take on) leadership roles, whether it's in your family, sports or work team or a group of friends. You will thrive in such leadership positions as you are comfortable communicating with a crowd. And yet no matter how high you rise, you will not become carried away with the ego trip that often comes with positions of influence – you always have your feet (the base of the mountain) on the ground. For those who are willing, directly connecting with a mountain offers either a challenge or a retreat.

Your Connection Type lends itself so beautifully to leadership positions because you are mid-intensity. This means that you are able to equally prioritise both tasks and people. You don't overlook people to get the job done but you don't get carried away with emotion and lose sight of what is important.

You have great insight into the needs of a group and you are able to communicate in a way that resonates with a group. However, this confidence and grit can come across as stubbornness or inflexibility without relational awareness. Your capacity to 'keep calm and carry on' could be unrelatable for more sensitive connectors, with the mountain seeming intimidating and perilous. You have considerable energy for human connection because you don't carry the emotional energy of others with you. Some of the more intense connectors in your life may take this personally, wondering where your loyalties lie. You seem to care about everyone in the group equally. This can be wonderful for leadership but may cause issues in friendships and romantic relationships.

You could benefit from finding deeper ways to connect with your more sensitive or intense loved ones. Don't be afraid to share your emotions with those you trust, as it can create a deeper connection and bring you relief. Admitting that you carry a heavy load will not undermine your strength. Talking about your feelings with others can be a positive source of connection. Admitting that you don't have all the answers will enhance rather than undermine your leadership of others. It takes courage to say, 'I don't know, but I'm going to work hard to find out.'

Being a natural leader can be both a power and a curse. You need to balance your natural inclination to lead others with your certainty that you know the right way for them. Although there may be a well-worn path that you have faith in, there are (metaphorically speaking) many ways to scale a mountain. Let others surprise you with their creative and unpredictable ways to succeed and prevail. Don't try to become an engineer with other people's lives. Your leadership will evolve if you try a 'softly softly' approach rather than the wrecking-ball approach! If someone feels that they have disappointed you, the connection will become unfulfilling on both sides. The best leaders and connectors travel with others on their journey rather than calling out instructions from the peak. See yourself as a Sherpa rather than the compass.

Conflict is one of your strengths. This is only something that can be said of connectors on the mid-line of intensity (Mountains, Shapeshifters and Coral types). You don't react to conflict impulsively or aggressively. You aren't afraid of difficult conversations because you don't become emotionally involved in them. You will workshop a disagreement until it is resolved. You are calm and measured but you definitely feel compelled to fix the conflict. If you are in a

BOUNDARY

relationship or a team with a different type of connector, it may be a positive opportunity to pause in the conflict and reflect on your response: what do I want to achieve from this conflict? How can I use this conflict to create a healthier connection? You don't explode in conflict. Having said that, if you regularly suppress conflict you could eventually transform from a mountain into a volcano. This instability could be your undoing. Your best asset in conflict is that you know which battles to pick. This differentiates you from higher intensity types who may be inclined to create storms in a teacup.

In the natural world, mountains are often beset by earthquakes and heavy rainfall. When you feel vulnerable, ashamed, sad or depressed, you are likely to feel like there is a landslide on the mountain. These natural phenomena can cause soil slips and more severe landslides. At your most vulnerable, you will feel like you are crumbling and unstable. Your frequency preference for human connection will decrease. You will lack the fuel for human connection because you don't 'feel like yourself' and you will take a step back from your social life. You will put on a brave face when you see others and, if you are forced into connection, you are likely to be distracted or you will numb yourself. You will shroud yourself in clouds when you need to retreat, avoiding contact with others.

Where to from here?

You need to be mindful of the point where leadership feels like the crushing weight of responsibility. As you are often the most resilient person in the group, people will rely on you and turn to you for guidance. It's the role of the leader to empower others, so if you're feeling overloaded it's likely that you're carrying the load for other people rather than showing them how to carry their own load.

Mountain types will benefit from sport and exercise to unwind. In fact, many of the Mountain types I know play an active role in sports and sports coaching. This may be because it's a combination of helping someone to do their best in a setting where the rules of the game are clear. It's mid-intensity, a pleasing combination of emotions and rules.

Communicate your human connection needs to those closest to you. At home and at work, it may help you to articulate how you operate to others. This will allow you to manage your human connections without causing offence to others.

Mountain types absorb the insight of the sky and convert it into practical strategies for change to improve the lives of others. Keep searching. Keep growing. Keep up the quest. Enjoy the fact that you are a natural leader. Seek out these opportunities to guide others to greater heights. Make sure you find your own Sherpa (whether this is a person or a conscious lifestyle) to support you on your way!

You gravitate towards leadership positions, often in sporting or community settings. You are the quintessential coach figure because you can see where other people need to go and you can help them get there. Develop a daily reflective or contemplative practice so you have a ritual for bringing the vision from the sky into your actionable 'on the ground' strategies. Practise saying 'I don't know,' and feeling comfortable when you don't always have all the answers. Opening up to emotional vulnerability will only strengthen your leadership.

Garden: Earth x Green

Garden types lie on the boundary between the Earth and Green quadrants. As the ultimate down-to-earth connector, Garden types make people feel calm and grounded. You are low-intensity and mid-frequency connectors. Gardens generally:

- Seem easygoing and relaxed
- Allow others to feel accepted so that they can be completely themselves in the presence of a Garden type
- Are humble and well respected
- Lead by supporting others
- Like to live day-to-day rather than reflect on big visions
- Are not demanding
- Value peace in connection; they believe that life is hard enough without having difficult or confronting relationships
- Would benefit from having goals in order to keep on track.

BOUNDARY

Characteristics

Imagine walking barefoot through a flowering garden. You feel calm and relaxed, enjoying the budding flowers and bees. The garden is peaceful and tranquil and immediately you are at ease. That's how people feel when they connect with you. You don't ask anything of them; you simply invite them into your presence and allow them to be, to take a moment to breathe.

It is effortless to connect with you. This is a gift that you offer to others because so many people ask a lot of the people they connect with. You give people the gift of your calm presence. You make people feel centred, balanced and less tense.

Recently I drove up to the Hunter Valley to give a presentation to a corporate offsite about company culture and high-performing teams. The Hunter Valley is beautiful wine country approximately two hours' drive north of Sydney. As soon as I stepped out of the car, I felt relaxed. I could hear birds chirping and felt the sunshine on my skin. I could see the horizon. My first instinct was that I wished I didn't have to leave at the end of my presentation – I wanted to stay the night.

This is how a Garden type makes people feel. You immediately put people at ease. It's not in your nature to make demands of anyone or to place expectations on conversation. You value peace and acceptance. When I think about Garden types, I visualise a comfortable chair on a verandah overlooking trees and flowers. I'm sipping a cup of tea and feel an easy silence. Even writing about Garden types makes me feel relaxed. It's intoxicating emotional energy to be around. Garden types are respite from a chaotic world.

The interesting aspect of Garden types is that you are often working in high-intensity contexts. I have met many first respond-ers and correctional services officers who are Garden types. It is the combination of Earth and Green that gives Garden types the ability to perform their job and then withdraw into an inner cave where they can recuperate and recover. Garden types don't recover when they are surrounded by connection. This is key. If you are a Garden type, you will have non-human sources of connection that renew you.

For Garden types, human connection is about being near each other and bringing comfort. You are not over the top or highly verbal. You like to observe and laugh along with the group. You are happy to talk if you're enjoying the conversation but you don't ever feel compelled to speak. As far as you're concerned, you communicate how you're feeling through your body language and your presence.

My grandfather was a Garden type. He was a police officer and he was humble, hilarious and mischievous. He was famous for practical jokes and would make my grandmother hysterical with laughter. He also loved a drink. He was Irish Catholic and lived for family and parties. He was quietly spoken until he'd had a few drinks, at which time he would regale everyone with funny stories from his life. He was the youngest of seven and his mother gave birth to him when she was aged forty-five. He loved horses and later in his life, he worked at the race track each morning from 4 am making sure the horses were fit to run.

He had a chair that he would sit in every afternoon and have a beer and a cigarette. If I sat with him, there was no expectation to talk but every now and then he would say, 'Did I ever tell you about the time . . .'

When I was in high school, he wrote me a moving letter that still makes me cry to this day when I read it:

> Because you are always in my thoughts, I decided to write to you as I have never really told you of my feelings towards you. I have trouble expressing my feelings, and in fact, apart from Nana when we were first married I don't think I have told anyone of my feelings.

I am sharing this because I hope it gives other Garden types the courage to share their feelings with people they love. This letter shapes my memory of my grandfather because even though he rarely shared his feelings with me verbally, I have them in writing. It is so special to me and I will keep the letter until the day I die.

BOUNDARY

He maintained his characteristic humour in the letter:

> **You are a bit of a desperate, you and your school mates, but you are very special to me. Although I try not to show it, I do enjoy you sitting alongside me in the car, changing the radio stations until you can find the worst music available.**

He finished the letter by saying, 'I pray that you are strong enough to know the salvation of humour and the warmth of accepting the sadness of others, without losing the joy within yourself.'

This could be a mantra for all Garden types and I hope that you can take this to heart, as I have. While you are steadfast in your emotions, other connection types may require more tenderness and demonstrative expression from you. Garden types shy away from high-intensity emotion and tend to keep the contents of their hearts private. For a Garden type, love almost goes without saying. It is like breathing. But it will always be meaningful for the people you love to hear it from you. Your challenge is to learn how to move towards others in your relationships. It is safe to let your guard down and share your emotions with those you trust. None of us is here forever and all that survives is the evidence of our love. Let's leave as much evidence of that as possible.

Where to from here?

You are down-to-earth and accepting. You make people feel safe. You are easy to be around, and are comfortable going with the flow of whichever group you're in. You may not think of yourself as a leader because you aren't as verbal or dominant as so-called typical leaders. However, your leadership style is very powerful because you lead by supporting others and stimulating them to grow. Your supportive and encouraging style of leadership means that you don't normally seek out formal leadership roles but play a key role in stabilising and defending the group. You are extremely loyal and everybody wants you on their team.

In terms of your ingredients for connection, you will thrive when you have a green sanctuary of connection you can withdraw into. This is your haven, so design it exactly as you want. You will also be nourished by different groups of people who understand the way you want to connect. Appreciate that all of us have different ways of opening up to others and connecting. Learn to identify high- and low-frequency connectors and high-intensity connectors (the opposites of your style) and try to meet them in the middle. To move towards the centre of human connection, you could try to stay a bit longer in each conversation. Say what's on your mind. Tell someone how you feel. You'll be surprised by how good it feels to connect this way.

You can optimise your connection with others by joining a regular low-intensity event such as a surfing class, an annual camping trip, a touch football team or a walking group. To improve connection with others, work on voicing your opinion; it matters.

The biggest challenge for a Garden type is that your focus on peace and comfort might keep you stagnant. To keep developing in your own life, create a one-year and five-year plan so you can make sure your 'flow' is heading in the right direction. To keep developing your relationships, explain how you feel to the people you love. I am not sure of the author but I am reminded of a great quote: 'A comfort zone is a beautiful place, but nothing ever grows there.' Make sure you know the difference between peace and avoidance.

The garden of your connection needs all the types in order to thrive (Light, Water, Earth and Green). You can connect with anyone! To keep the garden of your life flourishing, make sure you remove any weeds and make sure all the plants are healthy. Growing intuitively and wildly is exquisite but even nature has ways to renew and rejuvenate.

Coral: Water x Green

Coral types lie between the Green and Water quadrants and have characteristics of each, depending on the environment and context. Connecting with a Coral is like retreating to a quiet and nourishing haven. You are a mid-intensity and low-frequency connector. Like

BOUNDARY

snorkelling, connecting with Coral is relaxing and uplifting at the same time. Coral types generally:

- Are resilient and have a rich inner world
- Are able to sustain a complex inner ecosystem and feel fulfilled in their own company
- Feel strongly affected by changes to their environment; Coral types can be very sensitive and tend to absorb the emotional energy of others around them
- Feel vulnerable at the prospect of sharing their authentic self with others
- Thrive on intimacy with a select few
- Are shy at first, but can be surprisingly forthcoming once they open up.

Characteristics

Have you ever been snorkelling or scuba diving? Have you ever visited a coral reef? If so, you will understand the beauty and wonder of being underwater and witnessing the rich ecosystem that thrives there. It feels magical and calming all at once. It's captivating and it's also surprising. This incredibly colourful and complex coral reef is hidden below the surface of the water so it is not apparent until someone makes the effort to dive in.

This is what it's like to connect with you. You have a rich inner world that you spend most of your time in, which is invisible to the casual observer. A Coral type's comfort zone is the inner world, not the outer world. You may enjoy being in groups, but you will spend your time observing and reflecting.

So, what's it like for you to connect with others? Well, the best way to answer that is with another question: how should we conduct ourselves around coral when we're snorkelling? You are happy to connect with people who approach you in a thoughtful way, but you are very affected by people who are insensitive or aggressive. You don't like humour at someone else's expense and you feel pressured by clever conversation. Connection for you is not a game; it is an opportunity to be witnessed and respected.

You may have only recently become a Coral type. Coral types have often been Shapeshifter types in the past, so it is important for you to read that section as well. Over time (usually many years), your preference for frequency of connection with others declines and you start to focus on quality over quantity. You may find that you were once social, accommodating and adaptive in groups (a Shapeshifter), and that you now need to spend more time in your inner world than you did previously. This could be expressed through a new creative passion (cooking, art or music, for example), or a love of time with animals or nature. It is common for Shapeshifters to evolve into Coral types because my research shows that our frequency declines over time. Coral types are on the mid-line of intensity, directly below the Shapeshifter. So it's common for me to meet Coral types who used to be much more accommodating and adaptive. As I said earlier in the book, even though our frequency reduces over the course of our life, usually people stay within their type or quadrant.

Coral types lead by demonstrating resilience and non-judgement. You are a place to withdraw to for inspiration and renewal. You lead by example and speak quietly into the ears of the people you lead, to the point where they learn to trust you and ultimately may even internalise your ideas and approach.

As a low-intensity connector, you may find that you are overwhelmed by constant social activity and need quiet time to reflect. As such, you enjoy alternating between connecting with others and then retreating into your inner world.

You may have challenges with emotional boundaries: not knowing where your emotions end and someone else's begin. This is because you feel overwhelmed when people enter your underwater world and you may feel powerless to create boundaries between you and another person. You are likely to worry and internalise your fears.

This is the power and the challenge of being a Coral connector. Though people love to be absorbed by your connection and it is in your nature to connect in this way, you must consciously retreat after the connection in order to replenish.

BOUNDARY

When you connect with another person, you invite them to bathe in your connection. This translates as your acceptance of others and your tendency to be non-judgemental. Your primary imperative in connection is to calm and inspire. You create a safe space for others to connect.

Although day-to-day connections come easily to you, you need to ensure that you express how you feel rather than just going along with the group. You're very good at smiling, nodding and appeasing others while your real thoughts are hidden beneath the surface. For example, as you often offer solace to others in connection, some people might mistake this for a deeper connection. They could say, 'We just get each other' and 'It's so easy for us to be together'. They don't realise how much work you're doing below the surface!

As Coral types absorb others in their connection, there is often no clear separation between you and the people you're connecting with. If you haven't learnt ways to manage this, you may feel emotionally tossed around on a regular basis, as though the waters you inhabit are choppy and volatile.

In the face of conflict you are a true combination of Green and Water types. On the one hand you will retreat and withdraw, not wanting to confront the discomfort of the conflict. You will be upset rather than angry. On the other hand, you will be unable to forget the conflict and you will dwell on it until it is adequately resolved. You would prefer to avoid someone rather than confront a conflict. This might offend high-intensity connectors in your life who see conflict as a necessary way to process complications that arise in relationships.

In a similar way, when you are vulnerable you will take on elements of both Water and Green connections. You will respond to vulnerability (sadness, fear, anxiety or worry) like a Green type in that you will feel safest and most comfortable withdrawing from other people. You won't want to talk about it. At the same time, you will feel the emotion as powerfully as a high-intensity Water connector. In many ways you have the emotional complexity and colour of a high-intensity type but it's stored below the surface, just like a coral reef. The profound impact of too much sunlight or emotional pollution will be profoundly felt by a Coral type, who will experience the equivalent of coral bleaching, which occurs when corals become white in response to environmental factors such as high or low temperature, excessive light or the deprivation of nutrients.

Where to from here?

You need to feel free in your underwater paradise. In connection language, that means you need to inhabit your inner world more than anything else, and then invite people into your inner world every now and then. Unlike other types, you actively invite people into your world, rather than meeting them out in the real world. For this reason, you need to choose the people who you invite in with care. Share with others how you see the world. Ask them for their views and let them know when you need time out.

Even though you are nourished by solitude, you will find your alone time even more rewarding if you also have restorative rituals that allow you to connect with yourself, such as meditation or mindfulness. You will benefit from a healing daily practice. You will be nourished by pets, nature, cooking, gardening, music and self-care routines.

Coral types learn and grow through psychological safety. You need to feel like you are in a safe space before you can be productive, create and work happily alongside other people.

You will thrive if you structure your time around a rhythm of connection and withdrawal into your haven. Make sure you stay connected to your inner rhythms and understand the inner flow that sustains you. If you are connected to this flow, you are better able to absorb others in your nourishing connection. You can optimise your connection by inviting someone to share an activity you like. Try, 'I've noticed there's an opportunity to go to . . . Would you like to come with me?'

Here is a mantra for a Coral type to live by: 'To take care of others, start by taking care of yourself.'

BOUNDARY

part four
Who do you click or clash with?

chapter 13

Connection Type compatibility

Now that you know and understand your Connection Type, we are ready to talk about whether you click or clash with other types. You can see the nature of your connection with other types in the following Connection Compatibility Table:

Connection Type: Light types – Spark, Star, Sunlight

Connection style and values	Most compatible with	Will clash with
High frequency, high intensity. People-focused, big picture, enthusiastic, dynamic, ideas-oriented, high energy. Core values in connection: setting the tone, talking and sharing openly, telling the truth.	Dawn: you feel seen and championed by them. They admire your energy and courage. Shapeshifter: you are able to collaborate and work towards common goals without being competitive. They love bouncing off your energy.	Other Light types if you both become competitive in any way. Green types because you think they are too reserved and they think you talk too much.

Connection style and values	Most compatible with	Will clash with
	Water types: you feel you can open up to them and be yourself. They see you as human sunshine and love your company. Mountain: you respect their steadfastness and their leadership style, and they love learning from you.	Earth types because you think they are change resistant and that they put up an emotional barrier. They think you give too much away and are too self-centred. Water types if you are offended by the amount of time they need to spend alone and they find you too demanding.

Connection Type: Water types – Elixir, Ripple Effect, Ocean

Connection style and values	Most compatible with	Will clash with
Low frequency, high intensity. People-focused in a one-on-one setting, supportive, build relationships, emotion-oriented. Core values in connection: awareness, empathy, clarity; want everyone to feel heard and understood.	Other Water types: you will have a deep respect for each other and understand what the other needs from connection. Light types: you are warmed and energised by their company. They feel they can be vulnerable with you and you will be able to hold their energy. Dawn: they love your sensitivity and awareness while you love their ability to	Other Water types in times when you both feel as though you can't raise the spirits of the other. You may feel you can't get out of the pool you have created for each other. Light types, if you feel they want to spend more time with you than you are able to give. You see them as boundless in their energy for human connection whereas you need more space. They may be offended

Connection style and values	Most compatible with	Will clash with
	see the best in you. They remind you of who you are when you forget. Coral: you find them captivating, and they see you as calm and present. Shapeshifter: you appreciate their understanding and they admire your depth.	by your need for time away and need to be reassured that constant time together for you is not a measure of your love. Tree types may be too closed off for you emotionally and your combined low frequency may mean that you are unable to reach each other. They may experience you as being emotionally volatile and demanding. Earth types because you consider their practical, no-nonsense attitude to be unemotional and they consider you to be overly sensitive. You will see Shapeshifters as being so accommodating and chameleon-like that you can't relate or establish a clear connection to them, while they will fear drowning in your emotional depths. You will admire the leadership of Mountain types but will resent the fact that they need to be social in a number of different groups. They will feel like they can never please you.

Connection Type: Green types – Shades, Observer, Tree

Connection style and values	Most compatible with	Will clash with
Low frequency, low intensity. Task-focused, work independently, organised, reserved, to the point, detail-oriented.	Other Green types: there will be an ease and an appreciation of silence and boundaries that you will both find refreshing.	Other Green types if there isn't enough spark to connect. There may be too much unsaid between you, with neither of you inclined to talk.
Reserved and professional communication style. Economical with language.	Shapeshifter: they will respect your need for space and be comfortable for you to connect with when you're up for it.	Water types: you may experience them as being too emotionally volatile and demanding. You may be too closed off for them emotionally and your combined low frequency may mean that you are unable to reach each other unless you work hard at it.
Connection values: respect, patience and comfort.	Garden: they are easygoing and undemanding but a bit more social than you are, so you will appreciate that they give you a reason to socialise.	Light types: they are a mystery to you. You find them overbearing and too talkative. They find you enigmatic and hard to connect with.
	Coral: you will have a mutual understanding where they respect your boundaries and you respect their sensitivity.	Earth types: you will generally have an affinity but you may not be able to keep up with them socially.
	Meeting Place: they will bring fun and joy to your life while you are the anchor or root system that makes them feel safe.	Shapeshifters will be comfortable for you but your natural reserve means that they don't have a lot of material to collaborate with, and this is their preferred mode of connecting.

Connection Type: Earth types – Meeting Place, Foundation, Rock

Connection style and values	Most compatible with	Will clash with
High frequency, low intensity. Task-focused in groups, come together to achieve a common goal, logical, systems-oriented, data-oriented, process-oriented, approaches problem-solving in a linear way. Connection values: pragmatism, good humour, ease, loyalty, putting the group first.	Shapeshifters: they will respect your pragmatic approach to getting things done and your ability to support the team. You will appreciate their adaptive nature and will see them as an asset to the team. Other Earth types: you will trust and respect each other, knowing that the team comes first, that the rules must be followed, and that you both want to have a good time. Mountain: you will admire their leadership qualities and they will admire your down-to-earth practicality. Together you are a good team. Spark: you will love the warmth and care they bring to your life. You will make them feel safe and protected. Garden: they are a haven for you and you are a trusted support for them.	Ripple Effect and Ocean types because you consider them to be overly sensitive overthinkers. They consider your practical, no-nonsense attitude to be unemotional and unfeeling. They don't like how you shield yourself from emotional vulnerability and will feel like they 'can't get through to you'. Some Star and Sunlight types because you think they love the sound of their own voice and are overly dramatic. You think they bring everything back to them. They will see you as too task-focused and inflexible; set in your ways of thinking. You will clash if you have a conflict because you will become dismissive and they will become aggressive.

Connection Type: Shapeshifter

Connection style and values	Most compatible with	Will clash with
Mid-frequency, mid-intensity. Chameleon in social situations, can read a group, work out what it needs and then become it. Very accommodating and adaptable. Connection values: harmony and collaboration.	Although you are compatible with all other types, you prefer to bounce off the high energy and frequency of Light types: Spark, Star and Sunlight. You appreciate the teamwork and consistency that Earth types bring and will enjoy working with them. You respond well to Mountain leaders and partners as they share your mid-intensity and bring leadership to connection.	No one. It's not in your nature to clash. Although as you are mid-frequency, you will prefer to connect with other mid- and high-frequency types.

Connection Type: Dawn

Connection style and values	Most compatible with	Will clash with
Mid-frequency, high intensity. Champion of highest potential, sees the best in other people and organisations. Connection values: a combination of insight and empathy.	Light types, because you will form a mutual admiration club with each other. You will see the best in them and they will value and reward your loyalty by always putting you first. You will be loved.	Foundation and Earth types because you will perceive them to be blunt and emotionally unaware. They will see you as being too sensitive. Green types because their reserved

Connection style and values	Most compatible with	Will clash with
	Water types, because you draw them out of their depths to the surface and bring the warmth of your connection. They give you access to the depths of their expression and sensitivity. You value their judgement.	communication style will leave you feeling frustrated. You can communicate with anyone except people who don't want to communicate!
	Shapeshifter: you are matched in your mid-frequency and they will admire your ability to read and champion people. You will admire their ability to harmonise and collaborate.	
	Meeting Place: they will bring a practical joy to your day-to-day life. You will offer them a higher perspective on life.	

Connection Type: Mountain

Connection style and values	Most compatible with	Will clash with
High frequency, mid-intensity. A beacon for others and a natural leader with a powerful presence. Connection values: a combination of leadership and down-to-earth strategies.	Light types. You love learning from them – they have so many ideas! And they respect your steadfastness and your leadership style. Shapeshifter: you are both mid-intensity connectors and they admire your ability to carve out a path for others. You collaborate well with them – you trust and admire their ability to connect universally. Earth types: you have a mutual respect – they admire your leadership qualities and you admire their down-to-earth practicality. Together you are a good team.	Mountain types don't tend to clash with people; you just gravitate more towards the people you consider to be like-minded. Ripple Effect and Ocean types because they consider your focus on practical, down-to-earth strategies to ignore the complex nature of people. You will see them as impossible to reach or as people who don't seek solutions and only want to talk. Observer and Tree types because you cannot relate to their low frequency. You will be friendly with each other but it won't go beyond that for you.

Connection Type: Garden

Connection style and values	Most compatible with	Will clash with
Easygoing and relaxed, accepting and humble. Connection values: peace, acceptance and non-judgement.	Green types because you are able to draw them into human connection in a gentle way. You are easygoing and undemanding but a bit more social than them, so you give them a reason to socialise. Earth types: you are a trusted support for them and they are a safe haven for you. Shapeshifter: you will create a very even and laid-back connection together. You are both mid-frequency so tend to have the same appetite for human connection. Spark: you will enjoy the warmth and animation of the Spark connection. They will feel accepted by you.	Your connection style means that you will rarely clash with anyone, unless you have an extremely good reason. You may feel some discomfort in the presence of Star and Sunlight types because you see their tone-setting and truth-sharing as being overly intrusive and demanding. They disturb the peace of your connection. They will see you as too quiet and not giving enough away. Ripple Effect and Ocean types will find your reserved communication style and low intensity hard to connect with. You will see them as warm but too emotional.

Connection Type: Coral

Connection style and values	Most compatible with	Will clash with
Very sensitive to their environment but resilient over time. Captivating and uplifting in one-on-one connection. Connection values: inviting, restorative, nurturing.	Your compatibility will be dependent on where you are located on the spectrum. For example, if you are closer to the centre you will be more drawn to higher frequency connectors like Meeting Place, Mountain and Spark types. They will find you mysterious and captivating. You will admire their gregarious nature and their ability to lead others. If you are further down towards the lower arrow, you will be more aligned with Observer and Ripple Effect types. You will feel safe and respected in their connection and they will see you as their sanctuary.	Like a Shapeshifter and Mountain, your mid-intensity means that you rarely clash with anyone. You don't seek out conflict or aggression and you tend to avoid and withdraw when faced with confronting or provocative interactions. Having said that, your low frequency and tendency to withdraw might mean that you don't connect naturally with Light (Star and Sunlight) and Earth types (Foundation and Earth) types. They are higher frequency and more social.

chapter 14

Who do you instantly click or clash with?

As I explained at the very start of the book, there are three different ways to experience a click and three different ways to experience a clash. We can click or clash with a person, a group or a place. A click creates belonging and a clash creates loneliness.

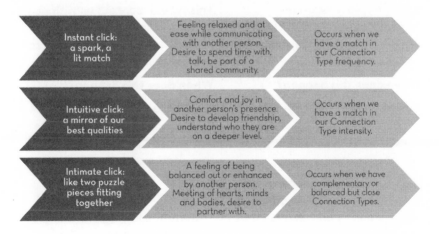

Instant click: a spark, a lit match	Feeling relaxed and at ease while communicating with another person. Desire to spend time with, talk, be part of a shared community.	Occurs when we have a match in our Connection Type frequency.
Intuitive click: a mirror of our best qualities	Comfort and joy in another person's presence. Desire to develop friendship, understand who they are on a deeper level.	Occurs when we have a match in our Connection Type intensity.
Intimate click: like two puzzle pieces fitting together	A feeling of being balanced out or enhanced by another person. Meeting of hearts, minds and bodies, desire to partner with.	Occurs when we have complementary or balanced but close Connection Types.

Instant clash: like trying to light a wet match	We feel like it is hard work, forced and unnatural to connect with another person.	This clash occurs when we have opposite levels of frequency and intensity in our Connection Type.
Intuitive clash: a mirror of our most challenging or suppressed qualities	We feel competitive or defensive in another person's company. They get on our nerves and under our skin. We overreact in response.	This clash occurs when someone acts out our most challenging qualities.
Intimate clash: a person triggers our trauma or negative past experiences	We feel triggered by this person and behave uncharacteristically when we are around them. They bring out our worst.	This clash occurs when someone activates trauma from our past.

The three clicks and clashes

How we click	How we clash
1. Instant click: a glimmer	**1. Instant clash: like trying to light a wet match**
This type of connection with a person, place or group immediately feels comfortable. We are cheerful, upbeat and feel a sense of belonging.	This type of connection with a person, place or group immediately feels effortful, forced and unnatural.
When does this happen?	**When does this happen?**
An instant click happens with people, places and groups that match the frequency of our Connection Type.	We have a cold clash and therefore experience loneliness with people, place and groups that don't match the frequency or intensity of our Connection Type.
High-frequency connectors have instant clicks with other high-frequency connectors and mid-frequency connectors who are in an animated mood.	High-frequency, high-intensity connectors (Light types) have cold clashes with low-frequency, low-intensity connectors (Green types) and vice versa. Low-frequency, high-intensity connectors (Water types) have

How we click	How we clash
Mid-frequency connectors have instant clicks with other mid-frequency connectors. Low-frequency connectors have instant clicks with other low-frequency connectors.	cold clashes with high-frequency, low-intensity connectors (Earth types). Mid-frequency connectors such as Shapeshifters, Mountain and Coral types have good range, so generally respond well to friendly and positive connectors, wherever they are located on the model.

2. Intuitive click: a mirror of our best qualities

An intuitive click is an experience of wanting to develop a friendship, connect deeply and spend extended time with a person, place or group.

When does this happen?

We have an intuitive click with people, places and groups that match the intensity of our Connection Type. This is often a match in both frequency and intensity (i.e. when we share the same Connection Type), but frequency isn't a necessity for an intuitive click – it relies on intensity.

2. Intuitive clash: a mirror of our most challenging or suppressed qualities

This type of clash prompts a feeling of judgement, competitiveness or defensiveness in the company of a person, place or group. We overreact in response.

When does this happen?

This clash occurs when someone we know expresses a part of us that we are uncomfortable with, or haven't come to terms with, or we are actively suppressing. In order to provoke this reaction in us, this person usually comes from the same quadrant as our Connection Type and/or will match our intensity. For example: Light types will intuitively clash with other Light types; Water types will intuitively clash with other Water types; Green types will intuitively clash with other Green types; Earth types will intuitively clash with other Earth types.

How we click	How we clash
3. Intimate click: like two puzzle pieces fitting together	**3. Intimate clash: a person triggers our trauma or negative past experiences**
In an intimate click, we experience a feeling of being balanced out or enhanced by another person. They smooth out our edges or even see potential in these edges and make us feel like a better version of ourselves. We respond by wanting to partner with them.	In an intimate clash, another person provokes a fight/flight/freeze/fawn response in us.*
When does this happen?	When someone represents a threat to us, we feel on edge, unsafe or uncomfortable in their presence. Or we could feel aroused, curious and excited in their presence. Either way, our senses are heightened and we are on high alert.
This click occurs when someone is a balance for our Connection Type but not the opposite of our Connection Type. The term 'opposites attract' should be rephrased as 'balances attract'! We are looking to partner with someone who enhances our connection – if our frequency is high, we will want someone to balance it; if our intensity is low, we will want someone to balance it. If we are mid intensity we will want someone to enhance us through their low or high intensity.	**When does this happen?**
	This clash occurs when someone's behaviour activates (triggers or reminds us of) our past traumatic experiences. In this clash the other person will offer the same type of connection as the person or group who originally activated this pattern.

The instant click: a glimmer = a match in frequency

We experience an instant click when we meet someone, arrive in a place or join a group and we immediately feel at ease. We breathe

---

* Like fight or flight, the fawn response is another automatic reaction some people might use in order to please, appease and pacify a threat. It was identified in the work of Dr Pete Walker: pete-walker.com/codependencyFawnResponse.htm a sigh of relief. We smile more. We are cheerful. Our body language is more open. This openness leads to an enjoyable connection and we experience a feeling of liking that person, place or group. A feeling of ease, novelty or comfort tells us that we are experiencing belonging. An instant click occurs when we have a match in frequency. We experience this click when someone responds to us in a way that communicates: your connection is welcome here. Your connection needs will be met here. Frequency is the most immediate form of connection because it relates to how often we talk and how fast we talk.

This means that, on first meeting, we will socialise and communicate easily with a person or place with our level of frequency.

An instant click is a delightful experience. It could be walking into a fitness class and feeling boosted by the high energy, or entering a restaurant and instantly loving the ambience. It could be paddling out past the waves on a surfboard and inhaling the salty air, or calling a trusted friend for a chat.

If you are a high-frequency connector, you are an extravert. This means you feel most like yourself and seek out belonging primarily through a lot of human connection. You will have an instant click with someone who talks as much as you and as fast as you.

If you are a mid-frequency connector, you're an ambivert and seek out belonging from a combination of human connection and time alone. You communicate this preference to others through the rate and pace of your conversation. You will be looking for a match in how someone talks.

If you are a low-frequency connector, you are an introvert. This means that you feel most like yourself and experience belonging primarily when you are on your own. You communicate this preference to others through the amount that you talk. You are more reserved in conversation and usually do not initiate conversations. You have an instant click with other people who respect the way you like to communicate and create comfort with you because they speak as much as you do.

Instant clicks in real life

Instant click at work: two high-frequency connectors

Two new work colleagues start in the same roles on the same day. They are both high frequency and they communicate this to each other by being chatty and open. They speak as fast as each other. When one person finishes answering a question, they ask the other person the same question to invite their response. They tell jokes and are both light-hearted. There are few pauses in their conversation. They may or may not end up being friends, but both feel comfortable and any nerves they may have felt on their first day are calmed by the connection.

Instant click socially: two mid-frequency connectors

At after school pick-up, two mid-frequency connectors stand and wait for their children to leave the classroom. They are both looking at their phones. One glances up and recognises someone she knows. 'Oh hi,' she says. The other parent looks up and smiles. 'Hi, how are you going?' The conversation that follows is relaxed – not fast paced – and both are content with the pauses between their questions. They talk casually about the weekend until their children run out of the classroom.

Instant click with a place: low-frequency connector

A low-frequency connector (an introvert) travels out of the city and after a couple of hours arrives in a country town. The horizon opens up before him and he finds himself breathing deeply as he feels relief driving alongside green paddocks. He looks forward to the weekend ahead where he will be in the country on his own with his dog. 'Why don't I live here?' he wonders to himself.

Instant clicks: high-frequency types

High-frequency types will experience an instant click with people, groups and places that match their high frequency. They are:

- Light types: Spark, Star, Sunlight
- Mountain types
- Earth types: Meeting Place, Foundation, Rocks

These connectors will talk frequently and quickly to a variety of different people, 'working the room' at a social event. They will want to live in cities and join a variety of social groups.

Instant clicks: mid-frequency types

Mid-frequency types will experience an instant click with people, places and groups that match their mid-frequency and, depending on their mood that day, they may also enjoy the high-frequency connection of Light, Mountain and Earth types.

Mid-frequency types are:

- Dawn types
- Shapeshifter types
- Garden types

If mid-frequency types are feeling overwhelmed with connection, these types will prefer to be on their own.

Mid-frequency types want to live in cities, but away from the centre – close to the ocean or mountains. They will also thrive in large regional centres. They will enjoy a combination of human connection and time alone or with animals. At a social event, mid-frequency connectors will find a small group of people they are comfortable with and stay in conversation with them.

Instant clicks: low-frequency types

Low-frequency types will experience an instant click with people, places and groups that match their low frequency. They are:

- Water types: Elixir, Ripple Effect, Ocean

- Coral types
- Green types: Shades, Observer, Tree

Low-frequency types thrive when there is no expectation for them to talk or engage in human connection and usually have their most comfortable conversations when there is no eye contact or pressure to talk, such as when driving with someone in the car or riding a bike alongside someone. These types experience belonging away from big cities, or in quiet suburbs. They will enjoy living in coastal towns or the country.

We've just discovered the people and types we experience an instant click with. Who do we instantly clash with?

The instant clash: trying to light a wet match = opposite levels of frequency and intensity

An instant clash is the opposite of an instant click. We experience an instant clash when we meet someone, arrive in a place or join a group and immediately feel like it's hard work and unnatural to be there. We start plotting our exit and mentally calculate how long we have to stay in that place or conversation. During an instant clash, we don't have any hard or inflamed feelings towards the people we're connecting with; we just feel that it's an effort to be there.

An instant clash feels like we're trying to light a wet match. The conversation is stilted and forced. Even though we may experience an instant clash as awkwardness, we need to reframe this experience as loneliness for both parties because there is a gap between how we want to connect and how we are connecting.

An instant clash simply results when there is a mismatch in our frequency and our intensity: for example when the high-frequency, high-intensity connector and the low-frequency, low-intensity connector meet for the first time. Frequency is the first signal of our Connection Type because it relates to how often we talk and how fast we talk. Intensity is a deeper signal of how we connect because it relates to how we bond with others. Generally we struggle to connect most and will have instant clashes with the opposites of our frequency and intensity.

Instant clashes in real life: Light and Green types

One example of an instant clash is a high-frequency/high-intensity connector (Light type) talking to a low-frequency/low-intensity connector (Green type). The Light type will feel like they are carrying the conversation while the Green type will just want the Light type to stop talking!

The Light type will perceive the Green type to be inexpressive and aloof. The Green type will perceive the Light type to be 'over the top', 'too much' or in love with the sound of their own voice. The Green type may feel like they can't keep up with the pace of the conversation, so will give short answers and leave pauses in the conversation. The Light type will keep desperately trying to establish a connection through conversation but the Green type will want to take the focus away from conversation and just engage in pleasant time together. The Light type is trying to establish a quick connection through conversation. The Green type doesn't establish connection through conversation. Both will be uncomfortable and lonely.

I want to share a story about two people who made the most unlikely connection after an instant clash: my father-in-law and me. Bill is a Green Observer type. He is low frequency and low intensity. He values respect, comfort and getting to the point in conversations. He is task-driven. He develops connection through positive, shared experience over time.

You know me now. I am a Light type. I am high frequency and high intensity. I value high energy and enthusiasm in conversation. I am people-driven. I develop connection through animated conversations.

The first time I met Bill, I kept trying to talk to him. He kept looking at me like I was a mosquito, with body language to match. At one point I think he may have even physically startled when I asked him a question. My sister-in-law started laughing and said, 'Ali's trying to talk to Dad.' The whole family joined in the laughter, as though attempting to engage Bill in conversation was hilarious.*

---

* To be clear, I wasn't asking overly intense questions; I was asking him how long he had lived in the area!

Over time, I learnt to moderate my conversation with Bill, but I still never felt I could figure him out. He was always respectful, but I never felt as though he liked me. This is a typical example of an instant clash. We were just different in our approach to connection.

After about ten years (not joking), Bill started being more comfortable around me. He would crack jokes in my presence, and we began doing crosswords together whenever I visited their house. This warmth and comfort grew until eventually I felt completely at ease in his company. It took around eleven years to experience this click.

Recently I said to Bill, 'Do you know that for the first ten years of knowing you, I thought you didn't like me?'

Bill looked at me and replied, 'What makes you think I like you now?'

Jokes aside, we have turned an instant clash into a deep respect and (from my side anyway) love for each other. The positive experiences we have shared over time have created a meaningful connection between two very different connectors. For anyone living through an extended instant clash, my advice for you is to hang in there and aim for some moments of meeting in the middle, but don't expect the other person to ever fundamentally change. With patience, care and people in common, you may even eventually turn a clash into respect and love. And even though Bill and I have opposite Connection Types, I would trust him with my life.

Instant clashes aren't inflamed

Instant clashes do not involve an emotional charge and usually occur when our Connection Type is the opposite to another person's. Flip to the Ality Connection Type model printed on the inside cover and see, for example, that Sunlight and Star types will have cold clashes with Observer and Tree types, since these types are found opposite each other.

An instant clash happens when our point of connection with another person is so remote that we don't take it personally. We both accept that there is no way we could click even if we tried. It's not because we don't like each other; it's because this person's Connection

Type is so removed from ours as to make this person a stranger to us emotionally. An instant clash signifies the absence of connection.

When we experience instant clashes, it is less inflammatory than the intuitive or intimate clashes that we will explore later. When we have an instant clash, we tend to just avoid these people in the future. We simply don't want to continue the conversation with them because we don't feel a 'glimmer' of hope that we will ever get on. We don't hold anything against that person, just like we don't hold anything against a wet match – we see it for what it is and move on, trying to find another match that will catch light. We probably don't even give most of our instant clashes a second thought and just accept that we are not going to be particularly close. For example, a Light type will experience an instant clash in connection if they meet someone who is quite reserved and gives one-word answers and does not express a lot of interest in talking. Light types will very quickly realise that this person doesn't want to build a connection in a Light-type way. One of them will find a way to exit the conversation to relieve the discomfort. This is an instant clash with no hard feelings.

It's often useful to make light of instant connection clashes. When I'm giving a workshop and people are wearing stickers signifying their Connection Types, I make the joke that they can use the stickers to work out who they want to sit next to at lunch. Once a man piped up in response, 'Yeah. I won't be sitting next to you!' Far from being offended, I loved it – the model at work! Funnily enough, joking about this instant clash opened the way for us to genuinely connect. It's almost as if talking about our unlikely connection produced a connection. I did sit with him at lunch (to continue the joke), and we had a great chat. Naming the instant clash can transform an instant clash into a click.

When I work with organisations, I often observe that the high-performing teams acknowledge each other's Connection Types and even the instant clashes. For example, the high-frequency types will say, 'Oh Mira can only stand to be in a Zoom meeting for 30 minutes and then she tunes out,' or 'Jun doesn't do Friday night drinks – he's over us by then!' The low-frequency types feel understood and appreciate that they don't need to explain themselves. Equally, they might know that their high-frequency co-workers like to chat when they get to work in the morning and so they accommodate them. There's a desire to meet the connection preferences of the other people in the team without having to be the same.

Instant clashes in real life

Instant clash at work
In the course of my work I have been told by a Green connector that when they see a Light connector walking towards them and smiling, they will think: 'I am about to lose twenty minutes of my life.'

Instant clash socially
A woman arrives late for a social lunch. She takes the last seat remaining at the end of the table, next to a low-frequency, low-intensity connector. The latecomer is high frequency and high intensity: a Light type. She is bubbly at first, asking questions of the woman next to her: 'How have you been?' 'Are you going away for the holidays?' 'How's work?'

The woman gives short answers and the conversation doesn't seem to go anywhere. The Light woman says, 'Oh there's someone I haven't seen in ages, I'm just going to go and say hello!'

Instant clash with a place
A low-frequency, high-intensity connector (Water type) walks into a nightclub with his date. The music is pumping so loudly that the floor is vibrating. He has to shout to order their drinks. He starts feeling like he has a headache. After they finish their drink, he yells to his date: 'Do you want to get out of here?'

Instant clashes between opposite types

Light types

High-frequency/High-intensity types will experience an instant clash with people, places and groups that do not match their high frequency and high intensity i.e. their opposites:

- Low-frequency/low-intensity Green types: Shades, Observer, Tree
- Garden types

Light types will experience loneliness when they are in a quiet and slower paced environment. They will have an instant clash with unpopulated areas in the country with limited human connection.

Green types

Low-frequency/low-intensity types will experience an instant clash with people, places and groups that do not match their low frequency and low intensity i.e. their opposites:

- High-frequency/high-intensity Light types: Spark, Star, Sunlight
- Dawn types

Green types will experience loneliness when they are overwhelmed by crowded and loud environments. They will have an instant clash with multiple social engagements and relentless conversation.

Water types

Low-frequency/high-intensity types will experience an instant clash with people, groups and places that do not match their low frequency and high intensity i.e. their opposites:

- High-frequency/low-intensity Earth types: Meeting Place, Foundation, Rock
- Garden types

Water types will experience loneliness when they are surrounded by ongoing low-intensity human connection, for example a group holiday on tour. They thrive when they can move at their own pace and withdraw into their sanctuary. Their home must be peaceful and quiet.

Earth types

High-frequency/low-intensity types will experience an instant clash with people, groups and places that do not match their high frequency and low intensity i.e. their opposites:

- Low-frequency/high-intensity Water types: Elixir, Ripple Effect, Ocean
- Dawn types

Earth types will experience loneliness when they are on their own for too long or when they are forced into deep, emotional conversations. They are task-driven and enjoy the stimulation of busy areas.

Mid-intensity connectors such as Shapeshifters, Mountain and Coral types are adaptive and accommodating by their nature so rarely experience clashes on first meeting any other Connection Types. Mid-intensity types are usually versatile with the environments they find comfort in because their connection is flexible.

The good news is: we can recover from an instant clash, so we shouldn't abandon a connection with someone just because of this one-off experience. A way to overcome an instant clash is to name it when it's happening – like my husband did. He turned an instant clash into a click because he had the courage to name what was happening in our connection. After that, in the early days of our relationship I remember describing it as a slow burn.

The point to remember about instant clashes is that there are no hard feelings, only discomfort. We feel like the connection is hard work, unnatural and awkward. One way to overcome an instant clash is to acknowledge to yourself what is happening, and to do your best not to take the clash personally. If you are forced into continuing the connection, just know that over time your connection will soften and become more comfortable.

An instant clash can also be overcome if you focus on a common goal or objective. For example, if you have an instant clash with an in-law, the key would be to focus on your mutual love for their child (your partner). Or if you have an instant clash with a co-worker, the focus needs to be on your common goal to elevate the team. The key is: with a bit of mutual respect and a desire to focus on a common goal, we can turn instant clashes into something sustainable and mutually rewarding. I have learnt so much from my instant clash with my father-in-law. I now find myself wanting to emulate him in many ways. His humility, his measured responses, his lack of drama and his sense of commitment to his family inspire me and I appreciate the beauty of his Green-ness. Everyone has beauty in their Connection Type if we take the time to look and listen.

The biggest breakthrough that this work has offered is that it's impossible to take connection 'personally': the way someone connects is just a reflection of their belonging needs. We've been conditioned to believe that when we have an instant clash with someone, they don't like us. Let's change our language from 'They don't like me', to 'We have different connection needs'. And remember that when someone is offensive or dysregulated in their behaviour, they are feeling lonely.

chapter 15

The intuitive click: how we choose friends

In this chapter we discover who we seek out as friends.

My best friend and I started our friendship in Year 7. We were twelve years old and we went to the same high school. We didn't have an instant click because our frequency is a bit different. She is a mid-frequency connector and I am a high-frequency connector. I had initial clicks with people who were as outgoing as me. But then we started playing netball in the same team and took the same train home from school in the afternoon. After a few months, we felt very comfortable in each other's company.

I still remember the moment that cemented our friendship. We were on our own, walking from school to the train station one afternoon and I said, 'Um, do you have your period yet?'

My heart was racing as I asked the question. To me this was an experience I wanted to share with someone. I was longing for another person to understand and relate to what I was going through.

I remember thinking, *I hope she says 'yes'*.

She took a second to answer – this was a vulnerable disclosure for a twelve-year-old girl. Then she said, 'Yes. Do you?'

I breathed a sigh of relief. 'Yes! I do!'

It was like a valve had been released and both of us felt permission to connect in the way we had been needing to. We have been best friends ever since. Her mum used to describe us as 'joined at the hip'. This is an intuitive click because the intensity of our Connection Type matches. My question was my way of establishing whether she could match my intensity.

I'm not suggesting that it's appropriate for adults to ask deeply personal questions of other adults in order to strike up a friendship. Adult friendships have very different dynamics and we need to give other people the freedom to share who they are with us. This trust can take longer to build than it does between twelve-year-olds.

We experience an intuitive click when we want to spend an extended amount of time with someone or in a place. We feel comfort and joy in their presence. We feel most like ourselves and we feel like we can express ourselves freely and unreservedly. We feel seen, heard and understood. We relax. Time seems to stand still or speed up because we don't notice it passing. This suspension of time leads to a deeply fulfilling connection and we experience a feeling of strong belonging. It feels like coming home. An intuitive click is like a mirror of our best qualities. It brings out the best in us, and helps us express the best version of ourselves; how we want to be perceived in the world.

This experience of deep belonging may not have its source in another person; it may have its source in an animal or in a particular place, by reading books, playing an instrument, making art, meditating, cooking or exercising. Look for intuitive clicks in the sense of belonging you feel, not in another person.

We experience this type of click when someone responds to us in a way that communicates:

- All of you is welcome here
- You can be yourself
- Your connection needs will be met here.

Intuitive click = match in intensity

An intuitive click or friendship occurs when we find a match in the intensity of our Connection Types.

Intensity is the deepest form of connection because it relates to how we bond, how we feel close to someone and how much we disclose to another person.

This means that we will develop friendships with people and feel connected to places, experiences and groups that match our level of intensity. Generally we struggle to connect most over time with the opposites of our intensity.

Intuitive clicks and clashes

Type	Will have an intuitive click with	Will have an intuitive clash with
Light types: Spark, Star, Sunlight	Other Light types Dawn types Water types	Earth types Green types Garden types
Water types: Elixir, Ripple Effect, Ocean	Other Water types Light types Dawn types	Earth types Green types Garden types
Earth types: Meeting Place, Foundation, Rock	Other Earth types Green types Garden types	Light types Water types Dawn types
Green types: Shades, Observer, Tree	Other Green types Earth types Garden types	Light types Water types Dawn types
Shapeshifter, Mountain and Coral types	As these types are mid-intensity, they have good range to adapt to either high-intensity or low-intensity connectors. They will connect best over time with other mid-intensity connectors such as Shapeshifter, Mountain	These types will find it more effort to adapt to Connection Types on the extremes of high- and low-intensity connection, such as: Star Sunlight

Type	Will have an intuitive click with	Will have an intuitive clash with
(cont)	and Coral types. They may also develop friendships and intuitive connections with other types that are close to centre (mid-intensity) such as Spark, Elixir, Shades and Meeting Place types.	Ripple Effect Ocean Observer Tree Foundation Rock

If you are a high-intensity connector, you connect and bond through highly engaged and honest conversations where you can disclose your emotions to someone who will make you feel psychologically safe. You experience belonging during these types of conversations. You will have an intuitive click with someone who wants to engage in these types of conversations as much as you do.

If you are a mid-intensity connector, you bond through a combination of light and entertaining conversation *and* shared positive experience over time. You have an intuitive click with people who can entertain you in conversation and also connect with you through shared enjoyable activities. If mid-frequency types are feeling overwhelmed with connection, these types will prefer to be on their own.

If you are a low-intensity connector, you feel most like yourself when you are on your own. When you do connect with other people, you will seek out shared positive experiences with no pressure to talk.

The feeling of having a lot in common doesn't refer to superficial aspects of life. It refers to sharing a common intensity.

Intuitive clicks in real life

Intuitive click at work: two high-intensity connectors

Two high-intensity people are allocated to a project. They have a meeting to discuss it. They spend the first 15 minutes of the meeting bonding about their histories – how they came to be working in the same organisation and what they studied at university. They agree to meet for coffee the following week because they enjoy talking to each other.

Intuitive click socially: two low-intensity connectors

Two dads who are friends are at a children's party with their kids at a park. One of the dads yells out to the other, 'We need another player on our basketball team! Are you up for it?' The dad stands up, smiles and says, 'I can't be the sort of dad that says no to basketball.' They don't speak a lot but they like each other and feel upbeat in each other's company.

Intuitive click with a place: high-intensity connection

A high-intensity screenwriter has a place in the mountains where she goes to write, explaining to a friend, 'I feel creative there. I feel inspired there.'

Intuitive click at work: low-intensity connectors

The manager explains the task to his employee. The employee nods and then asks, 'When do you need it by?' The manager responds and the employee says 'I'll have it for you then.' This is a low-intensity conversation because it is to the point and task-focused. It lacks emotion and doesn't involve personal disclosures or unnecessary additions.

Intuitive click socially: two high-intensity connectors

'How was your holiday?'

'Oh my god, it was terrible – we all had the flu and had to stay inside! We almost killed each other!'

This is a high-intensity response because the person is connecting using honest, no-holds-barred conversation to disclose their true experience. They equally expect the other person to disclose their true experience.

Intuitive click with a place: low-intensity connection

'Do you two ever go anywhere else on holiday?' the adult children ask their older parents. 'Don't you get bored?'

'No, we love it! We love the restaurants and the walks and the place where we stay – it suits us perfectly.'

This is an intuitive click with a place because it simply feels right.

Now we're going to talk about intuitive clashes: when someone gets under our skin.

chapter 16

The intuitive clash: when someone gets under our skin

If an intuitive click is a mirror of our best qualities, an intuitive clash is a mirror of our ... ahem ... most challenging qualities. Except it's not an accurate mirror, it's one of those mirrors that distorts our reflection to make us look disfigured.

We experience an intuitive clash when another person's behaviour provokes a competitive, judgemental or defensive reaction in us. Think about someone who really gets on your nerves. It may be someone at work, in your family or from your social circle. You may find yourself having strong reactions to this person:

> 'How could they?!'
> 'What the...?!'
> 'Are they serious?!'
> 'What is wrong with them?!'
> 'How do they sleep at night?!'
> 'Can you believe...?!'

When we have an intuitive clash with other people, we tend to tell long and involved stories (whether it's in our own head or out loud to others) about why they are so annoying/outrageous/obnoxious/mean/narcissistic/unstable/unreliable/stupid etc.

I don't like to be the bearer of bad news, but we generally experience an intuitive hot clash with people who are acting out and expressing a part of us we are uncomfortable with or haven't come to terms with. They represent a part of us we are actively suppressing. To be clear, it doesn't mean that our behaviour is as extreme as this person's behaviour in whatever way they irritate us. Usually, this person is manifesting a more extreme version of a quality we dislike in ourselves or have suppressed. Intuitive clashes with another person are just a signal of something we need to work on emotionally.

I'm going to give some examples to illustrate this in action:

Example 1: the intergenerational clash

Miriam is a fifty-year-old woman who has an intuitive clash with the teenaged Kitty, who is confident with her sexuality. Miriam had to suppress her sexual desires when she was a teenager, so she didn't act on them. Her social and cultural background meant that she would have been ostracised from her family if she had expressed herself sexually. Miriam chose to prioritise belonging with her family and community over realising her sexual desires. For this reason, the sexually confident teenager Kitty produces an intuitive clash in her. It's not that Kitty is wrong or bad, but the older woman feels repelled by her behaviour.

Example 2: the mirror at work

Thirty-year-old Gianna has an intuitive clash with twenty-one-year-old Yan from her work because 'She's so dumb and incompetent!' When asked why she is so irritated by her behaviour, she replies: 'I guess because she can't do anything for herself. She can see what needs to be done but she's too lazy to do it.' She pauses. 'I guess they are things that sort of annoy me about myself, to be honest. I need to change some things in my life and I know what I need to do, but I'm just not doing them.'

Example 3: the jealous clash

Robert is offended by the fact that his friend Igor keeps posting his extravagant overseas holiday on Instagram. 'Doesn't he know he's showing off?' But then he says 'I guess I'd like to go overseas. Maybe I'll look at flights.'

Example 4: the humiliated clash

A man is angered by another person at work who constantly interrupts him and talks over him in meetings. This is a reminder of his experience of being dismissed and not listened to in his family. It makes him feel insecure, and that his ideas aren't valid or worthwhile.

Intuitive clashes don't necessarily come from negative behaviour – they simply shine a light on something we need to work on or heal in ourselves. An individual I worked with experienced low self-confidence that was intensified whenever he was asked to speak in public. His intuitive clash was prompted by someone he worked with who was an excellent public speaker. This colleague was kind and never did anything to diminish the confidence of my client. It was their mere presence that prompted the clash. Their gift for communication would shine a light on the insecurity in my client. Once we worked through and cleared the emotional history, my client was able to focus on developing his own style rather than comparing himself to his colleague.

An intuitive clash can occur, for example, between someone with a belief that flaunting money is unethical and another person with flashy belongings. Or, if someone is a people-pleaser and they have a belief that 'I am only lovable if I am meeting someone else's needs,' then they will have an intuitive clash with people who live on their own terms. You can see that someone doesn't have to be unkind or nasty to prompt an intuitive clash. Simply by existing, people can shine an uncomfortable light on the places in us that need to heal.

We need to see intuitive clashes as a process of being poked and prodded to change. If we resist the urge to take such clashes personally, we can take the heat out of our exchange. Intuitive clashes have a way of getting out of hand and lasting for years. They can even last for lifetimes if we don't have the awareness to see the clash for what it is: a signal that we need that we need to reconcile ourselves with an aspect of our personality we feel estranged from or that makes us uncomfortable.

By the way, an intuitive clash with another person doesn't mean that they are doing anything wrong; they are just living according to their Connection Type and may be totally unaware that they are triggering you.

In an intuitive clash we usually want the same things as this other person but have different ideas about how to realise them. Essentially, an intuitive clash causes us to question our ideas and how we approach life: is your way better than my way? Should I adapt or rethink my approach? In the moment, we are subconsciously concerned that this person's approach to life is more efficient, effective or enlightened than ours. For example, Miriam wants to be more sexually free. Gianna wants to be more proactive about her life choices. Robert wants to go on an overseas holiday. The people who they clashed with can be embraced as prompts for them to grow.

If we can reach this level of awareness, the intuitive clash can eventually become a click when we establish why this person threatens us to the point of competition, defensiveness or judgement.

Figuring out an intuitive clash

In order to leverage an intuitive clash for our own personal growth and benefit, we should pause and consider, 'what is the fear or desire underneath my reaction to this person?'

We can even have gratitude towards this person for the gift of clarity they are offering us. Their connection is nudging us towards the life we want, even though it can be an uncomfortable path to tread. To deal with an intuitive clash, we need to ask ourselves the following questions:

- In one sentence, what is it about this person's behaviour that is provoking me?
- What do they have that I wish I had?
- Is there some part of me I had to suppress that they are acting out?

- Is there something I can do to bring a bit more of what they represent into my life?

To produce an intuitive clash in us, the other person has the same approach to connection as we do.

> Light types have intuitive clashes with other Light types and Dawn types.
>
> Water types have intuitive clashes with other Water types and Dawn types.
>
> Green types have intuitive clashes with other Green types and Garden types.
>
> Earth types have intuitive clashes with other Earth types and Garden types.
>
> Mid-intensity types (Shapeshifter, Mountain and Coral types) have intuitive clashes with other mid-intensity types.

For someone to provoke us, they need to be on our wavelength of connection. This person is acting out a split-off part of our personality, which is why they are provoking a strong reaction in us. For them to enact an aspect of our personality, they must share our frequency and intensity.

Intuitive clashes in real life

Light type and Dawn type

Crystal has an intuitive clash with the husband of one of her friends (Jens) who is an investment banker and a Light type. Crystal is a Dawn type and is talking about her work as a nurse out at dinner one night. Jens responds by saying, 'What do nurses earn per year?' Crystal is taken aback but tells him her annual wage. He looks at his wife and laughs, saying, 'That's what I paid in tax last year.'

Crystal and her husband are horrified. In the car on the way home, they decide to never go out for dinner again with that couple. It's clear that Jens has been obnoxious and rude, but what is the lesson here for Crystal? If she asks herself these questions, she may be able to transform the awkward encounter into an opportunity for insight:

- In one sentence, what is it about this person's behaviour that is provoking me? *He is making me feel inadequate in terms of my abundance.*
- What does he have that I wish I had? *I would like more abundance and indulgence in my life. I feel overworked.*
- Is there some part of me I had to suppress that they are acting out? *Growing up, I was taught that I had to look after others. I come from a family of health practitioners. Money for the sake of money was considered to be selfish. This isn't a negative thing but sometimes it means I can overlook my own needs.*
- Is there something I can do to bring a bit more of what he represents into my life? *I can make sure that I focus on my own needs for wellbeing: exercise, taking baths, getting a massage every once in a while. I still don't want to go out for dinner with this person but he has shone a light on the areas where I deny my needs.*

Water type and Water type

One grandmother (Laurel, an Elixir type) has an intuitive clash with her Ripple Effect daughter-in-law, Uta, about the latter's approach to mothering. Laurel had three children of her own and is very perceptive when it comes to reading children's needs. Uta follows parenting books and blogs instead of trusting her gut and instinctively understanding what her child needs. Laurel has a strong negative reaction when Uta has nursery rhymes printed out and stuck around the house so she remembers to sing them. Laurel mutters to her husband when she gets home, 'I never had to remind myself with a printed-out sheet to sing a nursery rhyme! What's wrong with her?'

This is the reflective process Laurel might use for this intuitive clash:

- In one sentence, what is it about Uta's behaviour that is provoking me? *That she listens to other people – so-called experts – for parenting advice instead of trusting herself and my advice.*

- What does Uta have that I wish I had? *She openly accepts when she needs help – I'm not good at admitting my vulnerability.*
- Is there some part of me I had to suppress that Uta is acting out? *I wasn't always sure of myself when I was raising my children but I had to get on with it. There were a lot of times that I doubted myself but I had to soldier on because I had no other choice. I couldn't ask my own mother for advice because she was drinking all the time. I guess I wish I could have had someone to go to for help.*
- Is there something I can do to bring a bit more of what Uta represents into my life? *Maybe I can be a bit easier on myself and not try to be perfect all the time. I won't turn into my own mother if I admit that I struggle.*

Two sisters: Green type and Garden type

Two sisters, Gen and Claudia, are both Green types: Gen, twenty-one, is a Shades type and Claudia, twenty-three, is a Garden type. Gen is always 'borrowing' Claudia's clothes and asking her for money with no intention of paying it back. Gen doesn't have a job and relies on her hard-working older sister to pay for her when they go out.

This is how Claudia's reflective process looks when she experiences an intuitive clash with Gen:

- What is it about this person's behaviour that is provoking me? *She's always sponging off me with no intention of ever paying me back. She takes things without asking. She treats my stuff and my wallet like they're hers and doesn't realise how hard I have to work to pay for everything! Mum and Dad don't have any money for extras so she relies on me when we go out – it's so unfair.*
- What does she have that I wish I had? *She has no pressure. She can literally sit around all day and do whatever she wants. There are no expectations of her. I wish I could feel like that.*
- Is there some part of me I had to suppress that she is acting out? *I was always the responsible oldest one. I have to make my parents proud – they are so stressed about her. I could never slack off, as then there would be two of us letting down the family.*

- Is there something I can do to bring a bit more of what Gen represents into my life? *I don't know how everyone would react if I started being lazy. Maybe I can relax every once in a while. Like on my day off I can ask her to clean the house with me instead of just doing it on my own while she's asleep in the morning. Maybe she needs jobs at home, too.*

At the bar: Earth type and Garden type

A man is standing in a line at a busy bar. The person in front of him orders four drinks and the bartender says, 'That will be $48.' The person in front of him gets out his wallet at that point to pay.

Once the man has bought his own drinks he returns to his friends and says, 'It is not that hard to have your wallet out and your card ready when you order drinks! The guy ordering in front of me looked shocked when the bartender asked for money!'

This is the reflective process for an intuitive clash of this nature:

- In one sentence, what is it about this person's behaviour that is provoking me? *That they're not being thoughtful: there's a queue around them and all they are thinking about is themselves.*
- What do they have that I wish I had? *They don't consider other people. Sometimes I wish I didn't think so much about how everything affected the people around me and didn't have to please everyone.*
- Is there some part of me I had to suppress that they are acting out? *Actually, when I was growing up I was that kid who was in a world of my own – I didn't think much about how my actions affected other people; I just did what I wanted. I don't know when I stopped being like that.*
- Is there something I can do to bring a bit more of what they represent into my life? *Allowing myself to not be so hyper-vigilant all the time – it's okay and even healthy to let go of control.*

Mid-intensity types: Shapeshifter and Mountain type

A Shapeshifter artist can't stand it when people in his industry dress up and play the role of hipsters copying an artist from another era, like rockabilly. It really gets under his skin. He goes through the reflective process for an intuitive clash. Notice the Shapeshifter indecision:

- In one sentence, what is it about this person's behaviour that is provoking me? *That they can commit so strongly to a style – that they know who they are.*
- What do they have that I wish I had? *Clarity about who they are and confidence to claim an identity and say, 'That's my thing.'*
- Is there some part of me I had to suppress that they are acting out? *I don't know.*
- Is there something I can do to bring a bit more of what they represent into my life? *Think more about my style and how I am comfortable expressing myself.*

An intuitive clash is a fast lane to working out which parts of us need attention. If someone were to lightly poke our arm and we didn't have an underlying injury, it wouldn't bother us. We may not even notice. But if we are sunburnt or have a bruise in that spot, then the poke is going to cause an acute negative reaction. This is the same process with an intuitive clash: it provokes us because we have an underlying vulnerability in that very spot. If you have someone in your life who provokes you emotionally, try using the questions above to prompt your insight. This will give you the distance from this person to realise that they don't have any particular power over you. They have a powerful impact because they represent an underlying pattern that you need to heal.

chapter 17

The intimate click: how we fall in love

Intimate clicks follow a very different pattern to instant and intuitive clicks. With friends and acquaintances, we are looking for people who match us in some way, either through our frequency or intensity. When we fall in love, we seek out romantic partners who complement or balance out our Connection Type. A complement is someone who contributes extra features to someone else to improve or enhance their quality. In the language of the Ality model, a complement is someone whose Connection Type is close to our type, but not the same in either frequency or intensity. We don't seek out lovers with exactly the same Connection Type as us because we consider this to be unnecessary duplication or a potential source of competition in the relationship. We want a partner in love to balance us out. We don't want a mirror: we want to form two pieces of a puzzle.

This means that opposites don't attract, because the most successful partnerships are with complements, not opposites. We enter into a romantic relationship with someone if we they balance us out and complement us. So we tend to choose friends who are the same as us, and lovers who complement us. For example, my close friends are all high-intensity connectors who connect through talking, while my husband is a Shapeshifter, a mid-intensity connector who bonds through shared positive experience and regular, low-intensity talking.

In my life partner, I was looking for someone as a balance rather than a reflection of my Connection Type. If I had been looking for someone who shared my type, I would have found another Light type. His Shapeshifter qualities balance out mine. When I'm talking about him, I often use phrases like, 'He centres me', 'He levels me' or 'He grounds me', which is interesting from the perspective of the Ality Connection Types. He connects me to the centre of the model.

His friends are also the same type as him with the same intensity: Shapeshifters and Mountain types, with some Sparks and Meeting Place types as well. Of course, most of our decisions about friends and romantic partners aren't made consciously. The Ality Connection Type model gives us an opportunity to make these decisions conscious and to recognise our patterns.

Who to choose as a romantic partner

All the happily married couples who have taken the Ality Connection Type assessment have complementary Connection Types. As the different couples demonstrate, there are many combinations that can produce a happy love relationship. However, there are some combinations that are more likely to work long term than other combinations.

To choose the best romantic partners, we should be looking for a person whose Connection Type is not the same type as ours, but also not an opposite or distant type on the model. The rule is: choose someone close to you on the model but not exactly the same type as you. To make this clear, a Sunlight type can fall in love with another Light type like a Spark, but two Sunlight types in the same relationship would be too much intensity and would eventually explode.

Couples who stay together

Here are some real-life examples of happy love relationships longer than ten years and their Connection Types.

Couple one: married for more than forty years

Connection Types: Female – Meeting Place; Male – Observer

Connection Types are indicated by the two circles. They are close together but not the same type; they match in intensity. The female's frequency is higher than the male's frequency.

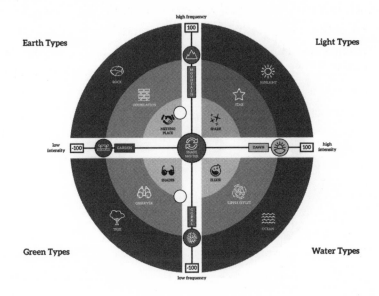

This is a low-intensity connection. The female of this Meeting Place–Observer couple told me: 'Our connection has always been based on the same values and principles and the love and strength of family. Also, he was cute and I rather fancied him. I would describe our relationship as a very good friendship, supportive of each other yet maintaining an independence of self. Agreeing on the major issues, annoyed by the minor issues. Respectful of each other's needs and being prepared to compromise.'

Couple two: married for more than forty years

Connection Types: Female – Dawn; Male – Spark

Connection Types are indicated by the two circles. They are close together but not the same type. They have the same frequency. The male has a lower intensity than the female.

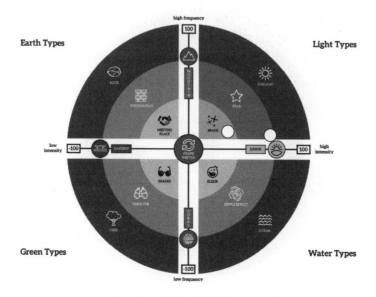

This is a high-intensity connection. When asked to describe his wife, the male Spark said: 'Can I use terms like "something magical" or "one of the seven wonders of the world"? She has always inspired me to reach my highest potential. Our relationship energises my life.'

The female Dawn put it this way: 'He is like breathing. I see him like my background canvas without who I could never paint the pictures of my life.'

Couple three: married for more than ten years

Connection Types: Female – Shapeshifter; Male – Coral

Connection Types are indicated by the two circles. They are close together but not the same type. There is a match in intensity.

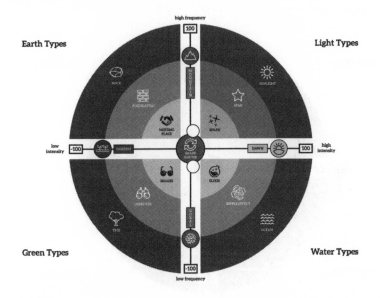

The female Shapeshifter (mid-intensity connector) of this couple said, 'I would describe our relationship as stable; stable because there is no second-guessing or games. We have genuine admiration and respect for each other and want the best for each other. This keeps our connection strong, and passionate, and always evolving.'

Couple four: married for more than ten years

Connection Type: Female – on the cusp of Star and Sunlight; Male – Shapeshifter

Connection Types are close but not the same. There is a match in frequency.

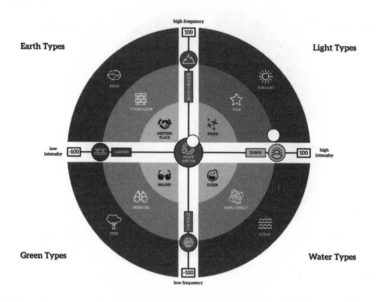

This is the connection of my husband and me. I am high intensity; he is mid-intensity. When describing our relationship I use phrases like, 'He centres me', or 'He brings me down to earth', which is interesting when you look at where we are located on the model. When I asked him how he would describe our connection he started singing 'You Raise me Up' by Josh Groban. He always deflects my intense questions with humour!

We have a match in frequency, which is great because we need as much human connection as each other. We both have the same enthusiasm for socialising and being part of a community. Funnily enough, I am mid-intensity when I describe our relationship to others. My true high-intensity feelings for my husband are too deep to share in public.

Couple five: married for more than fifteen years

Connection Types: Female – Shades; Male – Meeting Place

Connection Types are indicated by the two circles. They are close together but not the same type. There is a match in intensity.

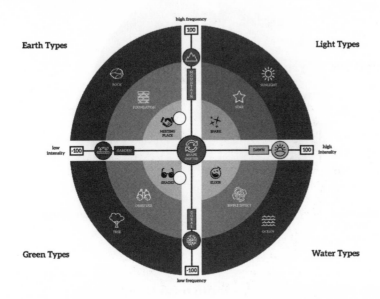

This is a low-intensity connection. The couple knew each other as friends for several years before coming together romantically. They are united by their three children and are strong supports for each other. Their relationship is drama-free and pragmatic.

Couple six: married for more than fifteen years

Connection Types: Female – Ripple Effect; Male – Elixir

Connection Types are indicated by the two circles. They are close together but not the same type, and they match in frequency. The female Ripple Effect of this couple described the relationship in the following way: 'We are a haven for each other. We both work extremely hard and our relationship is the fuel that sustains us. When we have a break we withdraw into the sanctuary of our family. After twenty years together we have built a life we are both proud of.' We can see the low-frequency match coming through in her choice of language; the haven and the sanctuary are places to withdraw from the world.

Both individuals respect the other's need to become immersed in work and then return to the family.

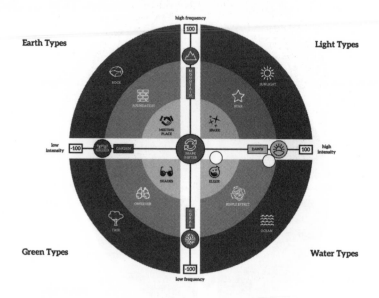

Couple seven: together for more than twenty years

Connection Types: Male – Star; Male – Sunlight

Connection Types are indicated by the two circles. They are close together but not the same type; there's a match in frequency. This male–male couple reinforces the data on intimate clicks, indicating that we can draw conclusions about Connection Types that apply to all couples. The Sunlight male says: 'we are both high energy and together we go at a million miles an hour. We have three children and a dog and we're always on the move and having fun.' This high-frequency and high-intensity connection is unstoppable, drawing to itself other people like a magnetic force. These two men are fuelled by, as Carl Jung described of extraversion, 'the capacity to endure bustle and noise of every kind, and actually find them enjoyable, constant attention to the surrounding world, the cultivation of friends and acquaintances . . . The psychic life of this type of person is enacted, as it were, outside himself, in the environment.'[26]

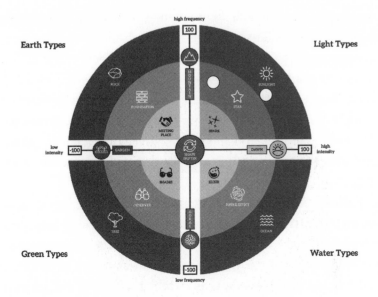

Couple eight: together for more than five years

Connection Types: Female – Star; Female – Sunlight

Connection Types are indicated by the two circles. They are close together but not the same type; they match in frequency. This female–female couple reinforces the data on intimate clicks, indicating that we can draw conclusions about Connection Types that apply to all couples.

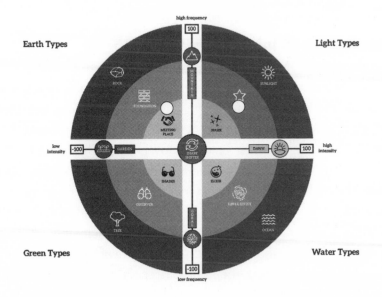

This couple are a match in frequency, with one high-intensity female and one low-intensity female. The high-intensity person said: 'Our connection has always been electric. The embers of our connection lay dormant and sat quietly but constantly for years, across miles of distance between each other. Once we were in the same space, the wind caught the embers and the fire blazed and burned ferociously. I would describe our relationship as deep, free, loving, equal, passionate, loyal and we are unapologetically and fiercely protective of each other's hearts.'

Her partner said: 'I have always found her alluring, captivating and enchanting, even through many years of platonic friendship. I have never been so inexplicably drawn to someone. When our window of opportunity presented itself, our connection as lovers expanded on this and I would describe it now as dazzling, powerful and unwavering. Our relationship is the perfect mix of fun, laughter, joy and ease and intense loyalty, love, desire and devotion. She also always laughs at my jokes and tells me I look good, so I think this helps.'

Not only is this a beautiful reflection on this relationship, it is also symbolic of the nature of their mutual connection with language like 'the wind caught the embers and the fire blazed' and 'When our window of opportunity presented itself': this is perfect for a combination of Light and Earth types.

Reflecting on an intimate relationship

The difference in how high-intensity and low-intensity connectors describe their intimate clicks is characteristic of each type's way of relating to their emotions. High-intensity connectors feel their emotions in a more profound way whereas low-intensity connectors are more consistent in their emotions over time. The low-intensity connectors emphasised the friendship element of the intimate click whereas the high-intensity connectors emphasised the high emotion of the click.

Starting a new romantic relationship can be incredibly exciting, with many powerful emotions flooding through your brain and body. If you are embarking on a romantic partnership (or if you are in a romantic relationship now), it might be useful to ask yourself the following questions relating to frequency and intensity:

Compatibility in love: frequency and intensity

Frequency compatibility

- Do we experience belonging in ways that serve us both or is one of us usually connecting according to how the other wants to connect?
- Do we want to go out and socialise as much as each other?
- Is this dynamic sustainable enough to allow room for other important relationships in my life?
- Is my partner threatened by or jealous of the way I connect with others?

Intensity compatibility

- Do I feel as though I can openly, effectively and safely communicate with this person? Or do I feel dismissed or ashamed for the way I communicate?
- Are our patterns of connection aligned with how I want to live my life, i.e. do we talk to each other and spend time together in a way that makes me feel confident, respected and valued?
- Does our relationship bring out the best in both of us?
- Does our relationship support the highest potential of us both?

The intimate partners we choose can be among the most significant life decisions we ever make. I hope that understanding your Connection Types combined with the questions above help you make these choices. Compatibility is not about shared interests; couples will have intimate clicks instead of intimate clashes if they have

Connection Types that are close to each other on the model. We can come from the same quadrant but it's better if we're not the exact same type: for example we can both be Light types but not both Sunlights. My research shows that couples close to each other on the model with a match in either frequency or intensity will work very well.

Now we've talked about how and why we have intimate clicks, it's time to talk about how and why we have intimate clashes.

chapter 18

The intimate clash: triggers and traumas

An intimate clash feels like love and hate; war and peace; attraction and repulsion; fear and desire, and (emotional) violence and passion all in one connection, which sounds like a contradiction, I know. We experience intimate clashes with people who trigger a response in us that feels unsafe, dangerous or threatening because of our conditioning, past experiences or trauma. An intimate clash triggers a strong negative and defensive reaction to another person and at the same time we find this person extremely attractive. The most powerful, life-defining, explosive clashes are intimate clashes. We use language like: 'You ruined my life', 'I have wasted the last five years with you', 'It's all your fault' and 'I wish I'd never met you'. If we could replace the word 'you' in these phrases with 'my childhood trauma' then we would get to the truth of what's going on.

It's easy to become confused between an intimate click and an intimate clash, especially in the beginning. An intimate click initially feels like desire, as we're swamped with the excitement of high passion and complete immersion in another person. In an intimate click we are looking for another to balance us out, so we expect some resistance. Passion is not a straight line. We don't expect perfect harmony all the time because we want to find a counterweight in the connection.

But we need to know the point when resistance and balance turns into a toxic connection. There's a difference between an intimate click and an intimate clash and it's generally found in the nature of the arguments. In an intimate clash, arguments are more regular and are hurtful to the other person. The arguments in an intimate clash have the tone of: you must change who you are, if you want to continue the relationship. They can even verge on abuse. To help you differentiate between the experiences of an intimate click and a toxic intimate clash, refer to the following table.

Intimate click	Toxic intimate clash
• Occasional arguments about minor issues that leave us feeling irritated and upset, with a desire to make peace after the fact. • We are physically attracted to the other person and regularly seek out their affection. This can also feel like all-consuming desire in the first twelve months. • We feel like the connection is healthy and sustainable. • We treat the other person as a separate individual with their own priorities.	• Constant arguments about important issues that leave us feeling torn apart and burnt, with a (temporary) desire to 'hurt' the other person. Arguments may involve emotional or physical abuse. We say and do destructive things that are difficult to recover from. The peace-making process is as heated as the argument. In an argument during an intimate clash, you feel enraged and disempowered because the trigger makes you feel like you are a child. • We are consumed by a desire for the other person as though they are an addiction; we have an uncontrollable urge to connect with them. • Deep down, we know that the connection doesn't bring out our best. For example, we may lose other relationships that were previously important, and we may give up parts of our life that we previously cared about.

Intimate click	Toxic intimate clash
	• We treat the other person as though they are an extension of us. Giving attention to anything outside the relationship is considered to be disloyal.

Intimate clashes can burn us for life. Even if we had an intimate clash with someone many years ago, we will still remember aspects of it vividly. When we think of this person, it will cause our heart to race or we feel a kind of emtional shudder.

An intimate clash usually starts with our initial attraction to a person, which could be physical, mental or emotional. There is something about this individual that instantly draws us in or arouses our interest. Our antenna is up and the first impression this person makes on us has a powerful effect. This effect could be positive or negative – what matters is that they have made an impact.

Another way to understand an intimate clash is a negative attraction. This again sounds like a contradiction. There is enough similar and familiar energy that you are drawn into this person's emotional orbit, but there is something significant that repels you at the same time. This push–pull response to a person is a result of our conditioning or past trauma. On the one hand the feeling is familiar but on the other hand the feeling is traumatic. An example is a relationship between a woman who grew up with constant financial worries and a man who is highly successful and wealthy. On the surface everything is positive but behind closed doors he is unkind and psychologically abusive towards her. She is attracted to him and he gives her a sense of safety that she never had, but the abuse eats away at her sense of self. She is drawn to him and repulsed by him.

An intimate clash makes you feel like you are the same age you were when your original trauma took place. Usually our traumas occur when we are children, so usually an intimate clash triggers childhood trauma. An emotional trigger occurs when our internal reaction to a person or event is inflamed and makes us feel like we are re-experiencing the trauma all over again. An example of an emotional trigger might be someone serving you dessert if you are overcoming an eating disorder or being in a carpark alone at night if you are scared of being alone in the dark. The event triggers your trauma. It seems to be out of proportion to the event, compared to the way that other people are responding.

We can also experience intimate clashes with ourselves when certain situations trigger our deepest, most painful emotions, as per the table below. Similarly, new traumatic experiences tend to activate our old traumatic experiences and create momentum so that an emotional snowball can become an emotional avalanche. It's also worth noting that the traumatic experiences of our children can trigger our own traumas.

Intimate clash	Common traumatic emotions that are triggered
• We have bad luck such as a parking ticket or a minor car incident, such as a blown tyre.	• Unworthiness – I don't deserve to be happy; good things don't happen to me.
• We aren't invited to a party or picked for a team, or our child isn't invited to a party or picked for a team.	• Rejection, abandonment: I am unlovable.
• We are humiliated in public.	• Shame: I am bad or wrong.

In terms of Connection Types, an intimate clash typically occurs between types who are distant from each other on the model. An intimate clash always starts with an instant click because we are initially attracted to the other person. Rather than the instant click being the result of a match in frequency or intensity, the instant click happens when someone represents 'the answer' to solving our trauma or completing us in some way. Over time there is something in our connection that activates our trauma. In fact, we are often attracted to certain people and have an intimate clash with them because we share the same childhood traumas. Seen from a distance, we can see these people as fellow travellers into the same type of trauma.

If you are currently in the grips of an intimate clash with another person, ask yourself: do we share the same type of childhood trauma?

I can make this clearer with an example. Imagine a man whose father routinely made negative comments about his body when he was growing up. The father would weigh his son and keep telling him that he had work to do when his weight would show on the scales. The son developed a belief that his body was imperfect and disgusting. This young man grows up and is in his twenties, and we find him in a football locker room. His teammates are all joking around after their showers. One of them comes up to the man, pokes his stomach and says, 'Better hit the weights!' This is an example of an intuitive clash.

Our guy laughs it off publicly but is overwhelmed with shame. On the way home from football, he stops at a fast-food drive-through and eats to make himself feel better.

Back home, his girlfriend notices the fast-food wrappers in the kitchen bin. She says, 'I thought you were trying to lose weight. You'll always be fat if you don't even watch what you eat.'

The man turns around and grabs his girlfriend's shoulders. 'If you think I'm fat, then just leave!' he shouts.

His behaviour is violent and a total overreaction. Yes, her comment was rude and insensitive, but he had an overblown response. This is an intimate clash.

What I haven't shared yet is that the girlfriend has a mother who struggles with obesity. The girl is triggered by seeing fast-food wrappers in the bin. She was really talking to her mother when she made the comment to her boyfriend.

This is how triggers and intimate clashes work. One small comment or action can be like a knife through an open wound, and we respond as such. Rather than focusing on the comments or the people who make them, it would be much more healing for this man to explore the wound that is his body image. When it comes to emotional power, a person's only 'power' over us in an intimate clash is the fact that they have set off an emotional chain of events.

An intimate clash is the match that sets fire to our childhood trauma.

How to respond to an intimate clash

Once we have developed the awareness that we are part of an intimate clash, the healthy response is to remove ourselves from the connection. It may be difficult to cut the ties because of the deep emotions involved.

The next step is to separate the other person from the entire cascade of emotions that their behaviour triggers in us. Nevertheless, they must be held responsible if they have used physical violence or coercive control behaviours, which are crimes.

It is an empowering approach to separate a person from the emotions they stir up in us, because we all have the power to clear through our emotional history with the help of a professional. The more we have worked to process and become conscious of our emotional history, the less likely we are to be gripped by triggers, and the more likely we are to use a strategy to work through the triggers when they arise. We all have some degree of emotional trauma and after we have engaged in this process, when we are triggered (because we all are, because we are human) we have the tools and support network to clear the new trigger. Once we identify the basis for an emotional trigger in our history, we reclaim our power away from the person who is currently triggering us.

Triggers are like lighthouses – they send out a signal so that we can avoid big and potentially threatening emotions.

There is a big difference between an intimate clash and stagnating in your relationship. We are all constantly evolving and it is impossible to expect that our romantic partner will evolve in the exact same way or at the exact same time. Compatibility = attraction + comfort + commitment. Over time, our romantic relationships become less about acute attraction and more about commitment and companionship. As a relationship matures we need to ask different questions. Instead of: am I attracted to you? or do you light me up and cause my heart to quicken? we need to ask: do we both want this to work? Do we enhance each others' lives? Are we equally committed to the relationship? Are we both friends and lovers?

In contrast, an intimate clash triggers our trauma such that we may not feel psychologically or physically safe in that person's company. An intimate clash is different from a long-term relationship that needs love and attention to grow.

The following section reveals some Connection Type combinations that ended in separation or divorce. You can see that in these relationships the Connection Types were distant from each other on the model. Also, there was no match in either frequency or intensity.

Couples who separate due to intimate clashes

Here are some combinations of the Connection Types of romantic couples who did not stay together.

Couple one: divorced within ten years

Connection Types: Female – Ocean; Male – Star

Connection Types are distant, so they do not match in frequency or intensity.

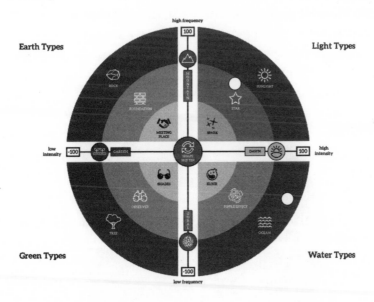

Couple two: divorced within ten years

Connection Types: Female – Sunlight; Male – Observer

Connection Types are distant, so they do not match in frequency or intensity.

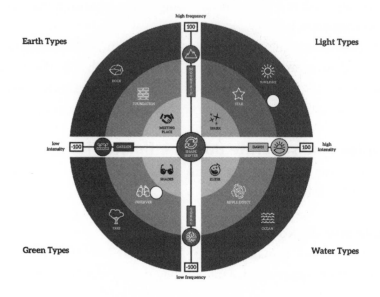

Couple three: together for one year, did not marry

Connection Types: Female – Sunlight; Male – Shades

Connection Types are distant and do not match in frequency or intensity.

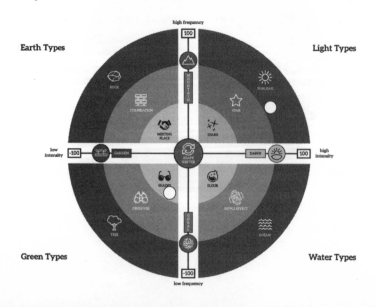

Couple four: together for two years, did not marry

Connection Types: Female – Ripple Effect; Male – Foundation

Connection Types are distant, so they do not match in frequency or intensity.

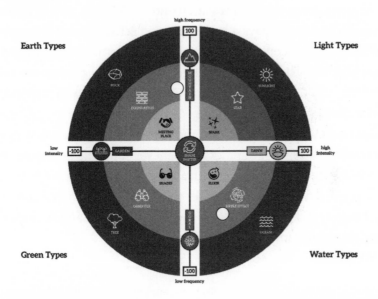

Reflecting on intimate clashes

We can gain some insight into triggers through our relationship patterns. If you experience intimate clashes with a series of different people throughout your life who exhibit the same or similar behaviours, it may be because there is something familiar in this pattern for you. Is there a person in your early childhood with a characteristic shared by these people? You may be attempting to heal that old connection through these relationships. Learning to identify the signs and patterns of this type of personality will help you to minimise these clashes in the future.

Although it can be unsettling to experience intimate clashes, the people with whom we have them are among the greatest teachers in our lives because they instruct us about our intimate traumas and they show us where we need to heal. In terms of their impact on our lives, these people can be just as powerful as the people we establish lasting intuitive and intimate clicks with – the people we end up befriending and marrying.

The good news about intimate clashes is that the way forward is always within us, and that we can overcome them with therapeutic interventions. Even though I research and work in the area of human connection and hence have a highly attuned sense of what is happening when I meet people, I have experienced intuitive and intimate clashes that blindsided me. Hopefully my intimate clashes are now behind me, and I am able to draw on my toolbox of how to respond to intuitive clashes. There are a variety of ways to seek therapy and I am keen for us all to explore every avenue that effectively and safely helps us to reach greater self-awareness. Whenever someone gets under my skin and I am gripped by an intuitive clash, I remove myself from the situation if I can or make time after to reflect on the interaction and reset. I then try to sit and focus on breathing, to hold and sit with the feeling, no matter how uncomfortable it is.

I ask myself:

> **Where do I feel this in my body?**
> **What is this feeling trying to tell me?**

This process doesn't completely relieve the pain, fear or discomfort, but it does help to diminish the powerful emotion to the point where I am able to talk about it calmly.

Then I schedule a session with a professional and talk it out. I *always* feel better afterwards, and I *marvel* at how the most unlikely people can set up opportunities for growth and expansion in me. For example, I've learnt over time that the behaviour or offhand remarks of others in social situations that trigger something I'm challenged by or that I'm working on emotionally.

If we can get to the point where we realise that every other person in the world is a small mirror into parts of ourselves, we transform the way we experience human connection. Some parts of us are delightful and we perceive other parts to be disfigured, but all parts deserve our love.

Using this approach we can transform our childhood trauma into a protective force. Once we have identified and integrated our pain, it can be converted into a force for good. We can transmute the pain and trauma into power and resilience, and can use the wisdom of the experience to guide ourselves through future pain and trauma. An intimate clash can become a hero's journey if we find our way back home to ourselves.

In summary, there are three different types of clicks and three accompanying types of clashes:

Instant click: when we feel an immediate rapport with a person, group or place because we share the same frequency.

Intuitive click: when we want to develop a friendship or spend extensive time with a person, place or group due to a match in intensity.

Intimate click: when we feel like another person is a puzzle piece that matches us: they balance us out because they are close to us on the model with a match in frequency or intensity.

Instant clash: when we find it hard, forced or unnatural to make a connection with an individual, group or place.

Intuitive clash: when someone else's behaviour repeatedly gets on our nerves or under our skin, and we overreact in response.

Intimate clash: when an intimate relationship or an incident triggers our childhood trauma, resulting in us feeling on edge, unsafe or uncomfortable.

Beyond click or clash: radical honesty and acceptance

When my husband broke the first-date taboo by telling me he didn't feel connected to my topic of conversation, he was *telling the truth*. When he called me and I agreed that our date was awkward, I was *telling the truth*. We set a precedent in our relationship that we would always be radically honest with each other. It would have been easier – and more polite – if we hadn't told the truth that night. But then we probably wouldn't be married either.

The trick is being honest and respectful at the same time, to express how you are feeling while still honouring the other person. This approach to communication is normally reserved for intimate relationships but I'm proposing that we can't ever achieve trust with anyone until we are radically honest.

> **The key is to use truth to serve the relationship, not to serve ourselves.**

Radical honesty is telling our truth even when it's hard or uncomfortable (and in relationships there is only *our* truth, not *the* truth). Clearly we need to choose who we use radical honesty with. The lovely lady we buy bread from at the bakery doesn't need to know about our headache and it's appropriate to just smile and say that we're well, and to ask if she is well, too. Sharing our struggles with her would not serve the connection.

> **We use radical honesty when the connection will benefit from our openness.**

Radical honesty can turn an unlikely connection into a lifelong relationship. My husband and I are a perfect demonstration of the fact that human connection is not about sameness, instant clicks, chemistry or common interests. We don't only connect with people we're the same as, or with people who make us feel comfortable.

This also applies in the work context. I recently worked with an organisation's executive leadership team. On days one and two, I coached each member of the team in one-on-one 90-minute sessions. On day three, I facilitated a full-day workshop with the whole team.

At the start of the workshop I said that the day was unlikely to be successful if the research is anything to go by. According to a study from consulting firm McKinsey, most leadership initiatives fail and this is because there is a 'one size fits all' design method. Facilitators come in and offer ideas and strategies that overlook the organisational context, separate reflection from real work, underestimate mindsets and fail to measure results.[27]

I said that, unless they were willing to bring radical honesty to the room that day, it was likely that any new strategies would only have a momentary impact. The next thing I said was that their team was dysfunctional.

Real crowd-pleaser, huh?

But, I continued, 'Every relationship and every team is dysfunctional in some way.' Our work together was about identifying how they were uniquely dysfunctional and understanding their blind spots and patterns.

That team rose to the occasion in an exceptional way. All of them shared their vulnerability about their role, including the loneliness of leadership and feeling like they would be judged if they spoke openly. It was incredible to see what happened to the entire team as one person after the other spoke with radical honesty. After eight hours (with breaks, obviously), we came out of the room with several action items that have fundamentally shifted the way the team operates. Each member of the team signed the new contract we created, and the team went from being a group of separate colleagues to being a cohesive whole. The way we connect with each other creates a new world and a new future.

Radical acceptance

The final stage of this work is embracing radical acceptance in the way we connect. This is the idea that the source of suffering in our relationships is trying to change the other and being attached to the way we want them to be. The moment we surrender and accept people as they are we are more likely to adjust our expectations of their behaviour. In my experience, when we adjust our expectations and accept the way people are, this gives them freedom to meet us in the middle. Radical acceptance is the high point between control on the one hand and not caring on the other.

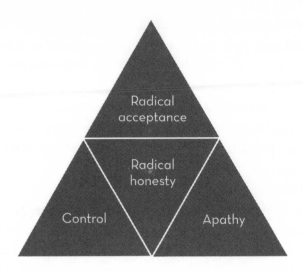

How to practise radical acceptance in relationships

1. Realise that people only change if they want to change.
2. Come to terms with the fact that someone may never change.
3. Make a commitment to accept this person as they are without trying to change them. This doesn't mean that you need to keep engaging with them. If an ongoing relationship is harmful to you, then create healthy boundaries around your contact with this person. This may mean limiting contact or ending a relationship altogether. To create healthy boundaries on your side, you must also commit to limiting the amount of time you think and talk about this person (otherwise, you are still 'letting them in').
4. Use radical honesty in your ongoing communication with others, always being guided by the questions: Will the connection benefit from my openness? What can I share that will serve the relationship long term?

Conclusion

Click or clash:
it's only the beginning

I went for a beautiful hike with my husband recently. As we walked along the Australian coastal track, it occurred to me that in the natural environment, all the elements coexist: the light, the water, the green and the earth. In fact, they don't just coexist; they need each other.

We are the same. We need each other to make up the human ecosystem. The combination of elements creates connection and belonging. So it's time to start celebrating each other as interdependent parts of the human ecosystem. That's the best foundation for human connection; to see everyone as an equally vital part of the human ecosystem and to see everyone as doing their best to belong.

In every group, a dynamic forms based on the emotional energy that each individual contributes. The Light types animate and express for the group, the Water types gently guide and care for the group, the Green types bring security and respect to the group and the Earth types protect the group and make sure everyone is having a good time. The Shapeshifters constantly adapt to whatever new energy the group needs. For every group there is a new combination of energy, making the potential group dynamics infinite!

I wish we could all see the beauty of our Connection Type when we look in the mirror. I wish Light types could see the transformative power of their enthusiasm and truth-telling; that Water types could see the transformative power of their empathy and awareness; that Green types could see the transformative power of the respect, trust and comfort they bring; that Earth types could see the transformative power of their loyalty and fun; and that Shapeshifters could see the transformative power of the harmony they embody. For now, you have this book to help give you deeper insight into the connection and love you bring to others.

Understanding my Connection Type has changed my life, and I don't say that lightly. Before I had this language and this model, I used to feel like relationships were pinball machines and we were the balls ricocheting around. We would be dropped into the relationship and then dart around unpredictably with no certainty about the outcome. I would meet people and then spiral into overthinking if we hadn't clicked, or I would over-analyse romantic relationships that clearly had no hope. I felt like there was no instruction manual!

I hope this model and knowledge of your Connection Type will become your guidebook, allowing you to navigate your relationships with other people, places and groups.

The point is, whether we're on a first date, in a job interview or trying to connect with our in-laws, we're not always going to get it right. We might clash; it might be an instant clash or an intuitive clash. With any given person, we might feel competitive or we might even be triggered. Whatever the case may be, I hope you now have a deeper understanding of what's going on, language to explain it, the determination to keep going and the tools to turn those less successful interactions into meaningful connections.

And isn't it worth the effort when it works out? Isn't an awkward first date worth the intimacy of a beautiful relationship? Isn't every disagreement worth the deeper understanding of each other once we make up? Isn't every sleepless night and tantrum worth the joy of raising a child? (Don't answer that if you're tired at the end of a long day with small children or teenagers.) Isn't moving house worth the peace we feel when we find our sense of place?

Knowing your Connection Type means that you will know which way to go in order to create belonging, and it also means that you can recognise and appreciate the needs of other people. It gives you an explanation for how you react in different situations. It gives you awareness about your type and why you seek certain friends and partners.

Once you discover your type, you have two choices:

1. You can celebrate and honour your type and laugh at your challenges, knowing that you will attract your chosen tribe just by being you.
2. Or, you can try to modify your type slightly in the hope of meeting other people in the middle.

Whether you use the Connection Type model to stick with who you are or to modify and mellow your type, I'd invite you to play around with it and use it as a conversation starter with the people in your life. In your own way, let everyone you love know how you feel about them. If there's anything worth living for, it's the radical honesty and radical acceptance of loving each other. One important application of this work is that we stop taking the behaviour of other people personally. Our needs in connection stem from our earliest family systems and so have been set long before any adult interactions. Someone's response to us is not a reflection of us, it's a reflection of that person's Connection Type.

We are all works in progress, and if we want to have flourishing relationships, we need to start with natural belonging. What brings you comfort and joy? A happy life comes from identifying what belonging looks and feels like for each of us, and pursuing it. If you're feeling lonely in any part of your life, remember that it only takes a series of tiny steps to invite belonging into your experience. Belonging is a mindset, not a person or a group. Tiny steps can be invitations to others – to go for a walk, to smile, to hold a hand, to share a meal. Sometimes it just takes one phone call and one question to change everything: was that awkward? If you have the courage to connect, I promise you it will be worth the risk.

And we need to get better at building belonging into our organisations and institutions. Recently I visited Dorrigo Hospital on the east coast of Australia to deliver a session on Connection Types to the nursing staff. At the aged-care facility, Highview, they have introduced a way of providing care to their residents that is based entirely on belonging. There is a cat onsite and the director of the hospital brings her dog into work each day to visit the residents, who have input into meal choices so they feel a sense of autonomy in what they are eating. There are gardens that the residents can walk in and tend. When one of them dies, the staff take them out the front door of Highview and have a guard of honour instead of the usual practice of transporting people through the basement of a hospital. What struck me when I was there was the special photography on the wall that was prepared as part of their Memories in Reflection project. On one side of the photo is the older person as they are now, looking into a mirror. In the mirror's reflection is the person as they were when they were younger. These photos capture the spirit of the person through an older and younger image in the same photo. This reminds the staff that the person they are caring for has lived a long and meaningful life. Highview is an example of how we can run organisations and institutions with belonging at their heart.

Visiting this hospital made me realise that while we can all do our best to build awareness of our own Connection Type and belonging needs, we also need to structure our organisations around belonging as well. We have moved from a world where we used to live together in villages and see our neighbours every day to a world where we look for connection through a screen rather than through a smile and we have to make an effort to see our friends and build community. Belonging needs to be government policy. Organisations need to approach belonging like kindergartens actively do. Leaders need to focus on belonging before performance. Every first day of work or school should include the question:

What is your Connection Type?

I dream of the Connection Type model being used in relationships, parenting, classrooms, organisations, universities, governments and legal institutions. And on first dates. Remember: the first step is belonging to yourself. All other relationships flow from there.

Endnotes

PART ONE

Chapter 1

1. M. D. Lieberman, *Social: Why our brains are wired to connect*, Oxford, Oxford University Press, 2013

2. L. Pavey, T. Greitemeyer and P. Sparks, 'Highlighting relatedness promotes prosocial motives and behavior', *Personality and Social Psychology Bulletin*, vol. 37, no. 7, 2013, pp. 905–17.

3. R. F. Baumeister and M. R. Leary, 'The need to belong: Desire for interpersonal attachments as a fundamental human motivation', *Psychological Bulletin*, vol. 117, no. 3, 1995, pp. 497–529.

4. J. Holt-Lunstad, T. B. Smith, M. Baker, T. Harris and D. Stephenson, 'Loneliness and social isolation as risk factors for mortality: A meta-analytic review', *Perspectives on Psychological Science*, vol. 10, no. 2, 2015, pp. 227–37.

5. C. M. Perissinotto, I. Stijacic Cenzer and K. E. Covinsky, 'Loneliness in older persons: A predictor of functional decline and death', *Archives of Internal Medicine*, vol. 172, no. 14, 2012, pp. 1078–83.

6. J. Holt-Lunstad, T. Smith and J. B. Layton, 'Social relationships and mortality risk: A meta-analytic review', *PLOS Medicine*, 2010, vol. 7, no. 7, e1000316.

7. T. Cruwys, S. A. Haslam, G. A. Dingle, C. Haslam and J. Jetten, 'Depression and social identity: An integrative review', *Personality and Social Psychology Review*, vol. 18, no. 3, 2014, pp. 215–38.

8. A. K. Saeri, T. Cruwys, F. K. Barlow, S. Stronge and C. G. Sibley, 'Social connectedness improves public mental health: Investigating bidirectional relationships in the New Zealand attitudes and values

survey', *Australian and New Zealand Journal of Psychiatry*, vol. 52, no. 4, 2018, pp. 365–74.

9. A. L. Kristjansson, I. D. Signfusdottir, T. Thorlindsson, M. J. Mann, J. Sigfusson and J. P. Allegrante, 'Population trends in smoking, alcohol use and primary prevention variables among adolescents in Iceland, 1997–2014', *Addiction*, vol. 111, 2016, pp. 645–52.

10. Planet Youth, Publications, https://planetyouth.org/the-method/publications/

11. G. Novembre, M. Zanon and G. Silani, 'Empathy for social exclusion involves the sensory-discriminative component of pain: A within-subject fMRI study', *Social Cognitive and Affective Neuroscience*, vol. 10, no. 2, 2014, pp. 153–64.

12. G. M. Sandstrom and E. W. Dunn, 'Social interactions and well-being: The surprising power of weak ties', *Personality and Social Psychology Bulletin*, vol. 40, no. 7, 2014, pp. 910–22.

Chapter 2

13. R. Dunbar, 'Coevolution of neocortical size, group size and language in humans', *Behavioral and Brain Sciences*, vol. 16, no. 4, 1993, pp. 681–94.

14. R. Dunbar, 'Dunbar's number: Why my theory that humans can only maintain 150 friendships has withstood 30 years of scrutiny', *The Conversation*, 13 May 2021, theconversation.com/dunbars-number-why-my-theory-that-humans-can-only-maintain-150-friendships-has-withstood-30-years-of-scrutiny-160676

15. Dunbar, 'Dunbar's number'.

16. A. F. Ward, K. Duke, A. Gneezy and M. W. Bos, 'Brain drain: The mere presence of one's own smartphone reduces available cognitive capacity', *Journal of the Association for Consumer Research*, vol. 2, no. 2, 2017, pp. 140–54.

17. D. Coyle, *The Culture Code: The secrets of highly successful groups*, 2018, Bantam Books.

18. F. Xinyuan, L. M. Padilla-Walker and M. N. Brown, 'Longitudinal relations between adolescents' self-esteem and prosocial behavior toward strangers, friends and family,' *Journal of Adolescence*, vol. 57, 2017, pp. 90–8; Z. Feng, A. Vlachantoni, X. Liu and K. Jones, 'Social trust, interpersonal trust and self-rated health in China: A multi-level study', *International Journal Equity Health*, vol. 15, no. 180, 2016; J. F. Helliwell and S. Wang, 'Trust and well-being', NBER Working Paper No. 15911, April 2010, revised December 2011, nber.org/papers/w15911

19. B. A. Austin, 'Factorial structure of the UCLA loneliness scale', *Psychological Reports*, vol. 53, no. 3, 1983, pp. 883–9; L. C. Hawkley, M. W. Browne and J. T. Cacioppo, 'How can I connect with thee? Let me count the ways', *Psychological Science*, vol. 16, no. 10, 2005, pp. 798–804; S. Cacioppo, A. J. Grippo, S. London, L. Goossens and J. T. Cacioppo, 'Loneliness: Clinical import and interventions', *Perspectives on Psychological Science*, vol. 10, no. 2, 2015, pp. 238–49.

20. Y. L. Michael, G. A. Colditz, E. Coakley and I. Kawachi, 'Health behaviors, social networks, and healthy aging: Cross-sectional evidence from the Nurses' Health Study', *Quality of Life Research*, vol 8, no. 8, 1999, pp. 711–22.

21. V. H. Murthy, *Together: Loneliness, health and what happens when we find connection*, Harper Wave, New York, 2020.

PART TWO
Chapter 4

22. T. Eurich, 'What self-awareness really is (and how to cultivate it),' *Harvard Business Review*, 4 January 2018.

PART THREE
Chapter 8

23. B. Hooks, *All about love: new visions*, William Morrow, New York, 2000.

Chapter 12

24. R. Eres and P. Molenberghs, 'The influence of group membership on the neural correlates involved in empathy', *Frontiers of Human Neuroscience*, vol. 7, 2013, p. 176.

25. ibid.

PART FOUR
Chapter 17

26. C. Jung (trns H. G. Baynes), *Psychological Types*, Harcourt, Brace & Co., New York, 1921.

Chapter 18

27. P. Gurdjian, T. Halbeisen and K. Lane, 'Why leadership-development programs fail', *McKinsey Quarterly*, 2014, mckinsey.com/featured-insights/leadership/why-leadership-development-programs-fail

Acknowledgements

I always read the acknowledgements in a book, so if you're reading this, thank you for reading this far!

My first thankyou is to the readers of this book and the participants in my workshops and presentations. Thanks for being part of this work. Just yesterday, two people made my day through their response to discovering their Connection Type. One person said it was profound to understand their type and the other said they felt 'emotionally recalibrated'. That lights me up – it's why I do what I do.

To John Daley, Matt Elliott and the whole team at The Change Room (Claire, Teena, Annie, Alisa, Holly, Philippa, Yela, Natarsha, Megan, Katie, Mini, Nam, Jeff, Mark, Nic, Andrew, Brett), thank you for listening to me deliver my Connection Type presentation one million times and still managing to act interested! The Change Room was one of the inspirations for why I developed this material. It has changed my life in so many special ways.

To Brody Smith, information designer extraordinaire! Thank you for helping me turn the Connection Type into an assessment. I could not have done it without you and it was thrilling to work with you.

To my editors, Izzy Yates and Clive Hebard from Penguin Random House Australia. You saw so many things that this book could be and helped me clarify and purify the message. Thank you for your enthusiasm for the Connection Types.

To the ICMI team, thank you for representing me as a speaker so I can share my ideas with the world. It is a pleasure to work with you! Thank you in particular to Viki Markoff for being a fairy godmother of this book and for weaving connections that brought it to life. To Sam Ferriere and your incredible marketing team. Sam, you have a gift for finding special people to collaborate with, and I love that you all get the vision!

Thank you to Janine Allis and Anthony Minichiello for your kind endorsements of the book – to have you consider and support my work is the highest honour.

To my father-in-law, Bill, thank you for being you throughout our ten-year 'instant clash'. I'm pretty sure you like me now . . . ? To my mother-in-law Jenny, thank you for your unwavering support and generosity. I love you both.

To my brothers and sisters – Paul, David, Bridget and Isabelle – thank you for educating me in what a high-intensity environment looks and feels like. We're all bouncing on the same wavelength and I love you all.

Paul, thank you for providing material on Light types in action. You are human Sunlight.

David Walker. I am singling you out and saying thankyou to *you*. Not just as part of a group, but to you alone. You are a marvel and you'll always be my beautiful little brother.

Isabelle you get your own special thank you because you have helped me shape some important ideas in the book. Even when you're at work, you take my calls about high intensity clashes and compatibility between high frequency and low frequency types.

You: 'Um, I'd better get back to work . . .'

Me: 'Wait! I want to talk to you about one more thing!'

I love you.

Bridget, you don't get a special mention because when I try to talk to you about my book you impersonate Stewie from *Family Guy* and say, 'How's the novel you've been working on?' JK: I love talking to you about my book and talking to you in general. I love you in general. And thank you to Cam for being you – I won't forget you, Cam! To Claudia, your mid-intensity goodness is a balm to my soul. To Clare and KA, thank you for your input into the book. You win the couples.

To Nana and Grandpa, Grandma and Poppa, you have all moved on to whatever afterlife awaits us but somehow I know you can feel this love.

To Mary and Jens, Vinnie, Lauren and Dominic, I love you! And to my entire extended family, thank you for being part of my earliest experiences of relationships, I love you: Ian, Kerry, Timothy, Hilary, Margaret, Drake, Anthony, Patrick, Melissa, Monica, Jessie, Angela, James, Jack, Mia and Ava.

To my sisters-in-law, Sophie, Anna and Claudia, thanks for being the big sisters I never had. I look up to you.

To my high-intensity friends, Hettie, Patrice, Sally, Ange, Arianne, Laura, Alice, Ellen, Jacqui, Abbey and Alissa (and Tim and Chris), I love talking to you! You make me feel like I belong in the world. And to all the other beautiful friends, new and old (Anna, Lara, Crystal, Karen, Sal, Toula, Bec, Al, Em, Gen, Imogen, every mum on Theo's soccer team, and so many others), thanks for making school events and school sport fun – you know who you are!

Thanks to (Ripple Effect type) Professor Leanne Piggott for being my mentor in work and life. I am very lucky and grateful to have you. Thank you to Professor Kim Rubenstein (a Spark) for being my PhD supervisor and an inspiration in social change leadership.

To my glorious father, Ross Walker (a Spark), you are the author of seven books (and counting) and a speaker, so I guess I'm just trying to be like you as much as I can. Is that the biggest acknowledgement I can give? Dad, you are a larger-than-life figure with so much expansive energy to share with the world. I am in awe of you and your generosity of spirit and always will be.

When I was younger, I used to write a lot. I would ask my mum (Anne Walker, a Dawn type) to read my work. As a mother of five children, she didn't have much time to drop what she was doing and read my writing, so she would always say to me, 'Put it on my pillow and I'll read it before I go to bed.'

I would gently place my writing on her pillow, eagerly anticipating her feedback in the morning. It always made me feel very special to think about someone reading my words before they were going to sleep. That is part of why I became an author, because I wanted to have that feeling again and again, as I imagined my words to be the last ones someone might read before they fall asleep. So my biggest thankyou, as always, is to my beautiful mother, who was the first to read my work and to make me believe I had something to say that people would want to hear. Mum and I have been having high-intensity conversations since I was . . . born, so she is a major part of how I created this model.

To Raph and Theo, who just asked me to skip to their part because they were bored watching me write acknowledgements to other people, you are literally sitting on either side of me pushing my elbows into my body as I try to type. Don't ever stop being this close. Raph, you are our Mountain type. You inspire me every day with your passion for life, your awareness and your insight. Theo, you are joy personified. You are teaching me how to play and to follow my instincts. You are living life as I always plan to live it, 'once everything is done'. You're probably a Spark or Star type but you're too young to take the assessment. I can't wait to discover more about you as you grow.

I wish I could freeze time. Raph is nearly ten and Theo is six and a half. How can life get any better?

Al, I belong with you. Every book I write has your hand and heart guiding it.

As one of five children, **Dr Ali Walker** developed an interest in group dynamics and human behaviour early in life around a very lively dinner table. Originally a criminal lawyer, Ali has a PhD in group dynamics from the Australian National University. Ali is a mediator and the founder of Ality, a company that designs personality assessments and wellbeing platforms to identify how we connect with others and our motivational drivers. She has delivered leadership programs and workshops to over 100,000 people throughout her career across organisations such as multinational companies, government departments, not for profits, universities, schools, hospitals, corrective services and juvenile justice facilities. Ali is also the author of *Get Conscious: How to stop overthinking and come alive.*

She lives in Sydney with her husband, two sons and groodle. She is a Light type: high frequency and high intensity.

Discover a
new favourite

Visit **penguin.com.au/readmore**